Constructive Controversy

Why do people make decisions based on their own perspective without considering alternative points of view? Do differences of opinion enhance or obstruct critical thinking? Is it wise to seek out people who disagree with you and listen to their objections to your conclusions? Focusing on the theory, research, and application of constructive controversy, this book analyses the nature of disagreement among members of decision-making groups, project teams, academic study groups, and other groups that are involved in solving problems. Johnson demonstrates that this theory is one of the most effective methods of enhancing creativity and innovation, decision-making, teaching, and political discourse. The book includes entertaining and intriguing examples of how constructive controversy has been used in a variety of historical periods to advance creativity, achieve innovations, and guide democracies. It will be welcomed by students in the fields of social psychology, management/business studies, education, and communication studies.

DAVID W. JOHNSON is Emeritus Professor of Educational Psychology at the University of Minnesota.

D1610518

Constructive Controversy

Theory, Research, Practice

DAVID W. JOHNSON
University of Minnesota

CAMBRIDGE
UNIVERSITY PRESS

CAMBRIDGE
UNIVERSITY PRESS

University Printing House, Cambridge CB2 8BS, United Kingdom

Cambridge University Press is part of the University of Cambridge.

It furthers the University's mission by disseminating knowledge in the pursuit of
education, learning, and research at the highest international levels of excellence.

www.cambridge.org
Information on this title: www.cambridge.org/9781107461505

© David W. Johnson 2015

First published 2015

Printed in the United Kingdom by Clays, St Ives plc

A catalogue record for this publication is available from the British Library

Library of Congress Cataloging in Publication Data
Johnson, David W.
Constructive controversy : theory, research, practice / David W. Johnson.
– 1 Edition.
    pages   cm
ISBN 978-1-107-46150-5 (paperback)
1. Group decision making.   2. Group problem solving.   3. Critical thinking.
I. Title.
HM746.J645   2015
658.4′036–dc23

                                                                    2015008282

ISBN 978-1-107-08981-5 Hardback
ISBN 978-1-107-46150-5 Paperback

Contents

Figures

Tables

Acknowledgments

I need to thank and recognize many people for their contributions and support to this book. First are all my students, colleagues, and friends, for their encouragement, support, and inspiration over the years. Second, of course, is my wife Linda, whose encouragement and support are directly related to the existence of this book. Third, my brother Roger, with whom I have collaborated my whole life. Brenda Bryant has been of immense help and assistance in completing the book. Finally, Dean Tjosvold and Karl Smith, who have pursued similar lines of work in business and engineering. The contribution of all these people and many more is immeasurable and significant.

I Underlying foundations of constructive controversy

INTRODUCTION

"NO! NO! NO! NO!" yelled one artist to another as he viewed what the other had painted during the day. "You do not understand! This is not what we are trying to do!" "It is you who do not understand!" the other replied. "This is what we talked about this morning!" "This is exactly what we are trying to achieve!"

Such heated discussions were common between two of the greatest painters of the early twentieth century. They had an intense creative collaboration filled with conflict. They dressed alike, in mechanics' clothes, and jokingly compared themselves to the Wright brothers (Orville and Wilbur). From about 1908 to 1912, they saw each other almost every day, talked constantly about the revolutionary new style they were developing, and painted as similarly as possible. Many of their respective works from those years were indistinguishable. In many cases, only art experts could or can distinguish between a painting by one or the other. They were deeply committed to their goal of creating a new style. Usually, they would meet for breakfast to discuss what they planned to paint during the day, and then spend all day painting separately. Each evening, they would rush to the other's apartment to view what the other had done, which they proceeded to criticize passionately. A canvas was not finished until the other painter said it was. They engaged in intense conflicts about the nature of the new style they were trying to create and the way in which they were expressing it in their paintings. One of the painters described it as climbing a mountain together, being roped together, knowing their survival depended on each other. The disagreements and conflicts over the nature and direction of their work were intense, spirited, illuminating, and remarkable. One of the painters stated that the things they said to

1

each other would never be said again, and even if they were, no one would understand what was meant anymore.

The two artists were Georges Braque and Pablo Picasso. The new style they were creating was Cubism. It was through their commitment to a mutual goal and their intense intellectual conflicts and arguments that they gained the creative insights necessary to do so. It is these two elements (commitment to a common goal and intellectual conflict) that provided the engine that powered their creativity, innovation, and productivity.

PHENOMENA UNDERLYING CONSTRUCTIVE CONTROVERSY

This book focuses on the theory, research, and applications of constructive controversy. It is one of the most effective methods of enhancing creativity and innovation, high-quality decision making, effective teaching, and constructive political discourse available. In order to present the theory and research on constructive controversy, however, it is first necessary to present the underlying frameworks of cooperation and conflict. Constructive controversy is a combination of cooperation and conflict, and while it can stand on its own, these two underlying phenomena are essential to understanding its basic nature. In this chapter, therefore, we will discuss the two underlying phenomena: cooperation and conflict. In addition, the work on constructive controversy represents a classic example of the interrelationships among theory, research, and practice, which we will also discuss in this chapter.

COOPERATION

Historically, there are scientists and others who believe that competition underlies most of human behavior (Johnson & Johnson, 1989). From the evolutionary lens of Darwin and others, on Earth there is a continual struggle for existence in which competitiveness, the striving for domination, and winning are at the very heart of nature and human existence. The fittest win the struggle for life and the weaker perish. What we see in the world today are the winners; the losers have disappeared. This is the basic law of biology: what you see existing in the world are the life-forms that have won the contest for survival. What you do not see are the life-forms that have lost, and consequently they are gone. It all started at least four billion years ago with the first primitive cells. If one of the first little cells had an advantage over the others, it would reproduce faster and prosper, while its rivals perished. This view of life dominates the thinking of many people. Species compete over habitat and food sources. Those who lose disappear. Out of the various types of humans, *Homo erectus* and Neanderthals (who had bigger brains than we do and were much stronger physically) lost (perhaps because of their inability to cooperate) and disappeared while we survived. Competition is seen as the basic underlying mechanism of life, and even today countries and cultural and religious groups seem to compete with each other to see who will survive and who will vanish. A question is, does competition to survive contain its own seeds of destruction? There can be no doubt that competition breeds competition, which tends to result eventually in mutual destruction (Johnson & Johnson, 1989).

There is a counterview to this social Darwinism (Johnson & F. Johnson, 2013). What is lacking from the competitive struggle for survival view is that beings of every level of complexity cooperate to live. Some of the earliest bacteria formed strings, where certain cells in each living filament die to nourish their neighbors with nitrogen. Some bacteria hunt in groups, similar to a pride of lions or a pack of wolves. Ants form societies of millions of individuals that can solve complex problems, from farming to architecture to navigation. Bees tirelessly harvest pollen for the good of the hive. Crows serve as sentries to guard the members of their flock. At every level of existence, cooperation is evident.

Human society may especially thrive on cooperation. Even simple acts, such as buying groceries at a store, draw on the labors of a small army of people (e.g., farmers, transportation companies, processing plants, grocery stores, inspectors, and so forth) from many different countries. The procedures for cooperation and coordination are passed on from generation to generation. Great ideas are generated, communicated to others, used, embellished, and transformed from the originators of the idea to future generations through socialization. What has made our branch of the human species so successful is that we are supreme cooperators, the greatest on Earth. Try cramming ten chimpanzees in an SUV for a four-hour drive and see what happens. Our incredible ability to cooperate is a primary reason we have survived in every ecosystem on Earth (from deserts to frozen wastes) and perhaps soon on ecosystems on other planets. Our cooperation extends beyond a group of people working to achieve a common goal; it includes large-scale, long-term views of the common good of our society and species as a whole. This does not make sense when viewed from a traditional Darwinian perspective. By helping others a person hurts his or her own chances to "win, flourish, reproduce, and survive." Your car breaks down and a stranger drives you to a gas station to get a tow truck even though it costs the stranger some money for gas and makes the stranger late for work. You donate $100 to a church drive to feed hungry people in another country rather than spend the money on yourself. Cooperation seems to happen spontaneously without too much thinking getting in the way. The first response of most people is to cooperate, but when they stop and think they tend to be more selfish. Even the cells in your body, rather than reproduce as much as they can, will multiply in an orderly fashion to create the lungs, heart, and other vital organs so that the body as a whole can function effectively.

Many everyday situations can be viewed as choices whether to cooperate or not. Suppose you want to buy a new refrigerator. You go to an appliance store and ask the salesperson which refrigerator is the best deal. The salesperson can interpret this either as the "best deal" for him or her and the store in general, maximizing their profit. Or the salesperson can interpret this as being the best refrigerator at the lowest price for you. If the salesperson recommends the refrigerator that gives you, and not the store, the best deal, then this is an example of cooperation. And it seems pretty amazing. Why would the clerk give up the store's profit for your benefit? That is cooperation against immediate self-interest. It makes no short-term sense. Yet even the lowliest creatures, such as bacterium, engage in such behavior.

This may be a fatal flaw in natural selection. Natural selection should motivate individuals to behave in ways that increase their own chances of survival and reproduction, not improve the fortunes of others. In a never-ending striving for food, territory, and mates in evolution, why would one individual ever bother to go out of his or her way to help another. The answer is that our ability to cooperate enhances our success in surviving and flourishing in the long term. In 1902, Prince Pyotr Alexeyevich Kropotkin (1842–1921), a Russian prince, published a book, *Mutual Aid: A Factor of Evolution*, presenting his view that besides the "Law of the Survival of the Fittest" there is in nature the "Law of Mutual Aid," which is far more important for the evolution of the species and the struggle for life. Kropotkin pointed out the distinction between the direct competition among individuals for limited resources and the struggle between organisms and the environment. It is the struggle between organisms and the environment as a whole that tends to induce cooperation among the organisms. He believed that the competitive form of struggle did exist, but argued that cooperation and mutual aid were more frequent and were being underemphasized. That is, it is not competition that is the most frequent and important factor in the ability to survive and evolve; rather it is cooperation and mutual aid. The two laws create an ongoing tension between what is good for the individual and what is good for others and society as a whole. A paradox of cooperation is that this tension may be greater in cooperative than in competitive situations. In competition, what is good for oneself and bad for others dominates behavior. In cooperation, all three concerns (what is good for oneself, fellow cooperators, and society as a whole) exist in the situation.

Theories of cooperation

Cooperation is such a central factor in human life that there are multiple theories about its nature (Johnson & Johnson, 1989), including cognitive-developmental theory, social cognitive theory, behavioral theory, and social interdependence theory. The dominant theory is probably social interdependence theory (Deutsch, 1949, 1962; Johnson & Johnson, 1989, 2009a).

Cognitive-developmental theory

The cognitive-developmental perspective is largely based on the theories of Piaget (1950) and Vygotsky (2012). To Jean Piaget (1950), cooperation is the striving to attain common goals while coordinating one's own feelings and perspective with a consciousness of others' feelings and perspective. When individuals cooperate in the environment, socio-cognitive conflict occurs that creates cognitive disequilibrium, which in turn stimulates perspective-taking ability and cognitive development. Cooperation in the Piagetian tradition is aimed at accelerating a person's intellectual development by forcing him or her to reach consensus with others who hold opposing points of view about the answer to the problem. Lev Semenovich Vygotsky (1978) and related social constructionist theorists claim that our distinctively human mental functions and accomplishments have their origins in our social relationships. Mental functioning is the internalized and transformed version of the accomplishments of a group. Knowledge is social, constructed from cooperative efforts to learn, understand, and solve problems. A central concept is the "zone of proximal development," which is the zone between what a person can do on his or her own and what the person can achieve while working under the guidance of older individuals or in collaboration with more capable peers. Unless persons work cooperatively, they will not grow intellectually.

Social cognitive theory

Social cognitive theory views cooperation as collective agency (Bandura, 2000), the shared belief in the collective power to produce desired results. In collective agency individuals have to work together to secure what they cannot accomplish on their own. From the social cognitive perspective, cooperation involves modeling, coaching, and scaffolding (i.e., conceptual frameworks that provide understanding of what is being learned) (Lave & Wenger, 1991). Ideally, the learner will cognitively rehearse and restructure information for it to be retained in memory and incorporated into existing cognitive structures (Wittrock, 1990). An effective way of doing so is explaining the material being learned to a collaborator. Finally, social cognitive theory places cooperation at the center of a community of practice, a group of people who share a craft or a profession.

Behavioral-learning theory

The behavioral-learning perspective assumes that individuals will work hard on those tasks for which they secure a reward of some sort and will fail to work on tasks that yield no reward or yield punishment (Bandura, 1977; Skinner, 1968). Cooperative efforts are designed to provide incentives for the members of the group to participate in a group effort. Skinner focused on group contingencies, Bandura focused on imitation, and others focused on the balance of rewards and costs.

Social interdependence theory

Social interdependence exists when the accomplishment of each individual's goals is affected by the actions of others (Deutsch, 1949, 1962; Johnson, 1970, 2003; Johnson & Johnson, 1989, 2005b). There are two types of social interdependence: positive (cooperation) and negative (competition). *Positive interdependence* (e.g., cooperation) exists when individuals perceive that they can reach their goals if and only if the other individuals with whom they are cooperatively linked also reach their goals. Participants, therefore, promote each other's efforts to achieve the goals. *Negative interdependence* (i.e., competition) exists when individuals perceive that they can obtain their goals if and only if the other individuals with whom they are competitively linked fail to obtain their goals. Participants, therefore, obstruct each other's efforts to achieve the goals. *No interdependence* (e.g., individualistic efforts) results in a situation in which individuals perceive that they can reach their goal regardless of whether other individuals in the situation attain or do not attain their goals.

The basic premise of social interdependence theory is that the type of interdependence structured in a situation determines how individuals interact with each other. The interaction patterns, in turn, determine outcomes. Positive interdependence tends to result in promotive interaction, negative interdependence tends to result in oppositional or contrient interaction, and no interdependence results in an absence of interaction. The relationship between the type of social interdependence and the interaction pattern it elicits is assumed to be bidirectional. Each may cause the other. Just as positive interdependence results in promotive interaction, promotive interaction may result in cooperation.

There are three constructs that are important markers for the types of social interdependence: substitutability, cathexis, and inducibility. *Substitutability* is the actions of one person substituting for the actions of another. *Cathexis* is the investment of psychological energy in objects and events outside of oneself. *Inducibility* is openness to influence. Essentially, in cooperative situations the actions of participants substitute for each other, participants positively cathect to each other's effective actions, and there is high inducibility among participants. In competitive situations the actions of participants do not substitute for each other, participants negatively cathect to each other's effective actions, and inducibility is low. When there is no interaction, there is no substitutability, cathexis, or inducibility.

It should also be noted that a great deal is known about the relative impact of cooperation and competition on a wide variety of variables (Johnson, 1970, 2003; Johnson & Johnson, 1974, 1989, 2009a). In essence, cooperation (compared to competition and individualistic efforts) promotes:

1. Greater effort to achieve: Cooperation produces higher achievement and greater productivity than do competitive or individualistic efforts. This finding is so well confirmed by so much research that it stands as one of the strongest principles in psychology and education. The more conceptual the task, the more problem solving required, the more desirable higher-level reasoning and critical thinking, the more creativity required, and the greater the application required of what is being learned to the real world, the greater the superiority of cooperative over competitive and individualistic efforts.

2. More positive relationships: *Cooperative learning creates more positive, committed, caring, and supportive relationships than do competitive or individualistic learning.* This is true when individuals are homogeneous and it is also true when individuals differ in intellectual ability, handicapping conditions, ethnic membership, social class, culture, and gender. Relationships among cooperators, in addition, are characterized by more professional and personal social support than are relationships in competitive and individualistic situations. True friendships develop from the joint effort required to achieve mutual learning goals.

3. Greater psychological health: Working cooperatively with others results in greater psychological health and higher self-esteem than does competing with peers or working individualistically. Personal ego-strength, self-confidence, self-reliance, ability to cope with stress and adversity, independence, autonomy, personal happiness, and general psychological health all result from cooperative efforts. Cooperative experiences result in higher self-esteem and more healthy processes for deriving conclusions about one's self-worth than do competitive or individualistic efforts. Working together to achieve mutual goals results in increased social competencies, the ability to build and maintain supportive and committed relationships, and mutual respect for each other as separate and unique individuals. Healthy social, cognitive, and psychological development results. Cooperative experiences are not a luxury. They are an absolute necessity for the healthy development of individuals who can function independently.

Social interdependence as a context for conflict

Once cooperation is clearly established among the relevant individuals, conflicts will occur. How the conflicts are managed determines whether cooperation is strengthened or weakened. There are two possible contexts for conflict: cooperative and competitive (in individualistic situations individuals do not interact and, therefore, conflict tends not to occur).

Competitive context

Conflicts usually do not go well in a competitive context. For competition to exist, there must be scarcity. Competition is inherently a conflict, as participants seek rewards that are restricted to the few who perform the best. Within a competitive context (Deutsch, 1973; Johnson & Johnson, 1989, 2005b; Watson & Johnson, 1972),

1. Individuals focus on differential benefits (i.e., doing better than anyone else in the situation). In competitive situations, how well a person is doing depends on how his or her performance compares with the performances of the others in the situation. There is a constant social comparison in which the value of one's outcomes depends on how they compare with the outcomes of others.
2. Individuals focus on their own well-being and the deprivation of the other participants. In striving to "win," individuals focus not only on what is good for them but also on what will prevent others from winning. There is a vested interest in others doing less well than oneself.
3. Individuals adopt a short-term time orientation where all energies are focused on winning. Little or no attention is paid to maintaining a good relationship. In most competitions, there is an immediate finishing line on which all attention is focused, with little or no concern about the future relationship with the other competitors.
4. Communication tends to be avoided, and when it does take place, it tends to contain misleading information and threats. Threats, lies, and silence do not help students resolve conflicts with each other. Competition gives rise to espionage or other techniques to obtain information about the other that the other is unwilling to communicate,

and "diversionary tactics" to delude or mislead the opponent about oneself.

5. There are frequent and common misperceptions and distortions of the other person's position and motivations that are difficult to correct. Students engage in self-fulfilling prophecies by perceiving another person as being immoral and hostile and behaving accordingly, thus evoking hostility and deceit from the other person. Students see small misbehaviors of opponents while ignoring their own large misbehaviors (this is known as the mote-beam mechanism). Double standards exist. Because preconceptions and expectations influence what is perceived, and because there is a bias toward seeing events in a way that justifies one's own beliefs and actions, and because conflict and threat impair perceptual and cognitive processes, the misperceptions are difficult to correct.

6. Individuals have a suspicious, hostile attitude toward each other that increases their readiness to exploit each other's wants and needs and refuse each other's requests.

7. Individuals tend to deny the legitimacy of others' wants, needs, and feelings and consider only their own interests.

Cooperative context

Typically, for a conflict to be managed constructively, it must occur within a cooperative context. For cooperation to exist there must be mutual goals that all parties are committed to achieving. Intellectual conflict is no exception. Within cooperative situations (Deutsch, 1973; Johnson & Johnson, 1989, 2005b; Watson & Johnson, 1972),

1. Individuals focus on mutual goals and shared interests.

2. Individuals are concerned with both self and others' well-being.

3. Individuals adopt a long-term time orientation where energies are focused on both achieving goals and building good working relationships with others.

4. Effective and continued communication is of vital importance in resolving a conflict. Within a cooperative situation, the communication of relevant information tends to be open and honest, with each person interested in informing the other as well as being informed. Communication tends to be more frequent, complete, and accurate.

5. Perceptions of the other person and the other person's actions are far more accurate and constructive. Misperceptions and distortions such as self-fulfilling prophecies and double standards occur less frequently and are far easier to correct and clarify.

6. Individuals trust and like each other and, therefore, are willing to respond helpfully to each other's wants, needs, and requests.

7. Individuals recognize the legitimacy of each other's interests and search for a solution that accommodates the needs of both sides. Conflicts tend to be defined as mutual problems to be solved in ways that benefit everyone involved.

CONSTRUCTIVE CONFLICT

One of the closely guarded secrets of cooperation is that it results in a great deal of conflict (Johnson & Johnson, 1989, 2005b, 2007). Cooperation does not mean compliance, conformity, acquiescence, or niceness. Rather, in deciding how best to accomplish a mutual goal, people disagree, criticize each other's conclusions and positions, engage in refutation and rebuttal, and even yell and scream at each other. Such intellectual arguments, for example, may involve which restaurant at which to eat dinner, what route to take when driving to a meeting, whether to fly or drive to a vacation spot, or how long a time-out for a young child should be. In essence, conflict pervades cooperation, primarily through juggling concerns for benefits for oneself, collaborators, and the society as a whole.

There is disagreement, however, over whether conflicts are beneficial or harmful. The view of many people seems to be that conflict tends to have negative consequences and should be avoided. Thus, discussions of conflict tend to present it as causing psychopathology, ending friendships, being fired from jobs or expelled from school, and even creating divorce, war, and social disorder. Furthermore, many psychological theories emphasize self-gratification, fulfillment of one's needs and desires, tension reduction, dissonance reduction, balance, good form, and equilibrium—all of which imply that life is better when it is conflict-free.

On the other hand, there are people who believe that conflict is desirable and has desirable outcomes. There is no doubt that conflict is often of personal and social value (Johnson & F. Johnson, 2013). Conflicts can stimulate curiosity and interest, solve problems, prevent stagnation, promote cognitive, social, and moral development, and are often part of the process of testing and assessing oneself. Conflicts can even be highly enjoyable as one experiences the pleasure of the full and active use of one's skills and abilities.

In addition, conflict gains and holds attention and interest. All drama, for example, hinges on conflict. When playwrights and scriptwriters want to gain and hold viewers' attention, create viewer interest and emotional involvement, and excite and surprise viewers, they create a conflict. A general rule for television shows is that if a conflict is not portrayed in the first 30 seconds, viewers will change the channel. Creating a conflict is an accepted writer's tool for capturing an audience. A general rule of modern novels is that if a conflict is not created within the first three pages of the book, the book will not be successful. By avoiding conflicts, individuals miss out on valuable opportunities to capture and emotionally involve themselves and others in the situation and enhance their creativity, productivity, and learning. The issue, therefore, is not how to eliminate or prevent conflict, but rather how to make it productive or, at the very least, how to prevent it from being destructive.

Conflict theorists have for hundreds of years posited that conflict could have positive as well as negative benefits. Freud, for example, indicated that extra psychic conflict was a necessary (but not sufficient) condition for psychological development. Developmental psychologists have proposed that disequilibrium within a student's cognitive structure can motivate a shift from egocentrism to accommodation of the perspectives of others and what results is a transition from one stage of cognitive and moral reasoning to another. Motivational theorists believe that conceptual conflict can create epistemic curiosity that motivates the search for new information and the reconceptualization of the knowledge one already has.

Organizational theorists insist that higher-quality problem solving depends on constructive conflict among group members. Cognitive psychologists propose that conceptual conflict may be necessary for insight and discovery. Educational psychologists indicate that conflict can increase achievement. Karl Marx believed that class conflict was necessary for social progress. From almost every field of social science, theorists have taken the position that conflict can have positive as well as negative outcomes.

Despite all the theorizing about the positive aspects of conflict, there has been until the past four decades or so very little empirical evidence demonstrating that the presence of conflict can be more constructive than its absence. Guidelines for managing conflicts tend to be based more on folk-wisdom than on validated theory. Far from being encouraged and structured in most interpersonal and inter-group situations, conflict tends to be avoided and suppressed. Creating conflict to capitalize on its potential positive outcomes tends to be the exception, not the rule. In the late 1960s, therefore, we began a program of theorizing and research to identify the conditions under which conflict results in constructive outcomes. One of the results of our work is the theory of constructive controversy.

Finally, the irony is that even though most people may have a negative view of conflict, they tend to seek out conflicts in which to participate. They may play tennis or participate in races, they may (a) attend rugby, football, or basketball games, (b) watch movies, plays, or television programs (all drama is based on conflict), (c) read mystery or romance novels or even classical literature, and (d) engage in inter-personal activities such as teasing. There is often a discrepancy between how individuals view conflict and how they choose to spend their time. Conflicts should be accepted as a natural part of life that are faced and resolved in constructive ways. A person might as well try to stop the Earth from turning on its axis so as to try to eliminate conflicts from his or her life. Conflicts arise no matter what a person does. Conflicts are especially frequent whenever individuals have goals they care about and are involved in relationships they value.

THEORY, RESEARCH AND PRACTICE

Constructive controversy is a classic example of the interaction among theory, research, and practice (see Figure 1.1). This relationship among theory, research, and practice is commonly talked about in the social sciences, but rarely seen. In this book the theory of constructive controversy is presented, the validating research is reviewed, and applications of the theory are discussed. Theory, research, and practice all interact and enhance each other.

Theory has a variety of functions. Theory (a) guides future research by telling us what we need to find out, (b) summarizes and subsumes research into meaningful conceptual frameworks by making sense of what we know, (c) generates further research that validates or disconfirms the theory and establishes the conditions under which the hypothesized relationships occur, and (d) guides practice by telling us what to do in applied situations. In order to be

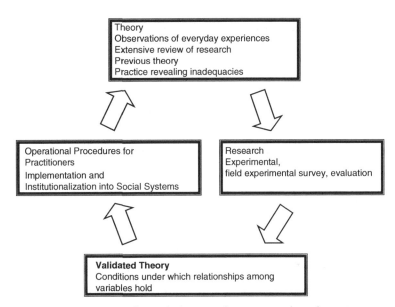

FIGURE 1.1 Relationship among theory, research, and practice

significant, a theory needs to be powerful by demonstrating considerable validity and generalizing across a wide range of individual differences, situational variables, cultures, and historical periods. A theory needs to be strategic by demonstrating implications for and applications to a wide range of problems and situations. Finally, a theory needs to be profound, so that individuals who know the theory understand more about the real world than do people who do not know the theory. Constructive controversy theory meets all of these criteria.

Research validates or disconfirms theory, thereby leading to its refinement and modification, or to its abandonment. The relationship between theory and research, however, is not unidirectional (Merton, 1957). Empirical research can shape the development of theory through the discovery of valid results that are unanticipated, the accumulation of research findings that the theory does not adequately explain, the clarification of the nature of theoretical concepts, and the demonstration of the relationship between the theory and new dependent variables.

Having a validated theory, however, does not signify that it will direct or even influence practice. There are many examples of validated theories that have never been applied. Effective practices can be derived from sound theories, but they can also be derived from unsound theories or from no theory at all (i.e., through trial and error or luck).

There is a two-way relationship between theory and practice. Practice may be guided by validated theory. Effective practice can be derived from validated theory; however, only if the theory is stated with sufficient precision that effective procedures can be deduced for practitioners to use. Operationalizing the theory in practical situations, moreover, can reveal inadequacies in the theory that lead to its modification and refinement. New research studies are then needed to validate the changes. The practical procedures are then modified to reflect the revised theory. This process is repeated over and over again.

PURPOSE OF THIS BOOK

The purpose of this book is to provide an integration of theory, research, and practice on constructive controversy for individuals who wish to deepen their understanding of conflict and how to manage it constructively. The book focuses on one type of conflict, that is, constructive controversy (i.e., conflict among theories, conclusions, opinions, and ideas). Chapter 2 deals with the definition of constructive controversy and other related concepts. Chapter 3 presents the theory underlying constructive controversy. Chapter 4 covers the process by which constructive controversy works, and Chapter 5 details the outcomes of constructive controversy documented by the research. Chapter 6 discusses the conditions mediating the effect of constructive controversy on the outcomes. Finally, there are five applications of constructive controversy that are discussed. Constructive controversy is used in organizational decision making (Chapter 7), educational organizations from first grade through graduate school (Chapter 8), the promotion of creativity, innovation, and problem solving (Chapter 9), the use of political discourse in democracies (Chapter 10), and the establishment and maintenance of world peace (Chapter 11). Each of these applications will be discussed. Chapter 12 summarizes the book.

SUMMARY

Constructive controversy is one of the most effective methods of enhancing creativity and innovation, high-quality decision making, effective teaching, constructive political discourse, and many other settings. Constructive controversy, however, is based on a foundation of cooperation and conflict. These two underlying phenomena are essential to understanding its basic nature. Constructive controversy is based on participants seeking to achieve a common goal that unites them in a cooperative effort. Yet constructive controversy structures and promotes intellectual conflicts in which people with different opinions or conclusions express their opinions and challenge each other's reasoning.

Social interdependence, cooperation and competition, is as old as the human species. Interdependence, however, carries the seeds of conflict. All competitions are inherently a conflict. Cooperation is riddled with conflicts, as diverse individuals and groups work together and have much different strategies and perspectives on achieving their mutual goals. When two parties are in conflict, they face the possibility that the relationship will be damaged and all potential for future cooperation will be ended. They also face the possibility that the conflict will produce new heights of creativity, problem solving, learning, insight, innovation, and friendship. Whether positive or negative outcomes result from a conflict within a cooperative context depends on the skillful use of an available procedure that is based on validated theory confirmed by considerable research. Constructive controversy provides such a theory and program of research.

In this chapter the two phenomena underlying constructive controversy, cooperation and conflict, are discussed. Based on the social Darwinism derived from Darwin's theory of evolution, a view developed that the basic nature of human interaction was competition. "The survival of the fittest," the striving for dominance and winning, was seen as the basic law of nature and of human existence. Most scientists now believe, however, that human nature is first and foremost cooperative. Beings of every level of complexity, from bacteria to humans, cooperate to live. Although the theory of natural selection states that individuals will behave in ways that increase their own chances of survival and reproduction, there are many instances where parties behave in ways that improve the fortunes of others. In human interaction there seems to be an ongoing tension between what is good for the individual and what is good for others and society as a whole. Conflicts, furthermore, are managed differently in a cooperative than in a competitive context.

There are multiple theories about the nature of cooperation (Johnson, 2003; Johnson & Johnson, 1989, 2009a, 2013). They include cognitive-developmental theory (e.g., Piaget and Vygotsky), social cognitive theory (e.g., Bandura), behavioral theory (e.g., Skinner), and social interdependence theory (e.g., Deutsch, Johnson, & Johnson). Of these various theories, it is social interdependence theory that is particularly relevant to constructive controversy.

When individuals take action, there are three ways in which what they do may be related to the actions of others. One's actions may promote the success of others, obstruct the success of others, or not have any effect at all on the success or failure of others. In other words, individuals may be (Deutsch, 1949, 1962; Johnson & Johnson, 1989): (a) working together cooperatively to accomplish shared learning goals, (b) competing against each other to achieve a goal that only one or a few can attain, or (c) working individualistically by oneself to accomplish goals unrelated to the goals of others. The basic premise of social interdependence theory is that the type of interdependence structured in a situation determines how individuals interact with each other and that, in turn, determines outcomes. Cooperation tends to result in promotive interaction, competition tends to result in oppositional interaction, and individualistic efforts tend to result in no interaction. Cooperation tends to result in greater effort to achieve, more positive relationships, and greater psychological health than does competition or individualistic efforts.

One of the secrets of cooperation is that it results in a great deal of conflict. Conflicts are especially frequent whenever individuals have goals they care about and are involved in relationships they value. A person might as well try to stop the Earth from turning on its axis as to try to eliminate conflicts from his or her life. There is disagreement, however, over whether conflicts are beneficial or harmful. The irony is that even though most people may have a negative view of conflict, they tend to seek out conflicts in which to participate. Conflicts arise no matter what a person does. There is no doubt that conflict is often of personal and social value. Conflicts can stimulate curiosity and interest, solve problems, prevent stagnation, and promote cognitive, social, and moral development. Historically, however, very little evidence existed that conflicts do in fact have positive outcomes.

Beginning in the late 1960s, therefore, we began a program of theorizing, research, and application that resulted in the theory of constructive controversy. The work on constructive controversy presented in this book represents a classic tale of the interrelationships among theory, research, and practice. This book reflects our cycle of reviewing the research literature, formulating and summarizing the theory, conducting a program of research to validate and refine the theory, creating operational procedures that operationalize the validated theory in practical situations, and implementing the procedures into multiple and diverse organizations. The purpose of this book is to provide an integration of theory, research, and practice on constructive controversy for individuals who wish to deepen their understanding of conflict and how to manage it constructively.

2 The nature of constructive controversy

INTRODUCTION

"Listen to me!" shouted Member A of a metro commission in charge of planning for suburban expansion. "Urban sprawl destroys more than one million acres (about the size of Rhode Island) of parks, farms, and open space every year. We do not want to turn more productive farmland as well as cherished parks and open spaces into strip malls, freeways, and houses that only the rich can afford! We have to limit suburban expansion!"

"Nonsense," replied Member B of the commission. "The population of Metro City keeps growing. Unless we develop the suburbs, large numbers of people are going to be forced to live in the same small area. The only way to prevent such overcrowding is to expand the suburbs. In addition, people get much more use out of houses and backyards than they do out of farmland, wetlands, or parks. Let's maximize the use of this land!"

"Look," replied Member A. "It isn't just land use. The more people who live in the suburbs, the more highways, sewage lines, phone lines, electrical lines, and so forth we need. Suburbs cost a lot of money. In addition, they steal jobs from the city, as malls are built far away from the city and businesses move to be nearer their customers. Expanding the suburbs is not a good idea."

"That may not be up to us," Member B commented. "If a farmer is planning to retire and he can sell his land to a developer at a price far above what it is worth as farmland, how do we stop him? Do we have the right to stop him? By the way, when population densities of cities go up and no new roads are built, the only possibility is that traffic will get worse."

This conversation continued through several meetings, until a decision was made as to how much suburb expansion the commission would recommend. Members' confidence in their decision was high due to the vigorous arguing of both sides of the issue.

LEVELS OF CONSTRUCTIVE CONTROVERSY

Engaging in intellectual conflict (i.e., constructive controversy) is important on many levels. On the personal level, individuals need to consider arguments for or against different options, such as decisions about changing careers, getting married, or buying a house. Individuals also need to understand how to reason rationally, to avoid such things as pseudoscientific thinking (i.e., beliefs in astrology, untested health practices) or believing in falsehoods (i.e., modern medicine does more harm than good). Also at the personal level, in psychotherapy, cognitive treatments involve replacing distorted arguments with more rational ones. At the educational level, students need to learn reasoning skills to achieve in math, science, social studies, and other subject areas. On a group level, members make decisions that entail looking at the pros and cons of different courses of action, such as whether to outsource jobs, begin a new product line, or build a new production facility. On a societal level, in a democracy the ability of citizens to think critically is considered to be paramount. In addition, citizens need to evaluate arguments and counterarguments about the issues confronting their society, such as the desirability of genetically modified foods, the solutions to global warming, and whether to raise taxes to improve the infrastructure. Thus, at all levels of human interaction the competency to engage in constructive intellectual conflict is essential.

Yet, learning how to manage intellectual conflicts constructively does not seem to happen automatically. In many homes, children are taught to never disagree with their parents, police officers, and other figures of authority. In many schools, students are taught to never disagree with their teachers (or with each other). In many organizations, members are taught to never disagree with their boss or with each other.

The clearest evidence of individuals avoiding intellectual conflict comes from schools. A large-scale observational study of classrooms in British primary schools (called ORACLE) conducted in the 1970s (Galton, Simon, & Croll, 1980) found that it was common practice for children to sit together at a table. That did not mean, however, that they were working together or even interacting. Instead, the children at any table worked in parallel on individual tasks. They might talk as they worked, and even talk to each other about their work, but they typically did not work together. Even when students were given joint tasks to complete, their interactions were rarely productive (Alexander, 2006; Bennett & Cass, 1989; Blatchford & Kutnick, 2003; Galton, Hargreaves, Comber, Wall, & Pell, 1999; Kumpulainen & Wray, 2002).

In the early 1990s the Spoken Language and New Technology (SLANT) project observed the interaction of children ages 8 to 11 years in ten primary school classrooms (Wegerif & Scrimshaw, 1997). Although students worked together in small groups at the computer, most of the interactions were not task focused, equitable, or productive. Some groups were dominated by one member so that other members became quiet and subdued and participated only marginally. In other groups the members tended to ignore each other, taking turns at the computer, each independently pursuing their own ideas. Some groups were characterized by unproductive, highly competitive disagreements and disputes (Fisher, 1993; Mercer, 1995). There were times when these competitive disagreements escalated, resulting in group members becoming increasingly hostile toward each other and engaging in vehement personal criticism.

There is evidence that students tend to be ineffective in using argumentative strategies, in adapting them to communicative circumstances, and in crafting convincing written arguments in school (Felton & Kuhn, 2001). The 2002 National Assessment of Educational Progress Writing Report Card showed that only 17 percent of fourth graders, 18 percent of eighth graders, and 31 percent of twelfth

Table 2.1 *Advocates of constructive controversy*

Date	Person	Quote
495–429 BC	Pericles (Athenian statesman)	*... instead of looking on discussion as a stumbling block in the way of action, we think it an indispensable preliminary to any wise action at all.*
470–399 BC	Socrates (Greek philosopher)	(Method of teaching emphasized creating disequilibrium and uncertainty through questioning.)
1608–1674	John Milton (English poet)	*Where there is much desire to learn, there of necessity will be much arguing ...*
1709–1784	Samuel Johnson (English author & lexicographer)	*I dogmatize and am contradicted, and in this conflict of opinions and sentiments I find delight.*
1727–1797	Edmund Burke (British statesman & orator)	*He that wrestles with us strengthens our nerves, and sharpens our skill. Our antagonist is our helper.*
1743–1826	Thomas Jefferson (3rd U.S. president)	*Difference of opinion leads to inquiry, and inquiry to truth.*
1775–1864	Walter Savage Landor (English author)	*There is no more certain sign of a narrow mind, of stupidity, and of arrogance, than to stand aloof from those who think differently from us.*
1806–1873	John Stuart Mill (English philosopher & economist)	*Since the general or prevailing opinion on any subject is rarely or never the whole truth, it is only by the collision of adverse opinion that the remainder of the truth has any chance of being supplied.*

Table 2.1 (cont.)

Date	Person	Quote
1819–1892	Walt Whitman	*Have you not learned great lessons from those who braced themselves against you, and disputed the passage with you?*
1835–1910	Mark Twain (American writer)	*It is best that we should not all think alike. It's difference of opinion that makes horse races.*
1859–1952	John Dewey (American philosopher & educator)	*Conflict is the gadfly of thought. It stirs us to observation and memory. It instigates invention. It shocks us out of sheeplike passivity, and sets us at noting and contriving ... Conflict is a "since qua non" of reflection and ingenuity.*

graders wrote argumentative essays that were judged to be skillful or better (Persky, Daane, & Jin, 2003). An essay was considered skillful if it offered a thesis and some supporting reasons and examples, but lacked clear transitions among arguments and did not necessarily consider alternative viewpoints. It is found, however, that teaching students explicit strategies increases their writing performance (Ferretti, Andrews–Weckerly, & Lewis, 2007; Ferretti, Lewis, & Andrews–Weckerly, 2009; Graham, 2006).

It is not that children and young adults cannot engage in competent dialogue. Maybin (2006), for example, observed children's off-task talk in primary school and found that they use many varied language forms to discuss issues that concern them, including providing support for their views. Observational studies in homes, nurseries, and playgroups have shown that even preschool children will justify opinions, suggest alternatives, and reach compromises during free play with their siblings or peers (Dunn & Kendrick,

1982; Eisenberg & Garvey, 1981; Genishi & Di Paolo, 1982; Howe & McWilliam, 2001, 2006; Orsolini, 1993). Thus, while students tend to avoid constructive intellectual conflict in school, they often engage in it in non-school situations. The same is true of work situations. Employees tend to avoid intellectual conflicts at work, but not necessarily with their friends in leisure situations. In order to help individuals develop the competencies they need to engage in constructive intellectual conflict, instructional and work activities need to be designed to elicit intellectual conflicts. Such constructive controversies need to be structured carefully and frequently.

DEFINITION OF CONSTRUCTIVE CONTROVERSY

Constructive controversy exists when one person's ideas, information, conclusions, theories, and opinions are incompatible with those of another, and the two seek to reach an agreement that reflects their best reasoned judgment (Johnson & Johnson, 2007). The word "controversy" is derived from the Latin *controversia*, a combination of *contra*, which means "against," and *vertere*, which means "to turn." Hence, *controversia* means "to turn against" or "turned in an opposite direction." Constructive controversy involves what Aristotle called *deliberate discourse* (i.e., the discussion of the advantages and disadvantages of proposed actions) aimed at synthesizing novel solutions (i.e., *creative problem solving*). It is related to *critical discussion* in philosophy (van Eemeren & Grootendorst, 1999), which consists of participants assuming different points of view and using arguments, counterarguments, and refutations to resolve their conflicting opinions, and "elaboration," which refers to students generating connections among ideas and between ideas and prior knowledge (Wittrock, 1992). Related to controversy is *cognitive conflict* (which occurs when incompatible ideas exist simultaneously in a person's mind or when information being received does not seem to fit with what one already knows) (Johnson & Johnson, 2007).

Controversy also involves dissent and argumentation (Johnson & F. Johnson, 2013). *Dissent* may be defined as differing in opinion or conclusion, especially from the majority. Dissent often results in an argument. An *argument* is a thesis statement or claim supported by at least one reason and *arguing* is a social process in which two or more individuals engage in a dialogue where arguments are constructed, presented, and critiqued. Arguing is often called dialectical argumentation because a thesis and supporting reasons may be contradicted by an antithesis and its supporting reasons. A distinction has also been made between collaborative argumentation (the goal is to work cooperatively to explore and critique different ideas, positions, and conclusions) and adversarial argumentation (the goal is to "win" an argument as in a debate) (Brown & Renshaw, 2000; Gilbert, 1997).

Constructive controversy is a form of inquiry-based advocacy. *Advocacy* is the presenting of a position and providing reasons why others should adopt it. *Inquiry* is investigating an issue to establish the best answer or course of action; it involves asking questions and seeking to learn the necessary facts to answer the questions. Inquiry usually begins with a focal point, something that captures the participants' attention, holds it, and motivates them to investigate. Disinterested people do not inquire. The presentations create the focal point of the inquiry. *Inquiry-based advocacy*, therefore, is two or more parties presenting opposing positions in order to investigate an issue and establish the underlying facts and logic needed to reach a reasoned judgment about a course of action.

In many settings, individuals may grapple with controversial issues. Controversial issues are not the same as constructive controversy, although the controversy procedure may be useful in discussing them. A *controversial issue* is an issue for which society has not found consensus, and is considered so significant that each proposed way of dealing with the issue has ardent supporters and adamant opponents (Johnson & Johnson, 2007).

SUMMARY

Engaging in intellectual conflict is important on the personal level, the interpersonal level, the group level, the society level, and even the global level. At all levels of human interaction, the competency to engage in constructive intellectual conflicts is essential. Yet, learning how to manage intellectual conflicts constructively does not happen automatically. It happens through participating in structured constructive controversies. *Constructive controversy* exists when one person's ideas, information, conclusions, theories, and opinions are incompatible with those of another, and the two seek to reach an agreement that reflects their best reasoned judgment (Johnson & Johnson, 2007). It relates to deliberate discourse, creative problem solving, critical discussion, cognitive conflict, argumentation, and inquiry-based advocacy. In order to understand the nature of constructive controversy, the theory on which it is based must be discussed. That is the topic of Chapter 3.

3 Theory of constructive controversy

INTRODUCTION

Humans are unique as a species in being able to decide which evolutionary pathways on Earth will remain open and which will forever be closed. Human intelligence and creativity has given humanity the capacity to change the environment in which they live. This same capacity gives humanity the power to destroy the Earth. The legacy humanity has created is that if we want an animal or a plant to become extinct, we have the power to make it happen. No other creature has ever managed to do this. Even other branches of the human species did not seem to have this power. Neanderthals lived in Europe for over 100,000 years but did not significantly change the Earth's environment. *Homo Sapiens*, however, after having been on the Earth for only 40,000 years or so, may be creating global warming and the sixth major extinction in the history of the Earth (Kolbert, 2014).

There is a group of scientists who believe that global warming, the mass extinction of plants and animals, and other changes on the Earth have nothing to do with humans and their activities. It is a naturally occurring cycle. Other scientists believe that humans are responsible for the changes in the environment. Either way, regardless of the cause, the changes in the environment endanger the future of humanity. We should probably take action to ensure our long-term survival. It should be noted, however, that some scientists believe environmental change is too far advanced for anything to be done about it, and humanity is doomed and will become extinct regardless of what we now do.

Imagine that you are in charge of structuring a constructive controversy to determine the most appropriate course of action for humanity to take. When the "there is nothing we can do" position is taken off the table (as there is no use talking about it if the situation is hopeless), there are two (or more) alternatives left. One is that the future of humanity lies in its creativity and ability to find solutions to repair the damage that global warming and the sixth extinction are creating. The other is that the future of humanity lies in expanding beyond the Earth.

To structure the constructive controversy you organize two groups of scientists. The first group is assigned the position that what humans can destroy, they can rebuild. There are scientists who believe that humanity is the major cause of the changes in the Earth's environment and the ongoing extinction of its plants and animals. As the gradual destruction of the Earth's environment progresses, however, humans will find ways to reengineer the atmosphere by such methods as scattering sulfates into the stratosphere to reflect sunlight back out into space or shooting water droplets over the Pacific to brighten clouds. Or human creativity may come up with some other means of repairing the environment that no one has thought of yet. In addition, DNA banks may be used to recreate extinct plant and animal species. The essence of this position is that humans are geniuses at changing the Earth's environment to meet the short- and long-term goals of humanity and, therefore, we can equally be geniuses at making the Earth's environment safe again.

The second group of scientists is assigned the position that the Earth may be doomed, but humanity is not. These scientists may believe that humanity is the major cause of the changes in the Earth's environment and the ongoing extinction of its plants and animals. Richard Leakey, an anthropologist, for example, has warned that *Homo Sapiens* is not only the agent of the current extinction but also risks being one of its victims. Paul Ehrlich, a Stanford University ecologist, warns that in creating the conditions under which other species are becoming extinct, humanity is "sawing off the limb on which it perches." Scientists such as Leakey and Ehrlich believe that human ingenuity may be creating an environment that will no longer sustain human life. If humanity wants to survive, therefore, it will have to start colonizing other planets and moons. As soon as possible, we should start constructing colonies on Mars, Titan, Europa, the Moon, and asteroids, as well as sending colony ships to nearby star systems. The essence of this position is that as long as we keep exploring and expanding beyond the Earth, our survival is assured.

The results of such a constructive controversy would be very interesting. It should be noted that these are not the only two potential courses of action, but they are inclusive enough to start the problem-solving process. On the basis of the theory and research presented in the next four chapters, it could be predicted that the survival of humanity may depend on arguing the pros and cons of these and other positions to enable the creative problem-solving process to take place. Humanity has and will face challenges, and it is through the clash of differing positions that the ideal course of action may be revealed. This current challenge is no different.

THEORY OF CONSTRUCTIVE CONTROVERSY

The processes through which intellectual conflict leads to positive outcomes have been theorized about by developmental psychologists (Hunt, 1964; Kohlberg, 1969; Piaget, 1948, 1950), cognitive psychologists (Berlyne, 1966; Doise & Mugny, 1984; Hammond, 1965), social psychologists (Janis, 1982; Johnson, 1970, 1980; Johnson & Johnson, 1979), personality psychologists (Freud, 1930), communication experts (Smedslund, 1966), and organizational psychologists (Maier, 1970). From a social psychological perspective, perhaps the most developed theory is structure-process-outcome theory (Watson & Johnson, 1972).

Based on Kurt Lewin's (1935, 1948, 1951) field theory, structure-process-outcome theory posits that the structure of the situation determines the process of interaction, and the process of interaction determines the outcomes (e.g., attitudes and behaviors of the individuals involved) (Watson & Johnson, 1972). The quality of decision making, creative problem solving, learning, creativity, higher-level reasoning, and other outcomes of interest are determined not by the intrinsic capabilities of individuals, but rather by the pattern of interaction among individuals within a context of cultural, historical, communicative, and social influences. Thus, the way in which conflict is structured in situations determines how individuals interact with each other, which in turn determines the quality of the relevant outcomes. Conflict among group members' ideas, opinions, theories, and conclusions may be structured along a continuum (Johnson & Johnson, 2007). At one end of the continuum is constructive controversy and at the other end is concurrence seeking. Each way of structuring conflict leads to a different pattern of interaction among the individuals involved (see Table 3.1 and Figure 3.1).

Structure of situation

The structure of the situation contains (a) the role definitions and normative expectations that define what are appropriate and inappropriate ways for individuals to interact with each other in the situation, as well as (b) other situational influences, such as the number of people involved, spatial arrangements, hierarchy of prestige, social sanctions, power, and the nature of activities to be conducted (Watson & Johnson, 1972). Changes in any or all of these factors lead to changes in the processes of the system and the interactions of the members, which subsequently change the attitudes and behavior and the other outcomes of the individuals involved. Constructive controversy is structured by the following:

1. Establishing a cooperative context. Positive interdependence is structured by asking participants to come to a consensus that reflects their best reasoned judgment as to solution to the problem, the best course of action to take to solve the problem, or the best answer to a question or assignment.
2. Establishing the constructive controversy procedure. Participants (a) research and prepare a position; (b) present and advocate their position; (c) analyze, critically evaluate, and refute the opposing positions while rebutting criticisms of one's own positions; (d) reverse perspectives to communicate that they can see the issue from all points of view; and

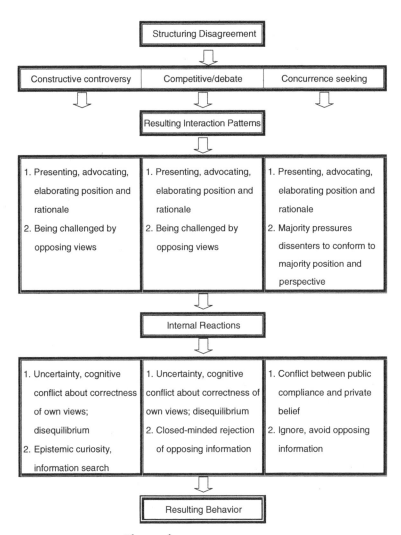

FIGURE 3.1 Theory of controversy

(e) synthesize and integrate information into factual and judgmental conclusions that are summarized into a joint position to which all sides can agree (Johnson & Johnson, 2007). This is an advocacy-based-inquiry procedure. In engaging in this procedure participants advocate a position and challenge opposing positions to gain increased understanding of the issue so that an agreement reflecting their best-reasoned judgment can be

Table 3.1 *Constructive controversy, debate, concurrence-seeking, and individudalistic processes*

	Constructive controversy	Debate	Concurrence seeking	Individualistic
Initial Conclusion	Categorizing and organizing information to derive conclusions	Categorizing and organizing information to derive conclusions	Categorizing and organizing information to derive conclusions	Categorizing and organizing information to derive conclusions
Oral Presentation	Presenting, advocating, elaborating position and rationale	Presenting, advocating, elaborating position and rationale	Presenting, advocating, elaborating position and rationale	No oral statement of positions
Level of Uncertainty	Being challenged by opposing views results in conceptual conflict and uncertainty about correctness of own views	Being challenged by opposing views results in conceptual conflict and uncertainty about correctness of own views	Being challenged by opposing views results in conceptual conflict and uncertainty about correctness of own view	Presence of only one view results in high certainty about the correctness of own views
Motivation	Epistemic curiosity motivates active search for new information and perspectives	Closed-minded rejection of opposing information and perspectives	Apprehension about differences and closed-minded adherence to own point of view	Continued high certainty about the correctness of own views

Table 3.1 (cont.)

	Constructive controversy	Debate	Concurrence seeking	Individualistic
Revised Conclusion	Reconceptualizing, synthesis, integration	Closed-minded adherence to own point of view	Quick compromise to dominant view	Adherence to own point of view
Relative Outcomes	High achievement, positive relationships, psychological health	Moderate achievement, relationships, psychological health	Low achievement, relationships, psychological health	Low achievement, relationships, psychological health

made. There is a reliance on argumentative clash to develop, clarify, expand, and elaborate one's thinking about the issues being considered. Advocacy and critically challenging the opposing positions are key elements in engaging in inquiry to discover what is the best course of action. In a controversy, participants have different perspectives and somewhat different information. This creates information interdependence between the advocates of the pro and con positions, where they have to discover how their information is complementary. Information interdependence also reduces competitive dynamics (e.g., competence threat) and increases cooperative dynamics (e.g., information exchange) as participants seek to expand their understanding of the issue (Buchs, Butera, & Mugny, 2004).

3. Adopting a number of roles that each participant needs to assume adequately. Examples are researcher, advocate, devil's advocate, learner, perspective taker, and synthesizer. Participants need to be able to research their positions and organize their findings into a coherent and compelling position. Participants also need to be effective advocates, persuasively presenting the best case possible for their positions. Participants need to be effective devil's advocates, critically analyzing opposing positions and pointing out their weaknesses and flaws in information and logic. No position should be unchallenged. Participants need to be able to learn thoroughly the opposing positions and their rationales. This facilitates their critical analysis as devil's advocates, but also facilitates their performance of the role of perspective taker. Finally, participants need to be effective synthesizers, integrating the best information and logic from all positions into a new, novel position that all participants can agree to.

4. Following a set of normative expectations that participants need to adhere to. Participants need to follow and internalize the norms of seeking the best reasoned judgment, not winning; being critical of ideas, not people; listening to and learning everyone's position, even if they do not agree with it; differentiating positions before trying to integrate them; and changing their mind when logically persuaded to do so.

Nature of concurrence seeking

Concurrence seeking exists when one person's ideas, information, conclusions, theories, and opinions are incompatible with those of another, and the two seek to inhibit discussion (to avoid any disagreement or argument), emphasize agreement, and avoid realistic appraisal of alternative ideas and courses of action (Johnson & Johnson, 2007). In concurrence seeking, individuals present their position and its rationale. If it differs from the dominant opinion, the dissenters are pressured by the majority of members to conform to the dominant opinion, and if the dissenters do not, they are viewed as non-team players who obstruct team effectiveness and, therefore, they are subjected to ridicule, rejection, ostracism, and being disliked (Collins & Porras, 1994; Freese & Fay, 2001; Nemeth & Goncalo, 2011). If they concur, they often seek out confirming information to strengthen the dominant position and view the issue only from the majority's perspective (thus eliminating the possible consideration of divergent points of view). Thus, there is a convergence of thought and a narrowing of focus in members' thinking. A false consensus results, with all members agreeing about the course of action the group is to take while privately some members may believe that other courses of action would be more effective.

Concurrence seeking is close to the *groupthink* concept of Janis (1982), in which members of a decision-making group set aside their doubts and misgivings about whatever policy is favored by the emerging consensus so as to be able to concur with the other members. The underlying motivation of groupthink is the strong desire to preserve the harmonious atmosphere of the group on which each member has become dependent for coping with the stresses of external crises and for maintaining self-esteem. Concurrence seeking is structured by the following:

1. Establishing a cooperative context (i.e., structuring positive interdependence). Participants are to come to an agreement based upon the dominant position in the group.
2. Establishing the concurrence-seeking procedure. The dominant position is determined. All participants are encouraged to agree with that position. Both advocacy of opposing positions and critical analysis of the dominant position are avoided. Participants are to "be nice" and not disagree with the

dominant position. Doubts and misgivings are to be hidden, and outward conformity in supporting the dominant position whether you believe in it or not is encouraged.

3. Assigning a number of roles (such as supporter and persuader) that each participant needs to assume adequately. Participants need to be supporters of the dominant position. They need to be persuaders of dissenters to adopt the dominant position.

4. Conforming to a set of normative expectations. Participants need to follow and internalize the norms of hiding doubts and criticisms about the dominant position, being willing to quickly compromise to avoid open disagreement, expressing full support for the dominant position, never disagreeing with other group members, and maintaining a harmonious atmosphere.

Other forms of decision making and learning

In learning and decision-making situations there are two other ways in which the situation may be structured. *Debate* exists when two or more individuals argue positions that are incompatible with one another and a judge declares a winner on the basis of who presented his or her position the best and who argued against the opposing position most persuasively (Johnson & Johnson, 2007). *Individualistic efforts* exist when individuals work alone at their own pace and with their set of materials without interacting with each other, in a situation in which their goals are unrelated and independent from each other (Johnson & Johnson, 2007).

A key to the effectiveness of conflict procedures is the mixture of cooperative and competitive elements within the procedure (see Table 3.2). The greater the cooperative elements and the less the competitive elements, the more constructive the conflict (Deutsch, 1973). Cooperative elements alone, however, do not ensure maximal productivity. There has to be both cooperation and conflict. Thus, controversy is characterized by both positive goal and resource interdependence, as well as by conflict. Debate has positive resource interdependence, negative goal interdependence, and conflict. Within concurrence seeking, there is only positive goal interdependence,

Table 3.2 *Nature of decision-making procedures*

	Controversy	Debate	Concurrence seeking	Individualistic
Positive goal interdependence	Yes	No	Yes	No
Resource interdependence	Yes	Yes	No	No
Negative goal interdependence	No	Yes	No	No
Conflict	Yes	Yes	No	No

and within individualistic learning situations there is neither interdependence nor intellectual conflict.

SUMMARY

Structure-process-outcome theory posits that the structure of the situation determines the process of interaction, and the process of interaction determines the outcomes (Watson & Johnson, 1972). The way in which conflict is structured in situations determines how individuals interact with each other, which in turn determines the quality of the relevant outcomes. Conflict among group members' ideas, opinions, theories, and conclusions may be structured along a continuum (Johnson & Johnson, 2007). At one end of the continuum is constructive controversy and at the other end is concurrence seeking. Each way of structuring conflict leads to a different pattern of interaction among the individuals involved. The structure of the situation contains (a) the role definitions and normative expectations that define what are appropriate and inappropriate ways for individuals to interact with each other in the situation, as well as (b) other situational influences, such as the number of people involved, spatial arrangements, hierarchy of prestige, social sanctions, power, and the nature of activities to be conducted (Watson & Johnson, 1972). Constructive controversy is structured by (a) establishing a cooperative context (i.e., structuring positive interdependence),

(b) establishing the constructive controversy procedure, (c) establishing a number of roles that each participant needs to assume adequately, and (d) establishing the normative expectations that participants need to adhere to. The constructive controversy procedure involves (a) researching and preparing a position, (b) advocating it, (c) refuting the opposing positions while rebutting criticisms of one's own position, (d) reversing perspectives, and (e) synthesizing the positions into a joint position to which all sides can agree (Johnson & Johnson, 2007). Two other ways of making decisions involve debate and individualistic efforts.

In the next chapter the processes of constructive controversy and concurrence seeking will be discussed in more detail.

4 The processes of constructive controversy and concurrence seeking

INTRODUCTION

How tornadoes, hurricanes, and cyclones work was once one of the great scientific mysteries, especially in the nineteenth century. The word "tornado," however, was created sometime in the late sixteenth century. It was a combination of two words *tronada*, which means thunderstorm, and *tornar*, which means to turn, twist, return. British sailors seem to have used it first. There was a mysterious quality to these storms, and people were intrigued. In the first half of the nineteenth century, there was a great "Storm War" over the nature and causes of tornadoes. On one side of the conflict was James Espy and on the other side was William Redfield.

Building on the ideas of John Dalton, Espy in the early 1800s developed the idea of what is now known as convention, in which heat creates columns of rising air that pump warmth and humidity into the cold air aloft. Clouds then form and rain falls. He believed that the mechanism that fueled tornadoes was a rapidly rising column of hot air within the mysterious black funnel of the tornado. He did not believe that the funnel cloud was rotating. Rather, he believed that the winds were drawn into the central column from all sides in perfectly straight lines, like the spokes of a wagon wheel and from there they rose up in perfectly straight lines through the clouds to the sky. The updraft was created by the differences in temperature and pressure between the surface and the upper air. At the end of the 1830s, Espy was awarded the title "Storm King" by the reporters covering his appearances.

In 1821 William Redfield followed the aftermath of a severe storm and noticed that some of the trees were knocked down by a wind from the east while other trees were knocked down by winds from the west. While on the surface it looked as if two identical storms had passed each other in opposite directions, he proposed that the storm had been a gigantic whirlwind, spinning around a moving center like a top. When he published his views, he was scorned and criticized by James Espy, who believed that if a circular motion existed in a storm the outward motion would destroy the storm immediately unless there was some other unknown force preventing it. Redfield took the criticism personally. His response seemed to be marked by vindictive rage. He began mocking Espy's theory as nonsensical. Redfield engaged in personal attacks, expressing his view that Espy was a liar and a manipulator whose entire career was a sham. Redfield stated that the endorsements Espy received from the scientific establishment were fraudulent. Espy somehow wrote all of his endorsements himself and contrived to get them published.

Espy was shocked by Redfield's response and immediately wrote him a private conciliatory letter, in which he invited Redfield to come to Philadelphia and take part in his recently founded club, the "Franklin Kite Club." Redfield refused. He avoided Espy, refusing even to meet him. Espy later invited Redfield to tour with him, in which they could publicly present their competing theories and debate each theory's merits. Espy pointed out that there was a great deal of public interest in tornadoes and the debates would be well attended, ensuring considerable financial gain for Redfield as well as himself. Redfield angrily refused, implying he would not be seen on the same stage with someone so morally lacking as Espy. Throughout their lives, Espy kept making cooperative overtures to Redfield, trying to find ways to make money and gain fame through debates and side-by-side presentations of their conflicting theories. He was convinced, however, that he was "right" and Redfield was "wrong" and that in the debates he would win. Redfield stayed angry, competitive, and destructive and never consented to any of Espy's proposals.

Redfield died in 1857 of pneumonia. Espy died in 1860. By then the public was no longer interested in tornadoes. Until their deaths, both Espy and Redfield rigidly adhered to their theories without any real consideration of the validity of the other view. In 1856, however, William Ferrel proposed a theory that reconciled Espy's and Redfield's theories. He proposed that Espy was right in that the storms were powered by convection; but as the convection columns rise, they are deformed by the Coriolis effect (i.e., the rotation of the Earth causes a slight but continuous drag and deflection in the atmosphere), which changed the straight-line inflowing winds that Espy imagined into the spiraling whirlwinds described by Redfield. The theories of Espy and Redfield were not irreconcilable opposites, but two halves of the same process. Perhaps if the two men had interacted, discussed their theories and the data supporting them, tried to see where the theories were compatible and contradictory, they could have moved on to really understand the nature of tornadoes. Unfortunately, Redfield's refusal to discuss the nature of tornadoes with Espy, or even talk to him at all, probably prevented Espy and Redfield from discovering the complementarity of their theories and from actually understanding the nature of tornadoes.

Espy and Redfield represent the success of intellectual conflict to drive science forward. Unfortunately for them, it was a third party (i.e., Ferrell) who integrated the two positions into a much superior approximation of the "truth." What Espy and Redfield lacked was a process and procedure by which their differing theories could be discussed, understood, and creatively integrated into a new, more powerful theory. In this chapter the processes of constructive controversy and concurrence seeking are presented. The process of controversy would have made all the difference to Espy and Redfield.

PROCESS OF CONSTRUCTIVE CONTROVERSY

The process by which controversy results in such outcomes as high-quality learning and decision making, productivity, creativity, innovation, positive relationships, and psychological health is outlined in Table 4.1 and Figures 4.1 and 4.2. During a constructive controversy, participants proceed through the following process (Johnson &

Table 4.1 *Process of controversy and concurrence seeking*

Controversy	Concurrence seeking
Organizing what is known into an initial conclusion	Organizing what is known into an initial conclusion
Presenting, advocating, elaborating position and rationale	Presenting, advocating, elaborating dominant position and rationale
Being challenged by opposing views results in conceptual conflict and uncertainty about correctness of own views	Majority pressures dissenting group members to conform to majority position and perspective creating a conflict between public compliance and private belief
Conceptual conflict, uncertainty, disequilibrium result	Conflict between public and private position
Epistemic curiosity motivates active search for new information and perspectives	Seeking confirming information that strengthens and supports the dominant position and perspective
Reconceptualization, synthesis, integration resulting in consensus consisting of best joint reasoned judgment reflecting all points of view	Consensus on majority position, often false consensus due to members publicly agreeing while privately disagreeing

F. Johnson, 2013; Johnson & R. T. Johnson, 1979, 1989, 2000b, 2003, 2007, 2009a; Johnson, Johnson, & Johnson, 1976): forming an initial conclusion, advocating one's conclusion while being confronted with opposing conclusions from other people, becoming uncertain about the correctness of one's conclusion, searching for more information and a better perspective, coming to a new reconceptualized position. Each of these steps is discussed below.

Step 1: Organizing information and deriving conclusions

When individuals are presented with an issue, problem, or decision, they have an initial conclusion based on categorizing and organizing their current (but usually limited) information, experience, and

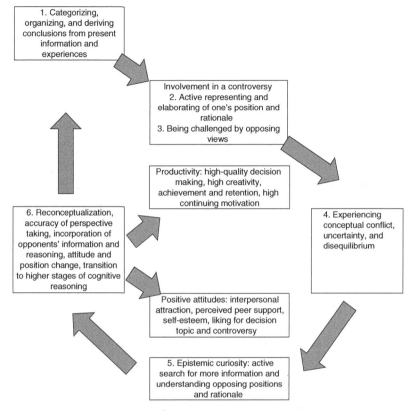

FIGURE 4.1 Process of controversy 1

perspective (Johnson & F. Johnson, 2013; Johnson & R. T. Johnson, 2007). They build this conclusion by identifying the decision to be made or the problem to be solved, thinking of the proper alternatives, adequately evaluating them, and choosing the most promising one. Individuals tend to have a high degree of confidence in their initial conclusion (i.e., they freeze the epistemic process). In building their conclusion, individuals must conceptualize by (a) forming concepts, (b) interrelating them into a conceptual structure, and (c) logically deriving conclusions.

Anything that interferes with the conceptualizing process is a barrier to problem solving, decision making, and learning. Three interrelated barriers are (a) uncritically giving one's dominant response to the situation, (b) mental sets, and (c) fixation on the first satisfactory solution generated. First, responses may be arranged hierarchically (Berlyne, 1965; Maier, 1970) and, when confronted with a problem, individuals may quickly respond with their *dominant response* (without thinking of, evaluating, and choosing among all the alternatives). Dominant responses based on physical states such as hunger can affect which stimuli a person attends to (Levine, Chein, & Murphy, 1942; McClelland & Atkinson, 1948), psychological states such as attitudes and beliefs (Allport & Postman, 1945; Iverson & Schwab, 1967; Shipley & Veroff, 1952), and one's general cultural frame of reference (Bartlett, 1932). The second barrier, *mental sets*, can cause the same words to have different meanings for different persons (Foley & MacMillan, 1943), the adoption of solutions that have been previously useful (Luchins, 1942), the perception only of what is expected (Neisser, 1954), and the interpretation of ambiguous events in ways that confirm expectations (Bruner & Minturn, 1955). The third barrier is individuals' tendency to become *fixated* on the first reasonable solution thought of – this is called *satisficing* (Simon, 1976).

These barriers reflect the facts that in many instances people are lazy cognitive processors (they do not actively process the information that is available or do not fully consider the alternative ways of understanding such information [Langer, Blank, & Chanowitz, 1978; Taylor, 1980]) and do not think divergently. *Divergent thinking* results in more ideas (fluency) and more classes of ideas (flexibility) (Guilford, 1956). To ensure that divergent thinking takes place and all major alternatives to the problem being considered are given a fair hearing, each alternative has to be presented in a complete and persuasive way.

Controversy involves assigning the major alternatives to advocacy subgroups and having each subgroup (a) develop its alternative in depth and (b) plan how to present the best case possible for its alternative to the rest of the group. Preparing a position to be advocated within a problem-solving group has clear effects on how well the position is understood and the level of reasoning used in thinking about the position. There is evidence that when individuals know that they will have to present the best case possible for Alternative A to the group as a whole, and try to convince the other group members to adopt Alternative A, they tend to understand Alternative A better than if they had simply considered it for their own use (Allen, 1976; Benware, 1975; Gartner, Kohler, & Reissman, 1971). Higher-level conceptual under-standing and reasoning are promoted when individuals know they have to teach each other a common way to think about problem situations (Johnson & Johnson, 1979; Murray, 1983). The way people conceptualize and organize material cognitively is likely to be markedly different when they learn material to teach to others compared to learning material for their own benefit (Annis, 1983; Bargh & Schul, 1980; Murray, 1983). Material learned to be taught has been found to be learned at a higher conceptual level than has material learned for one's own use.

There are conditions under which individuals will gather and organize facts, information, and theories into a rationale to support a thesis statement and there are conditions under which they will not. Three of the conditions that may affect the adequacy of a person's preparation are as follows:

1. **The presence of social and cognitive skills involved in formulating a rationale to support the thesis statement is the first condition.** The person needs the skills of searching out relevant evidence and organizing it into a coherent and logical rationale. Doing so as part of a team requires a wide variety of interpersonal and small group skills (Johnson & F. Johnson, 2013).
2. **The effort expended in doing so is the second condition.** The more the effort expended, the more the position is valued. Individuals generally have an enhanced regard for their own productions relative to others' (Greenwald & Albert, 1968), and the effort spent in preparing a position may be a source of enhanced regard for one's position (Zimbardo, 1965).
3. **The ego- or task orientation underlying the person's efforts is the third condition.** *Ego-oriented efforts* tend to focus on proving one is "right" and "better," while *task-oriented efforts* tend to focus on contributing to a process of making the best decision possible (Nicholls, 1983).

Thus, adequate preparation of the position to be advocated is dependent on four things. First, in being skilled in searching out relevant evidence. Second, in working with others to organize it into a coherent and logical rationale. Third, on being willing to expend considerable effort in doing so. Fourth, on being task-oriented.

Step 2:   Presenting and advocating positions

Step two in the constructive controversy process is presenting and advocating one's positions to others who, in turn, are advocating opposing positions. *Advocacy* is the presenting of a position and providing reasons why others should adopt it (Johnson & F. Johnson, 2013; Johnson & R. T. Johnson, 2007). The intent is to convert the other group members to one's position. *Conversion* requires that other group members become convinced that the presenter's position is the best of the available alternatives. Conversion is reached through a process of argument and counterargument aimed at persuading others to adopt, modify, or drop positions. Three of the immediate aspects of advocacy are cognitive rehearsal, reactance, and commitment. When individuals present their conclusion and its rationale to others, they engage in cognitive rehearsal and elaboration, which results in increased understanding of the position, discovery of higher-level reasoning processes, discovery of a greater amount of information and variety of facts, and changes in the salience of known information, thereby deepening their understanding of the problem or decision (Johnson & Johnson, 1989). Knowing that the presenting group member is trying to convert them, the other group members scrutinize the person's position and critically analyze it, as part of their resistance to being converted (Baker & Petty, 1994; Erb, Bohner, Rank, & Einwiller, 2002; Hewstone & Martin, 2008; Mackie, 1987). *Reactance* is an emotional reaction to pressure or persuasion that results in the strengthening or adoption of a contrary belief (Brehm & Brehm, 1981). Thus, advocacy can backfire if it creates resistance or reactance in the listeners. A way to minimize reactance is to portray oneself as being similar to the listening members (Silvia, 2005). Finally, advocating a position and defending it against refutation tends to increase a person's commitment to the position (Johnson & F. Johnson, 2013).

Advocating a position and defending it against refutation requires engaging in considerable cognitive rehearsal and elaboration. A number of research studies have found that individuals engaged in controversy (compared with those engaged in debate, concurrence seeking, and individualistic efforts) contributed more information to the discussion, more frequently repeated information, shared new information, elaborated the material being discussed, presented more ideas, presented more rationale, made more higher–level processing statements, made more comments aimed at managing their efforts to make high-quality decisions, made fewer intermediate-level cognitive processing statements, and made more statements managing the group's work (Johnson & Johnson, 1985; Johnson, Johnson, Pierson, & Lyons, 1985; Johnson, Johnson, & Tiffany, 1984; Lowry & Johnson, 1981; Nijhof & Kommers, 1982; Smith, Johnson, & Johnson, 1981, 1984). Disagreements within a group tend to result in a greater amount of information and variety of facts being exchanged as well as changes in the salience of known information (Anderson & Graesser, 1976; Kaplan, 1977; Kaplan & Miller, 1977; Vinokur & Burnstein, 1974). Group members, furthermore, tend to be more effective in teaching information to each other than are specially trained experts (Fisher, 1969; Sarbin, 1976). Individuals tend to be particularly prone to increase their commitment to a cause that they attempt to persuade another to adopt (Nel, Helmreich, & Aronson, 1969). Finally, for a presentation to be credible, and to have impact on the other participants in a controversy, a position must be persistently presented with consistency and confidence and, if possible, advocated by more than one person (Nemeth, Swedlund, & Kanki, 1974; Nemeth & Wachtler, 1983).

Explaining
An aspect of presenting a position is explaining the position and the reasons why others should adopt it. There is mixed evidence

concerning the value of explanations. Webb (1991, 1995) found that levels and elaborativeness of explanations in cooperative groups predicted more individual learning in mathematics, with the highest levels of achievement associated with giving explanations. Chinn, O'Donnell, and Jinks (2000) found in a study with fifth-grade students that the more complex the explanation given by a student, the greater the student's learning gains. There is also evidence that peer discussions promote achievement most effectively when students attempt to abstract general principles in conjunction with experimental testing of their hypotheses (Amigues, 1988; Heller, Keith, & Anderson, 1992; Howe, Tolmie, Greer, & Mackenzie, 1995; Linn & Elyon, 2000; Teasley, 1995). Buchs and Butera (2004) in the first study found that giving answers is more beneficial for recall performance than is listening to a partner give the answer, and that when students in a controversy had complementary information, they had better recall of the information about the issue than when they had the same information. Complementary information seemed to change the way students listened to each other. The evidence, however, is not consistent. Ploetzner, Dillenbourg, Preier, and Traum (1999) reviewed a number of studies and concluded that explaining to others was less effective in increasing achievement than was self-explaining and about as effective as listening (e.g., Bargh & Schul, 1980; Coleman, Brown, & Rivkin, 1997; Teasley, 1997). It may be that explaining increases achievement only when the student conceptually reorganizes the material so that the listener can understand it (Coleman et al., 1997). What is not discussed in the explanation literature, however, is whether the explanation being given challenges the thinking of the listener. The explainer will know that the listener will be listening critically and trying to find fault with it so that it can be refuted. This may increase the explainer's motivation to present a compelling explanation, which increases the likelihood that the explainer will cognitively reconceptualize the explanation while he or she is giving it.

Step 3: Being challenged by opposing views

In controversy, advocates of one position challenge the positions of opposing advocates (Johnson & Johnson, 1979, 1989, 2009a). Members critically analyze one another's positions in attempts to discern weaknesses and strengths. They attempt to refute opposing positions while rebutting attacks on their own position. At the same time, they are aware that they need to learn the information being presented and understand the perspective of the other group members. Hearing opposing positions tends to unfreeze the epistemic process. Individuals engaged in controversy become motivated to know, understand, and appreciate the others' positions. Hearing opposing views being advocated, furthermore, stimulates new cognitive analysis and frees individuals to create alternative and original conclusions. Even being confronted with an erroneous point of view can result in more divergent thinking and the generation of novel and more cognitively advanced solutions.

When a group member presents his or her conclusion or claim, other group members may respond with an evaluation of its validity by agreeing (thus encouraging continuation of the current thinking) or by disagreeing (thus encouraging a change in the current thinking). Disagreement can be expressed directly or indirectly through such strategies as questioning. Disagreement can create recognition of problems or difficulties in the proposed positions and motivate group members to address them. It can also create an awareness of a gap in understanding, which then motivates a search for more knowledge. A disagreement (even if wrong) may increase the attention of group members (De Dreu & West, 2001; Nemeth & Rogers, 1996). Disagreement may stimulate group members to consider more aspects of a problem from more perspectives and thereby increase the creativity of their thinking. Furthermore, disagreement can free others to express ideas opposed to the majority point of view (i.e., weakens the pressures to conform to majority opinion) (Johnson & F. Johnson, 2013; Nemeth &

Chiles, 1988), and disagreement, regardless of its validity, tends to legitimize differing positions, freeing all group members to express their ideas, including ideas that are unrelated to the specific disagreement (Nemeth & Chiles, 1988). Multiple studies have demonstrated that opposing views (Nemeth, 1986), disconfirmatory information (Toma & Butera, 2009), unfamiliar arguments (Garcia-Marques & Mackie, 2001), diverging evidence (Kruglanski, 1980), and counterintuitive findings (Berlyne, 1960; Piaget, 1985) can generate deeper information processing and more elaborate knowledge than being confronted by familiar arguments or confirmatory evidence. The more authentic the opposing view appears to be, the more effective it may be (Nemeth, Brown, & Rogers, 2001).

Some of the major issues in facing dissent are socio-cognitive conflict, argumentation, majority versus minority influence, and confirmation bias. Each is discussed below.

Socio-cognitive conflict

Socio-cognitive conflict theory states that social interaction represents the very context for progress and learning, precisely because the diversity in training, knowledge, and points of view across group or dyad members has the potential to create dissent and discussion. Dissent occurring during social interaction is called "socio-cognitive conflict" because it is both social (it entails disagreement between two or more persons) and cognitive (as disagreement leads each individual to question her or his own answer) (Doise & Mugny, 1984; Doise & Palmonari, 1984; Mugny, Perret-Clermont, & Doise, 1981). Dissenters tend to stimulate divergent thinking and the consideration of multiple perspectives. Members start with the assumption that the dissenter is not correct. If a dissenter persists, however, it suggests a complexity that stimulates a reappraisal of the issue. The reappraisal involves divergent thinking and a consideration of multiple sources of information and ways of thinking about the issue. On balance, this increases the quality of decision making and finding creative solutions to problems (Nemeth, 1995). On non-routine tasks, conflict over the nature of the decision may cause the group to evaluate information more critically (Postmes, Spears, & Cihangir, 2001) and break the tendency of groups to try to achieve consensus before all available alternatives have been thoroughly considered (Janis, 1971, 1972).

In order for argumentation to enhance conceptual understanding of content, there needs to be a focus in the discussions on resolving socio-cognitive conflict. Participants need to consider and evaluate diverse views (Nussbaum, 2008a). Participants need to use elaborative and metacognitive strategies to understand the conceptual principles being discussed. In the discussions, they need to implement the social and cognitive norms needed to spark their creativity. Finally, they need to take sufficient time to reflect on the issues being discussed and the conceptual principles and the various courses of action being proposed.

Argumentation

Being challenged by opposing views is the beginning of an argument. An important aspect of constructive controversy, therefore, is argumentation. Argumentation is a social process in which individuals work together cooperatively to establish the "truth" or best reasoned judgment about an issue (Golanics & Nussbaum, 2008; Johnson & Johnson, 2007). Argumentation is a cooperative activity, in which individuals work together to achieve a joint goal of constructing and critiquing arguments (Golanics & Nussbaum, 2008). There are two ways in which the word "argument" may be used. The first is as a product. An *argument* may be defined as a connected series of statements intended to establish a proposition (Johnson & Johnson, 2007). It consists of three parts, a thesis statement or claim, a rationale for the claim, and a conclusion (that is the same as the thesis statement). Thus, an example of the structure of an argument is, "My thesis is that global warming exists; because of A, B, and C, I conclude that global warming exists." Argument may be differentiated from *contradiction*, which is simply the automatic naysaying of any statement others make. The second use of the word "argument" is as a process in which two or more individuals engage in a dialogue where opposing arguments are constructed and critiqued to determine whether propositions are true or false. As a process, argumentation is a verbal, social, rational activity aimed at convincing a reasonable critic of the acceptability of a proposition (Van Eemeren, 2003; Van Eemeren, Grootendorst, Jackson, & Jacobs, 1996). While most of the empirical research on argument has been devoted to argument as product, everyday life may be far more characterized by the process of arguing.

Arguers may justify the acceptability of their position either by providing justification in favor of their point of view or by rebutting alternative standpoints (Van Eemeren, 2003). When engaging in an intellectual argument, arguers should assure themselves not only that their own claims are valid but also that alternative positions are not more sound or more correct than their own. From Aristotle and Quintilianus on, *confirmatio* (i.e., providing evidence in favor of one's claims) and *refutatio* (i.e., providing evidence against competing standpoints, in order to rebut them) have been considered as holding a comparable function in argumentative discourses (cf. Mosconi, 1990; Toulmin, 1958; Van Eemeren, 2003). Karl Popper (1962) stated that skilled arguers use conjectures to support their own claims and refutations to show weakness in opponents' arguments in order to undermine the opponents' positions (Baron, 2008; Ennis, 1993; Kuhn & Udell, 2007; Van Eemeren et al., 1996; Walton, 1985). Empirical research on argumentation, however, indicates that arguers share a strong preference for the choice of arguments that support their own points of view, and hardly even engage in rebutting possible alternative claims (Kuhn, 1991; Meyers, Brashers, & Hanner, 2000; Pontecorvo & Girardet, 1993). This is sometimes known as confirmatory bias in argumentation (Kuhn, 1991). While arguments may occur in any group, the greater the heterogeneity among members, the greater the amount of time spent in argumentation (Nijhof & Kommers, 1982).

An important part of the history of argumentation lies in the field of philosophy. Both the formal and dialectical nature of arguments were discussed by Aristotle (Walton, 2003), and contemporary philosophical work in argumentation emphasizes the use of the categories of claim, grounds, warrants (linking ground to claims), backing, rebuttals, and qualifiers (Toulmin, 1958). Walton's (1999) model of "The New Dialectic" analyzes rules of discourse and use of argumentation schemes in the context of specific sorts of dialogue, for example, persuasive discussions, inquiries, negotiations, and so forth (see Nussbaum, 2008b; Duschl, 2007). Van Eemeren and Grootendorst (1999) developed a model of critical discussion that prescribes rules of discourse that participants must follow. Proponents of both the product and process views of argumentation conclude that students benefit from encountering ideas that are different from their own, especially when other group members provide alternative perspectives on issues and present reasons and evidence as to the perspectives' validity (Chinn, 2006). Students need to engage in discussions in which they consider and evaluate diverse views (Nussbaum, 2008a).

Majority and minority influence
For constructive controversy to exist, a number of alternative courses of action or solutions (i.e., positions) must be proposed and advocated. These positions, however, are rarely supported by an equal number of group members. There often is one position that is supported by the majority of group members, while other positions tend to be advocated by a minority of members. Thus, a group may have a majority position and one or more minority positions. Sometimes, a group may have a number of minority positions without any majority position, at least initially. The literature concerning the differential effects of majority and minority influence on recipients' cognitive processes originates primarily from Moscovici's (1980) conversion theory and Mackie's (1987) objective consensus approach.

Majority influence on minority members In most groups, there is movement toward the majority opinion. Majorities start with positive judgments and expectations (e.g., they are correct and their approval is important). Majorities tend to exert more influence than do minorities

(Tanford & Penrod, 1984). Kalven and Zeisel (1966), for example, documented in a study of 225 juries that the majority position on the first ballot (i.e., held by 7–11 jury members) was the final verdict in over 85 percent of the cases. Such movement to the majority position is often based on information influence (group members believe that majority judgments give more accurate information about reality) and normative influence (group members want to be accepted and avoid disapproval) (Deutsch & Gerard, 1955). The majority may exert influence through arousing fear in other group members, such as the fear of being seen as a "non-team player" (i.e., being deviant) and/or the fear of being seen as a person who has poor judgment (i.e., who is wrong). Holders of minority positions may wish to abandon their positions and join the majority position in order to avoid being seen as deviant or as being wrong. Both can lead to ostracism and loss of respect. Especially in competitive groups, members may not wish to be seen as wrong, as it signifies they are "losers."

Majority influence also can operate through compliance and conformity (Moscovici, 1980). *Compliance*, which is accepting the dominant point of view, unfortunately, reduces cognitive reasoning and learning (Mugny, De Paolis, & Carugati, 1984; Mugny, Doise, & Perret-Clermont, 1975–1976), whether it is compliance due to unilateral decision in peer learning (Carugati, De Paolis, & Mugny, 1980–1981; Mugny & Doise, 1978) or to asymmetric adult–child relationships (Mugny, Giroud, & Doise, 1978–1979, Study 1). When exposed to a majority position, group members holding a minority position often conform to the majority position without a detailed scrutiny of its content (Nemeth & Rogers, 1996). They may even search for information to validate, confirm, and strengthen it (i.e., confirmatory bias), whereas those confronted with a minority opinion are more likely to generate more diagnostic disconfirmatory examples (i.e., disconfirmatory bias) (Butera, Mugny, Legrenzi, & Perez, 1996). Majority individuals tended to induce the use of confirmatory strategies even when the strategy proposed by the source was disconfirmatory (Legrenzi, Butera, Mugny, & Perez, 1991), and regardless of the targets' awareness that the solution proposed by the source was incorrect (Butera & Mugny, 1992). When faced with the majority position, individuals tend to view the issue from the perspective posed by the majority (i.e., excluding other perspectives), utilize the strategies proposed by the majority while ignoring other strategies for solving the problem (Nemeth & Kwan, 1987), utilize only the majority dimension of focus (Nemeth, Mosier, & Chiles, 1992; Peterson & Nemeth, 1996), agree with the majority position without considering other positions (Nemeth & Wachtler, 1983), recall less information (Nemeth et al., 1992), and show less creativity (Nemeth & Kwan, 1985). The attitudes formed following majority influence tend to yield to counter-persuasion unless there is a secondary task that encourages message processing (Martin, Hewstone, & Martin, 2007).

Movement to the majority position usually occurs early within the group discussion (Asch, 1956). Majority viewpoints seem to be considered seriously from the beginning. Majorities induce a concentration on the position they propose (Nemeth, 1976, 1986). Persons exposed to opposing majority views focus on the aspects of the stimuli pertinent to the position of the majority, they think in convergent ways, and they tend toward adoption of the proposed solution to the neglect of novel solutions or decisions. The quality of the solution or decision depends on the validity of the initial majority position. Majority influence often results in overt compliance without private or latent change to majority views (Allen, 1965; Moscovici & Lage, 1976).

Finally, much more stress is reported in majority influence situations than in minority influence ones, presumably because in the former individuals feared that they were wrong and that the majority would reject them, while in the latter individuals could deride the minority and their opposing views (Asch, 1956; Maass & Clark, 1984; Nemeth, 1976; Nemeth & Wachtler, 1983). The stress induced by the majority tends to narrow the focus of attention and increase the likelihood that the strongest and most dominant response would be engaged in (Zajonc, 1965). The more moderate stress experienced when facing minority opposition may stimulate individuals to consider more aspects of the situation and more possible conclusions.

Mackie's (1987) objective consensus approach predicts that group members infer that a position held by a majority of group members is more likely to be valid than a position held only by a minority. Therefore, group members generally expect to agree with the majority's opinion. But when it appears that the majority opinion is not valid, group members who hold minority positions are motivated to engage in careful scrutiny of the content of the majority's message (De Dreu & De Vries, 1996; Mackie, 1987). Thus, majorities as well as minorities can foster extensive and careful information processing under certain conditions (Shuper & Sorrentino, 2004).

Minority influence on majority members When alternatives to the majority position are presented by one or more group members (i.e., a minority), supporters of the majority position tend to feel (a) no pressure to conform to the minority position and (b) quite free to reject it, since minority positions are often perceived as invalid, undesirable, or even threatening. Hence, majority individuals may discount minority positions. Minority influence is based on conversion (Moscovici, 1980). At the very least, holders of the majority position may only respond to a minority position after giving it a deep scrutiny of its content, which includes both the minority position and the rationale for its validity. Minority positions have to be persuasive on their merits (while majority positions do not). Proponents of the majority position, after giving a minority position deep scrutiny, tend to utilize more strategies in completing tasks (Nemeth & Kwan, 1987), recall more information (Nemeth et al., 1992), demonstrate more flexibility in thought (Peterson & Nemeth, 1996), demonstrate more originality (Nemeth & Kwan, 1985), and more frequently detect correct solutions (Atsumi & Burnstein, 1992; Nemeth & Wachtler, 1983). When group members present minority positions, confirmatory biases in both inductive reasoning (Butera, Mugny, Legrenzi, & Perez, 1996; Legrenzi, Butera, Mugny, & Perez, 1991) and in information seeking (Maggi, Butera,

Legrenzi, & Mugny, 1998) tend to be reduced. When a minority dissents, there is a relatively unbiased search for more information on all sides of the issue; that is, individuals exposed to a dissenting minority view chose to read more articles than did those exposed to a dissenting majority view (Nemeth & Rogers, 1996). Finally, the presentation of minority positions tends to instigate systematic processing of its arguments, leading to attitudes that resist counter-persuasion (Martin et al., 2007).

There are several reasons why group members who hold minority positions have a difficult time influencing members who hold a majority position (Johnson & F. Johnson, 2013). First, there is skepticism. Minority positions are often considered to be incorrect and are dismissed by members who support the majority position. Minority positions also are often viewed negatively, sometimes with downright derision (Nemeth & Wachtler, 1983).

Second, members holding the majority position may be afraid to change their views. They may fear being wrong (the other majority members would then deride them and they may be perceived as "losers"), and they may fear losing membership in the majority (the other majority members would reject them) (Asch, 1956; Maass & Clark, 1984; Nemeth, 1976; Nemeth & Wachtler, 1983).

Third, group members who hold the majority position have to be converted through information and logic to believe in the minority position. That means they have to exert effort to learn new information and critically evaluate the validity of the minority's arguments. Minorities, compared with majorities, stimulate a greater consideration of their positions and, therefore, persons exposed to opposing minority views tend to exert more cognitive effort, attend to more aspects of the situation, think in more divergent ways, and detect more novel solutions and new decisions (Nemeth, 1976, 1986). On the balance, the novel solutions and new decisions tend to be more correct or of higher quality. In addition, members who initially supported the majority position are stimulated to reappraise the entire situation by considering minority positions, and their reappraisal may include alternatives other than those being proposed. In other words, their thought processes are marked by divergence and, hence, the potential for detecting novel solutions and decisions.

Fourth, minority influences may be latent, being detected in subsequent situations where individuals make solitary judgments (Moscovici & Lage, 1976; Moscovici, Lage, & Naffrechoux, 1969; Mugny, 1982; Nemeth & Wachtler, 1974). In other words, the effects of minority influences may be delayed as well as immediate.

Fifth, it may take some time for minority influence to be exerted. Movement to the minority position often occurs late in the group discussion (Nemeth et al. 1974; Nemeth & Wachtler, 1974, 1983). Minority viewpoints need time because it is the consistency and confidence with which the minority positions are argued that results in their receiving serious consideration (Moscovici & Faucheux, 1972; Moscovici & Nemeth, 1974). With consistency and confidence on the minority's part over time, individuals may ask, "How can they be so wrong and yet so sure of themselves?"

Finally, the relevance of the issue may affect the influence of minority positions. There is consistent evidence that the presentation of minority positions in high-relevance conditions may foster more extensive scrutiny of their content than the presentation of the majority position in low-relevance conditions (i.e., when it does not entail any direct consequence to the group members) (Martin & Hewstone, 2003; Mucchi-Faina & Cicoletti, 2006; Tomasetto, Mucchi-Faina, Alparone, & Pagliaro, 2009). There is less consistent evidence that the presentation of the majority position fosters more extensive scrutiny than the presentation of minority positions in high-relevance conditions (e.g., Martin et al., 2007). When an issue was of low relevance, participants exposed to the minority position developed more rebuttals than participants exposed to the majority position, whereas when the issue was of high relevance no difference between the numbers of rebuttals emerged (Tomasetto et al., 2009). Thus, it may be that it is only for low-relevance issues that minority influence may exert beneficial effects on decision making. Conversion theory, therefore, may not apply in high-relevance conditions.

In summary, majority influence may lead to compliance and conformity without critical analysis of the arguments or position, while minority influence may lead to critical analysis and deeper understanding by the majority members. When exposed to the majority position, many group members may engage in seeking confirmatory bias.

Confirmatory bias

When exposed to a majority position, group members holding a minority position often search for information to validate, confirm, and strengthen the majority position. *Confirmatory bias* is the tendency to generate arguments that support one's own claims, rather than rebuttals that challenge alternative standpoints (Klaczynski, 2000; Kuhn, 1991; Perkins, Farady, & Bushey, 1991). Sometimes known as confirmatory bias, it is a tendency to search for or interpret information in a way that confirms one's preconceptions. It involves testing ideas in a one-sided way – focusing on one possibility and ignoring alternatives. Searching only for evidence that confirms one's position is a widespread tendency that can be harmful to decision making. Confirmatory bias has been found in formal reasoning (Kahneman, 2003; Wason, 1960), selective exposure to information (Fisher, Jonas, Frey, & Schultz-Hardt, 2005), social perceptions (Zuckerman, Knee, Hodgins, & Miyake, 1995), and stereotyping (Leyens, Dardeene, Yzerbyt, Scaillet, & Snyder, 1999). Preference for arguments in support of one's own claims persists even among highly educated adults (Means & Voss, 1996; Sandoval & Millwood, 2005). There is considerable evidence that people prefer supportive to non-supportive information (Brock & Balloun, 1967; Ehrich, Guttman, Schonbach, & Mills, 1957; Freedman & Sears, 1963, 1965, 1967; Lowin, 1967, 1969; Mills, 1967; Sears & Freedman, 1967), especially when there is a choice (Frey & Wicklund, 1978) and decision irreversibility (Frey, 1981, 1986; Frey & Rosch, 1984).

In constructive controversies, confirmation bias must be reduced if an effective solution is to be found. The focus must be as much on rebutting opposing arguments as on presenting supporting information for one's own. Rate of rebuttals increases with age and education (Felton & Kuhn, 2001; Kuhn, 1991; Kuhn & Udell, 2003; Piolat, Roussey, & Gombert, 1999), with the acquisition of specific expertise in good thinking strategies (Hidi, Berndorff, & Ainley, 2002; Knudson, 1992; Kuhn, 1991; Kuhn, Shaw, & Felton, 1997), and as one's interest in and personal relevance of the issue increases (Kuhn & Udell, 2003).

Myside bias Closely related to confirmatory bias is myside bias. *Myside bias* is the tendency for people to evaluate evidence, generate evidence, and test hypotheses with a preference toward their own prior opinions and attitudes (Stanovich, West, & Toplak, 2013). Since critical thinkers should be able to decouple their prior beliefs and opinions from the evaluation of evidence and arguments, myside bias may be seen as a subclass of confirmation bias (McKenzie, 2004) and may be negatively related to active open-minded thinking (Baron, 2008). It is a form of egocentrism. Thus, the greater the myside bias, the less likely individuals are to make creative, well-formulated decisions or answers.

Step 4: Conceptual conflict, disequilibrium, and uncertainty

Individuals tend to experience conceptual conflict, disequilibrium, and uncertainty when faced with hearing other alternatives being advocated, having one's position criticized and refuted, and being challenged by information that is incompatible with and does not fit with one's conclusions (Johnson & Johnson, 1979, 1989, 2007, 2009b). In order to understand this step of the constructive controversy process, it is necessary to define conceptual conflict, disequilibrium, and uncertainty, and it is also necessary to discuss the conditions necessary for these three phenomena to occur.

Both the terms "cognitive conflict" and "conceptual conflict" are used to describe the internal conflict that leads to growth in cognitive reasoning and learning. In this article the latter term will be used. A *conceptual conflict* occurs when incompatible ideas exist simultaneously in a person's mind or when information being received does not seem to fit with what one already knows (Berlyne, 1957, 1966). An example is when the same amount of water is poured into two glasses – one is tall and skinny and the other is short and fat. The student knows that each glass holds the same amount of water but at the same time believes that the tall glass has more water in it. If more than one answer is possible, the potential for questioning the validity of one's own answer exists, resulting in possible cognitive conflict (see Berlyne, 1960; Limon, 2001; Piaget, 1985). Questioning the validity of one's own answer may then lead one to "decenter" from one's point of view and take seriously into account the other's position (Butera & Buchs, 2005). To account for the existence of different points of view, one must process and understand the elements that might explain why another person holds another position, which can result in an increase in knowledge. In sum, socio-cognitive conflict prompts individuals to reconsider their own point of view and to integrate others' points of view. Dewey (1910), Festinger (1957), Piaget (1964), and Berlyne (1965) have all discussed the importance of conceptual conflict in cognitive development and learning. Creating cognitive conflict in and of itself, however, does not necessarily promote conceptual change (Dekkers & Thijs, 1998; Dreyfus, Jungwirth, & Eliovitch, 1990; Elizabeth & Galloway, 1996), as group members may simply refuse to accept ideas in direct conflict with their own (Bergquist & Heikkinen, 1990). It is only within certain conditions, such as a cooperative context, that conceptual conflict may have significant effects.

Disequilibrium exists when there is an imbalance between (a) current knowledge and its associated cognitive frameworks and (b) what is encountered in the environment, such as the conclusions presented by others or what is witnessed (Piaget, 1964). Piaget theorized that people naturally strive to maintain a state of equilibrium by adapting old schemas (i.e., assimilating the new information into existing schemas) or developing new schemas that accommodate the information, thereby restoring equilibrium. The process of restoring balance is called *equilibration*. When new information does not fit into existing schemas, an unpleasant state of disequilibrium results, which motivates attempts to restore equilibrium, usually through *accommodation* (i.e., modifying or extending existing schemas to fit the new experiences). According to Piaget, cognitive development and learning depend on equilibrium being upset and the subsequent attempt to resolve the disequilibrium. Disequilibrium provides an opportunity to grow and develop cognitively. This process does not proceed at a steady rate, but rather in leaps and bounds.

Facing dissent may lead to the realization that a different point of view than one's own is possible, and therefore produces uncertainty (Butera, Mugny, & Tomei, 2000; Darnon, Doll, & Butera, 2007; Hardin & Higgins, 1996). *Uncertainty* is doubt about a conclusion or anticipated outcome (Johnson & Johnson, 2007). It applies to predictions of future events. It is a state of having limited knowledge about the nature of present reality and future outcomes. In constructive controversy, uncertainty is created when one's conclusions and opinions are challenged by opposing views expressed by other group members. There seems to be a human tendency to try to see reality accurately in order to be able to predict future outcomes. Uncertainty thus becomes at the very least uncomfortable and anxiety provoking. Under most conditions, resolving uncertainty becomes a priority for any group member. In other words, uncertainty unfreezes the epistemic process.

There is considerable research investigating conceptual conflict, disequilibrium, and uncertainty. The greater the disagreement among group members, the more frequently disagreement occurs, the greater the number of people disagreeing with a person's position, the more competitive the context of the controversy, and the more affronted the person feels, the greater the conceptual conflict, disequilibrium, and uncertainty the person experiences (Asch, 1952;

Burdick & Burnes, 1958; Festinger & Maccoby, 1964; Gerard & Greenbaum, 1962; Inagaki & Hatano, 1968, 1977; Lowry & Johnson, 1981; Tjosvold & Johnson, 1977, 1978; Tjosvold, Johnson, & Fabrey, 1980; Worchel & McCormick, 1963). It is interesting that the more the group members like each other, the more likely they are to disagree and argue with each other. Friends are more likely than nonfriends to engage in interaction where knowledge is shared, ideas are challenged, evidence is evaluated, and options are reasoned about (Azmitia & Montgomery, 1993; Hartup, French, Laursen, Johnston, & Ogawa, 1993; Miell & MacDonald, 2000), thereby creating greater conceptual conflict, disequilibrium, and uncertainty.

In order for conceptual conflict, disequilibrium, and uncertainty to be maximized, group members must (a) be free to express their opinions, (b) accurately perceive opposing information and reasoning, (c) not be overloaded with information, (d) see opposing information as useful, (e) be challenged by other group members, and (f) be challenged by valid information.

Freedom to express independent opinions
Exposure to more than one point of view decreases the tendency to conform to the majority opinion and to accept uncritically the opinions of others (Asch, 1956). Hearing opposing views being advocated gives participants the freedom to examine alternative and original solutions to problems without the stress of noncompliance to the majority opinion (Nemeth, 1986).

Misperceiving opposing information and reasoning
Seeking to understand the rationale supporting opposing positions is not a simple enterprise. There are a number of ways in which understanding information contradicting one's position and reasoning is subject to bias and selective perception. First, individuals tend to seek out, learn, and recall information that confirms and supports their beliefs (Levine & Murphy, 1943; Nisbett & Ross, 1980; Snyder & Cantor, 1979; Swann & Reid, 1981). Levine and Murphy

(1943), for example, found that individuals learned and retained information congruent with their positions better than they did statements that ran counter to their positions. Second, individuals with certain expectations will perceive some information and events but not others (Dearborn & Simon, 1958; Foley & MacMillan, 1943; Iverson & Schwab, 1967; Neisser, 1954; Postman & Brown, 1952). Third, individuals' preconceptions and perspectives affect the understanding and recall of information (Allport & Postman, 1945; Bartlett, 1932; Pepitone, 1950). Finally, individuals who hold strong beliefs about an issue are apt to subject disconfirming evidence to highly critical evaluation while accepting confirming evidence at face value (Lord, Ross, and Lepper, 1979).

Being overloaded with opposing information
Some danger of information overload and becoming confused with the complexity of the issues exists when we are required to learn opposing views and contrary information (Ackoff, 1967). There is a limit to the amount of information that human beings can process at any given time. If they are exposed to more information than they can handle, much of it will be lost. Sometimes, in the interests of accuracy or objectivity, so much information is packed into such a short period of time that nearly everything is lost. This is called *information overload*.

Perceiving usefulness of opposing position
There is evidence that if individuals are planning to use contrary information to improve the quality of their learning, problem solving, and decision making, they will learn and utilize the information (Johnson & Johnson, 1989). Jones and Aneshansel (1956), for example, found that when individuals have to learn information counter to their position because they have to be ready to argue from that viewpoint at a later time, they learn it better than will those who agree with the information and therefore already have such arguments at hand.

Being challenged by a valid or erroneous position

There is some question as to whether a challenge based on erroneous information and reasoning will have the same impact as will a challenge based on valid information and reasoning. As was discussed earlier, there are creative contributions made by being confronted with opposing positions, even when they are wrong. The value of the controversy lies not so much in the correctness of an opposing position, but rather in the attention and thought processes it induces. More cognitive processing may take place when individuals are exposed to more than one point of view, even if the point of view is incorrect (Nemeth & Wachtler, 1983). Subjects exposed to a credible but erroneous minority view generated more solutions to a problem and more correct solutions than did subjects exposed to a consistent single view. The advance to a higher-level reasoning process has been demonstrated to be sparked by being confronted with an opposing erroneous point of view (Cook & Murray, 1973; Doise, Mugny, & Perret-Clermont, 1976; Murray, 1974).

Summary

Hearing opposing views advocated stimulates new cognitive analysis and frees individuals to create alternative and original conclusions. When contrary information is not clearly relevant to completing the task at hand, it may be ignored, discounted, or perceived in biased ways in favor of supporting evidence. When individuals realize, however, that they are accountable for knowing the contrary information some time in the near future, they will tend to learn it. Too much information can result in information overload. Opposing views are more effective in promoting divergent thinking and effective problem solving when they are presented by a nonmajority. Even being confronted with an erroneous point of view can result in more divergent thinking and the generation of novel and more cognitively advanced solutions.

Step 5: Epistemic curiosity and perspective taking

The fifth step in the controversy process is group members experiencing epistemic curiosity, resulting in the search for more information about the topic being discussed and the attempt to find a more adequate perspective from which to view the issue. The conceptual conflict, disequilibrium, and uncertainty created by being exposed to opposing positions results in an awareness that one needs to learn the information in the opposing positions and understand the perspective of the other group members.

The uncertainty generated by "the disputed passage" tends to motivate *epistemic curiosity*, a desire to learn more about the topic being discussed (Berlyne, 1965, 1966). Epistemic curiosity, in turn, results in an active search for (a) more information and new experiences (increased specific content) and (b) a more adequate cognitive perspective and reasoning process (increased validity) in the hope of resolving the uncertainty. Divergent attention and thought are stimulated. When faced with intellectual opposition within a cooperative context, individuals tend to ask one another for more information, seek to view the information from all sides of the issue, and utilize more ways of looking at facts (Nemeth & Goncalo, 2005; Nemeth & Rogers, 1996). Epistemic curiosity depends on disagreement that inspires uncertainty. In a study involving low-achieving Israeli high school students, Schwarz, Neuman, and Biezuner (2000) found that learning partners who had different but incorrect conceptual strategies tended to use hypothesis testing to resolve their disagreements more so than did dyads, where one student initially used the correct strategy. In the latter case, the "right" student tended not to be uncertain and therefore the pair's hypothesis testing tended to be less effective. Discussions involving controversy compared to concurrence seeking or consensus were found to lead to perceiving more conceptual conflict and experiencing more epistemic curiosity (Tjosvold & Field, 1986).

Kang, Hsu, Krajbich, Loewenstein, McClure, Wang, and Camerer (2009) found that epistemic curiosity (i.e., a desire to learn new information and an anticipation of the rewarding information to be learned) was correlated with activity in caudate regions of the brain that had previously been found to be correlated with anticipated rewards across a wide variety of primary and secondary reinforcers (Delgado, Locke, Strenger, & Fiez, 2003; Delgado, Nystrom, Fissell, Noll, & Fiez, 2000), including social rewards such as benevolent reciprocity (Fehr & Camerer, 2007; King-Casas, Tomlin, Anen, Camerer, Quartz, & Montague, 2005), social cooperation (Rilling, Gutman, Zeh, Pagnoni, Berns, & Kitts, 2002), altruistic punishment (de Quervain, Fischbacher, Treyer, Schellhammer, Schnyder, Buck, & Fehr, 2004), and winning an auction (Delgado, Schotter, Ozbay, & Phelps, 2008). Kang et al. (2009) also found that individuals spent more scarce resources (either limited tokens or waiting time) to find out answers when they were more curious. The functional imaging also showed that curiosity increased activity in memory areas when participants guessed incorrectly, which suggests that curiosity may enhance memory for surprising new information. Kang and his associates (2009) did in fact find that higher curiosity in an initial session was correlated with better recall of surprising answers one and two weeks later. Howe and colleagues (Howe, Tolmie, & Rogers, 1992; Howe, Tolmie, Greer, & Mackenzie, 1995; Tolmie, Howe, Mackenzie, & Greer, 1993) found that dialogue in which other group members challenge and evaluate one's position and arguments results in one being motivated to reflect on the subject matter long after the group task is completed. They conclude that it is intellectual challenge that promotes ongoing epistemic curiosity, which in turn continually motivates new learning.

Interpersonal disagreement creates first an interpersonal conflict that becomes an internal conflict because it may make each individual doubt his or her conclusion. Arguments, therefore, are aimed at resolving both the interpersonal and the intrapersonal conflicts somewhat simultaneously. The resolution of the interpersonal conflict triggers the resolution of the intrapersonal cognitive or conceptual conflict (Ames & Murray, 1982; Doise, Mugny, & Perez, 1998; Gilly & Roux, 1984; Mugny et al., 1975–1976; Mugney et al., 1978–1979). This research has been conducted on both children and adults.

When children working on Piagetian tasks had interpersonal conflicts as to the correct answer, those who solved the conflict by searching for the correct answer tended to develop cognitively more so than did those who solved the conflict through concurrence or compliance (Carugati, De Paolis, & Mugny, 1980-1981; Mugny et al., 1978–1979).

When faced with intellectual opposition within a cooperative context, individuals tend to ask each other for more information, to seek to view the information from all sides of the issue, and to utilize more ways of looking at facts (Nemeth & Goncalo, 2005; Nemeth & Rogers, 1996). Conceptual conflict motivates *epistemic curiosity*, that is, an active search for more information in hopes of resolving the uncertainty. Individuals engaged in controversy (compared to persons involved in noncontroversial discussions, concurrence-seeking discussions, and individualistic efforts) are motivated to know others' positions and to develop understanding and appreciation of them (Tjosvold & Johnson, 1977, 1978; Tjosvold et al., 1980; Tjosvold, Johnson, & Lerner, 1981) and develop a more accurate understanding of the other positions (Smith et al., 1981; Tjosvold & Johnson, 1977, 1978; Tjosvold et al., 1980). Indices of epistemic curiosity include individuals actively (a) searching for more information, (b) seeking to understand opposing positions and rationales, and (c) attempting to view the situation from opposing perspectives. Finally, there is evidence that unfamiliar arguments (Garcia-Marques & Mackie, 2001), diverging evidence (Kruglanski, 1980), opposing views (Nemeth, 1986), disconfirmatory information (Toma & Butera, 2009), and counterintuitive findings (Berlyne, 1960; Piaget, 1985) can generate deeper information processing and more elaborate knowledge than being confronted by familiar arguments or confirmatory evidence.

Search for information

There is evidence that controversy results in an active search for more information. Lowry and Johnson (1981) found that individuals involved in controversy, compared with persons involved in concurrence seeking, read more relevant material, reviewed more relevant materials, more frequently gathered further information during their free time, and more frequently requested information from others. Smith et al. (1981) found that controversy, compared with both concurrence seeking and individualistic efforts, promoted greater use of relevant materials and more frequently giving up free time to gather further information. Johnson and Johnson (1985) and Johnson et al. (1984) found that controversy, compared with debate and individualistic efforts, promoted greater search for more information outside of class. R. Johnson, Brooker, Stutzman, Hultman, and Johnson (1985) found that individuals engaged in controversy had greater interest in learning more about the subject being discussed than did persons engaged in concurrence seeking or individualistic efforts. Beach (1974) found that small discussion groups working cooperatively consulted more books in writing papers for a college psychology course than did individuals in a traditional lecture-competition format. Hovey, Gruber, and Terrell (1963) found that individuals who participated in cooperative discussion groups during a college psychology course engaged in more serious reading to increase their knowledge and demonstrated more curiosity about the subject matter following a course experience than did individuals in a traditional lecture-competition course format. Students who engage in dialogue involving sharing, challenging, and evaluating tend to be motivated to reflect on the subject matter long after the task has been completed (Howe, Tolmie, & Rogers, 1992, Howe, McWilliam, & Cross, 2005; Tolmie, Howe, Mackenzie, & Greer, 1993).

Seeking to understand opposing positions

Individuals engaged in controversy tend to be motivated to know others' positions and to develop understanding and appreciation of them (Tjosvold & Johnson, 1977, 1978; Tjosvold et al., 1980; Tjosvold, Johnson, & Lerner, 1981). Attempting to understand opposing positions has benefits. Individuals involved in a controversy developed a more accurate understanding of other positions than did persons involved in

noncontroversial discussions, concurrence-seeking discussions, or individualistic efforts (Smith et al., 1981; Tjosvold & Johnson, 1977, 1978;
Tjosvold, Johnson, & Fabrey, 1980).

Perspective taking

In order to arrive at a synthesis that is acceptable to all group members, the issue must be viewed from all perspectives. Understanding
the information that the other advocacy teams are presenting is not
enough. The perspective from which opposing members are speaking
must also be clearly understood. Group members need to be able to
both comprehend the information being presented by their opposition
and understand the cognitive perspective their opposition is using to
organize and interpret the information. A *cognitive perspective* consists of the cognitive organization being used to give meaning to a
person's knowledge, and the structure of a person's reasoning.
Tjosvold and Johnson (1977, 1978) and Tjosvold, Johnson, and Fabrey
(1980) conducted three experiments in which they found that the
presence of controversy promoted greater understanding of another
person's cognitive perspective than did the absence of controversy.
Individuals engaging in a controversy were better able subsequently to
predict what line of reasoning their opponent would use in solving
a future problem than were persons who interacted without any
controversy. Perspective-taking skills are especially important for
exchanging information and opinions within a controversy, affecting
the amount of information disclosed, communication skills, accuracy
of understanding and retention of opposing positions, and friendliness
of the information exchange process (Johnson, 1971).

Karl Smith (Smith et al., 1981) compared the relative impact of
controversy, concurrence seeking, and individualistic efforts. Eighty-
four sixth-grade individuals were randomly assigned to conditions
(and to groups of four within the two group conditions) stratifying
for ability and sex. The study lasted for ten 90-minute periods. Two
issues were studied – the advisability of allowing logging, mining, and
the use of snowmobiles and motor boats in the Boundary Waters

National Park and the advisability of strip mining of coal. They found that individuals engaged in a controversy were more accurate in understanding their opponents' perspective than were persons involved in concurrence-seeking discussions or individualistic efforts. Johnson et al. (1985) also found that individuals in the controversy condition were better able to take the opposing perspective than were individuals participating in concurrence-seeking discussions.

Social projection

The opposite of perspective taking is egocentrism. Closely related to egocentrism is social projection – the expectation that others will behave as the person would behave in the situation (Krueger, 2013). Social projection theory states that, instead of thinking, "What is the other person's perspective and therefore how will the other person behave?," a person will think, "What would I do in that situation and, therefore, that is what the other person will do." The person assumes that other people's perspectives are identical to one's own. The theory assumes that the person has no information about what the other person might do. Social projection is assumed to be strongest when people see themselves and others as members of the same group (Robbins & Krueger, 2005).

In constructive controversy, individuals are members of the same group with the cooperative goal of making the best reasoned judgment about the issue, thus opening the door to social projection. The tendency for social projection to interfere with seeing the issue from a variety of perspectives makes it a form of egocentrism. Thus, social projection may be an obstacle to perspective taking and reaching a high-quality, creative decision or answer.

Step 6: Reconceptualization, synthesis, integration

When overt controversy is structured by identifying alternatives and assigning members to advocate the best case for each alternative, the purpose is not to choose one of the alternatives per se. The purpose is to create a synthesis of the best reasoning and conclusions from all the various alternatives. *Synthesizing* occurs when individuals integrate a number of different ideas and facts into a single position (Johnson & Johnson, 2007). It is the intellectual bringing together of ideas and facts and engaging in inductive reasoning by restating a large amount of information into a conclusion or summary. Synthesizing is often a creative process involving seeing new patterns within a body of evidence, viewing the issue from a variety of perspectives, and generating a number of optional ways of integrating the evidence. This requires seeing knowledge as *probabilistic*, that is, as available only in degrees of certainty. What should be avoided is seeing knowledge as *dualistic*, in that there is only right and wrong and authority should not be questioned, or *relativistic*, in that authorities are seen as sometimes right but that right and wrong depend on your perspective.

The dual purposes of synthesis are to arrive at the best possible decision and find a position that all group members can commit themselves to implement. When consensus is required for decision making, the dissenting members tend to maintain their position longer, the deliberation tends to be more "robust," and group members tend to feel that justice has been better served (Nemeth, 1977). When group members adapt their cognitive perspective and reasoning through understanding and accommodating the perspective and reasoning of others, a new, reconceptualized, and reorganized conclusion may be derived. Novel solutions and decisions tend to be detected that are, on balance, qualitatively better than the original positions.

It should be noted that reaching an agreement, or resolving the differences among positions, is not essential for learning and effective decision making (Howe, 2006; Howe, Rogers, & Tolmie, 1990; Howe, Tolmie, & Rogers, 1992; Howe, Tolmie, Thurston, Topping, Christie, Livingston, Jessiman, & Donaldson, 2007). Groups that do not resolve their differences are typically just as effective as groups that do resolve their differences. It is not resolution that is important, but going through the process of trying to achieve resolution.

Finally, Nussbaum and Schraw (2007) proposed the concept of argument–counterargument integration, in which the strength of an argument is a function of how well a conclusion accounts for counterarguments by refuting, discounting, or accepting the counterarguments, or by proposing a creative solution that eliminates possible objections. They do not, however, emphasize the benefits of discussing the opposing positions irrespective of integrating the various positions. They have applied their argument–counterargument integration model at the undergraduate level in a number of universities (Nussbaum, 2008b; Nussbaum & Schraw, 2007; Nussbaum, Winsor, Aqui, & Poliquin, 2007).

Incorporation of others' information and reasoning

A more accurate understanding of the opponent's position, reasoning, and perspective has been hypothesized to result in greater incorporation of the opponent's reasoning into one's own position. There is evidence that participation in a controversy, compared with participating in non-controversial discussions, concurrence-seeking discussions, and individualistic efforts, does result in greater incorporation of opponents' arguments and information (Johnson & Johnson, 1985; Johnson, Johnson, & Tiffany, 1984; Tjosvold, Johnson, & Lerner, 1981).

The critical question is: under what conditions will opposing information be incorporated into one's reasoning and under what conditions will it not be? Two conditions hypothesized to affect the incorporation of opposing information are (a) whether cooperative or competitive elements dominate the situation and (b) whether the participants disagree skillfully or unskillfully. Tjosvold and Johnson (1978) conducted a study utilizing 45 undergraduate individuals at Pennsylvania State University. Three conditions were included: controversy within a cooperative context, controversy within a competitive context, and no controversy. Subjects worked on resolving a moral dilemma by individually deciding what course of action should be taken, prepared for a discussion about the moral dilemma with a partner, discussed the moral dilemma with a person from another group, and were debriefed about the research study. The experimental session lasted 90 minutes. They found that when the context was cooperative there was more open-minded listening to the opposing position. When controversy occurred within a competitive context, a closed-minded orientation was created in which individuals comparatively felt unwilling to make concessions to the opponent's viewpoint, and closed-mindedly refused to incorporate any of it into their own position. Within a competitive context the increased understanding resulting from controversy tended to be ignored for a defensive adherence to one's own position.

Lowin (1969) and Kleinhesselink and Edwards (1975) found that when individuals were unsure of the correctness of their position, they selected to be exposed to disconfirming information when it could easily be refuted, presumably because such refutation could affirm their own beliefs. Van Blerkom and Tjosvold (1981) found that individuals chose to discuss an issue with a peer with an opposing position more frequently when the context was cooperative rather than competitive, and that individuals in a competitive situation more often selected a less competent peer to discuss an issue with. Tjosvold (1982) and Tjosvold and Deemer (1980) found that when the context was competitive, participants in a controversy understood but did not use others' information and ideas, but when the context was cooperative, the information and ideas provided by opponents were used.

In addition to whether a cooperative or competitive climate dominates the situation, the skill with which individuals disagree with each other also affects the degree to which opponents' reasoning is incorporated into one's own position. Tjosvold, Johnson, and Fabrey (1980) and Tjosvold, Johnson, and Lerner (1981) found that when individuals involved in a controversy have their personal competence disconfirmed by their opponent, a closed-minded rejection of the opponent's position, information, and reasoning results. The amount of defensiveness generated influenced the degree to which individuals incorporated the opponent's information and reasoning into their position, even when they understood accurately their opponent's position.

Attitude and position change
Involvement in a controversy tends to result in attitude and position change. Disagreements within a group have been found to provide a greater amount of information and variety of facts, and a change in the salience of known information, which actually resulted in shifts of judgment (Anderson & Graesser, 1976; Kaplan, 1977; Kaplan & Miller, 1977; Nijhof & Kommers, 1982; Vinokur & Burnstein, 1974). Controversy has promoted greater attitude change than did concurrence-seeking, no-controversy, and individualistic efforts (Johnson & Johnson, 1985; Johnson, Brooker, Stutzman, Hultman, & Johnson, 1985). Putnam and Geist (1985) found that the likelihood of an agreement requiring position change was highest when there were strong pro and con arguments followed by the development of qualifiers and reservations as ways of finding an acceptable consensus.

Transition from one stage of cognitive reasoning to another
Cognitive development theorists (Flavell, 1963; Kohlberg, 1969; Piaget, 1948, 1950) have posited that it is repeated interpersonal controversies (in which individuals are forced again and again to take cognizance of the perspective of others) that promote (a) cognitive and moral development, (b) the ability to think logically, and (c) the reduction of egocentric reasoning. Such interpersonal conflicts are assumed to create disequilibrium within individuals' cognitive structures, which motivate a search for a more adequate and mature process of reasoning. Murray (1972) and Silverman and Stone (1972) paired cognitively preoperational children with cognitively operational peers and had them argue until they came to an agreement or stalemate about the solutions to various problems. When tested alone after the interaction, 80 to 94 percent of the lower-level pupils made significant gains in performance compared to the very much lower rates of success reported in studies of more traditional training

attempts (Beilin, 1977; F. Murray, 1978). In Murray (1972) 8 out of 15 children who scored 0 out of 12 on the pretest had scores of 11 or 12 out of 12 on the various posttests.

There are several studies that demonstrate that pairing a conserver with a nonconserver, and giving the pair conservation problems to solve and instructing them to argue until there is agreement or stalemate resulted in the conserver's answer prevailing on the great majority of conservation trials and in the nonconserver learning how to conserve (Ames & Murray, 1982; Botvin & Murray, 1975; Doise & Mugny, 1979; Doise et al., 1976; Knight-Arest & Reid, 1978; Miller & Brownell, 1975; Mugny & Doise, 1978; Murray, 1972; Murray, Ames, & Botvin, 1977; Perret-Clermont, 1980; Silverman & Geiringer, 1973; Silverman & Stone, 1972; Smedslund, 1961a, 1961b). Inagaki (1981) and Inagaki and Hatano (1968, 1977) found that individuals (two-thirds of whom were nonconservers) who were placed in small groups and given a conservation task and who argued among themselves gave more adequate and higher-level explanations than did the control subjects who did not argue with one another. Experimental subjects showed greater progress in generalizing the principle of conservation to a variety of situations and tended to resist extinction more often when they were shown an apparently nonconserving event. The discussion of the task per se did not produce the effects. There had to be conflict among individuals' explanations for the effects to appear.

The impact of controversy on cognitive and moral reasoning has been found in pairs (Silverman & Geiringer, 1973; Silverman & Stone, 1972), two children against one child alone (Murray, 1972), and three children against two children (Botvin & Murray, 1975), in kindergarten, first, second, third, and fifth grades with normal and learning disabled children, although not with those disabled by communication disorders (Knight-Arest & Reid, 1978), with minorities and whites, and with middle and low socioeconomic status groups. Borys and Spitz (1979), however, did not find social interaction to be especially effective with mentally retarded institutionalized adolescents (IQ = 66, mental age = 10 years, chronological age = 20 years). With these individuals agreement was often reached quickly. Miller and Brownell (1975) found that nearly half the agreements were reached in less than 50 seconds and rarely took longer than 4 or 5 minutes. The advanced children did not prevail because of any greater social influence or higher IQ or because they were more skillful arguers. In arguments about best TV shows and other concepts that have no developmental or necessity attributes, the advanced children won only 41 of 90 arguments, lost 38, and stalemated 11 (Miller & Brownell, 1975). The advanced children seem to initiate discussion slightly more often, state their answer slightly more often, give good reasons more often, counter the others slightly more often, move stimuli more often, and appear slightly more flexible in their arguments than do the immature children, who tend to repetitiously focus on their original opinion and its justifications (Miller & Brownell, 1975; Silverman & Stone, 1972). Growth tended to occur only in the children who yield, which they do 60–80 percent of the time (Silverman & Geiringer, 1973). Growth tended to occur through actual insight, not through parroting the answers of the advanced peers (Botvin & Murray, 1975; Doise et al., 1976; Gelman, 1978; Murray, 1981). Change tended to be unidirectional and nonreversible. Children who understood conservation did not adopt erroneous strategies while nonconservers tended to advance toward a greater understanding of conservation (Miller & Brownell, 1975; Silverman & Geiringer, 1973). Even two immature children who argued erroneous positions about the answer tended to make modest but significant gains toward an understanding of conservation (Ames & Murray, 1982).

Similar studies have been conducted on moral reasoning. Typically, an individual who used lower-level moral reasoning to resolve a moral dilemma was placed in a cooperative pair with a peer who used a higher-level strategy, and the two were given the assignment of making a joint decision as to how a moral dilemma should be resolved. A controversy inevitably resulted. The studies utilizing this procedure found that it tended to result in initially immature individuals

FIGURE 4.2 Process of controversy 2

increasing their level of moral reasoning (Blatt, 1969; Blatt & Kohlberg, 1973; Crockenberg & Nicolayev, 1977; Keasey, 1973; Kuhn, Langer, Kohlberg, & Haan, 1977; LeFurgy & Woloshin, 1969; Maitland & Goldman, 1974; Rest, Turiel, & Kohlberg, 1969; Turiel, 1966).

Taken together, these studies provide evidence that controversies among individuals promoted transitions to higher stages of cognitive and moral reasoning. Such findings are important as there is little doubt that higher levels of cognitive and moral reasoning cannot be directly taught (Inhelder & Sinclair, 1969; Sigel & Hooper, 1968; Sinclair, 1969; Smedslund, 1961a, 1961b; Turiel, 1973; Wallach & Sprott, 1964; Wallach, Wall, & Anderson, 1967; Woholwill & Lowe, 1962).

Summary
Students arrive at a synthesis by using higher-level thinking and reasoning processes, critically analyzing information, and using both deductive and inductive reasoning. Synthesis requires that students keep

conclusions tentative, accurately understand opposing perspectives, incorporate new information into their conceptual frameworks, and change their attitudes and positions.

PROCESS OF CONCURRENCE SEEKING

When groups seek concurrence among group members' conclusions to make a quick decision, members avoid any disagreement or dissent, emphasize agreement among group members, and avoid realistic appraisal of alternative ideas and courses of action (Johnson & Johnson, 1979, 1989, 2007, 2009b). In other words, there is pressure for everyone to conform to the dominant, majority opinion in the group, so that there is a false consensus with members agreeing to a decision in which they do not really believe. The steps of concurrence-seeking process are as follows.

Step 1: The dominant position is derived

When faced with a problem to be solved or a decision to be made, the group member with the most power (i.e., the boss) or the majority of the members derive an initial position from their analysis of the situation based on their current knowledge, perspective, dominant response, expectations, and past experiences. They tend to have a high degree of confidence in their initial conclusion (they freeze the epistemic process).

Step 2: The dominant position is presented and advocated

The dominant position is presented and advocated by the most powerful member in the group or a representative of the majority. It may be explained in detail or briefly, as it is expected that all group members will quickly agree and adopt the recommended position. When individuals present their conclusion and its rationale to others, they engage in cognitive rehearsal and reconceptualize their position as they speak, deepening their understanding of their position, and discovering higher-level reasoning strategies. In addition, their commitment to their position increases, making them more closed-minded toward other positions.

Step 3: Members are confronted with the demand to concur and conform

Members are faced with the implicit or explicit demand to concur with the recommended position. The pressure to conform creates evaluation apprehension that implies that members who disagree will be perceived negatively and rejected (Diehl & Stroebe, 1987). Conformity pressure is also used to prevent members from suggesting new ideas, thereby stifling creativity (Moscovici, 1985a, 1985b). The dominant person or the majority of the members tend to impose their perspective about the issue on the other group members, so that all members view the issue from the dominant frame of reference, resulting in a convergence of thought and a narrowing of focus in members' thinking.

Step 4: Conflict between public and private positions

Any member who does not agree with the recommended position has a choice, concur with the dominant opinion, or disagree and face possible ridicule, rejection, ostracism, and being disliked (Freese & Fay, 2001; Nemeth & Goncalo, 2011). The advocacy by the most powerful person in the group or by the majority of members creates a conflict between public compliance and private belief. This conflict can create considerable distress when the dissenter keeps silent, and perhaps even more stress when the dissenter voices his or her opinion (Van Dyne & Saavedra, 1996). Dissenters realize that if they persist in their disagreement, (a) they may be viewed negatively and will be disliked and isolated by both their peers and their supervisors and/or (b) a destructively managed conflict may result that will split the group into hostile factions. Because of these potential penalties, many potential dissenters find it easier to remain silent and suppress their true opinions.

Step 5:   Members seek confirming information

Members concur publicly with the dominant position and its rationale without critical analysis. In addition, they seek out supporting evidence to strengthen the dominant position and they view the issue only from the dominant perspective (thus eliminating the possible consideration of divergent points of view). As a result, they are relatively unable to detect original solutions to problems (Nemeth & Wachtler, 1983). Thus, there is a convergence of thought and a narrowing of focus in members' thinking. Dissenters tend to adopt the majority position for two reasons: they assume that truth lies in numbers and so the majority is probably correct or they fear that disagreeing openly will result in ridicule and rejection, and therefore they pretend to accept the majority position to be liked and accepted.

Desire for agreement may reduce expression of new or different ideas. Members who have both supporting and conflicting information may only disclose the supporting information and resist insights that may generate new information that no one knows (Larson, Christiansen, Abbott, & Franz, 1996).

Step 6:   Public consensus

All members publicly agree on the answer, conclusion, or course of action the group is to take, while privately some members may believe that other answers, conclusions, or courses of action would be more effective.

SUMMARY

Constructive controversy and concurrence seeking are theoretically opposite ends of a continuum. Structuring them into a situation results in different processes of interaction. The process of constructive controversy consists of six steps: (a) organizing information and deriving conclusions, (b) presenting and advocating positions (includes explaining), (c) being challenged by opposing views (includes socio-cognitive conflict, argumentation, majority and minority influence, confirmatory bias, and myside bias), (d) conceptual conflict, disequilibrium, and uncertainty (includes freedom to express independent opinions, misperceiving opposing information and reasoning, being overloaded with opposing information, perceiving usefulness of opposing position, and being challenged by valid or erroneous position), (e) epistemic curiosity and perspective taking (includes search for information, seeking to understand opposing positions, perspective taking, and social projection), and (f) reconceptualization, synthesis, and integration (includes incorporation of others' information and reasoning, attitude and position change, and transition from one stage of cognitive reasoning to another). The process of concurrence seeking includes the following steps: (a) the dominant position is derived, (b) the dominant position is presented and advocated, (c) members are confronted with the demand to concur and conform, (d) there is conflict between public and private positions, (e) members seek confirming information, and (f) there is public consensus. Each of these processes tends to result in different outcomes. These outcomes are the focus of the next chapter.

5   The outcomes of constructive controversy

THE INKLINGS

Two of the most influential English writers of the twentieth century were J. R. R. Tolkien and C. S. Lewis. Tolkien wrote *The Hobbit* and *The Lord of the Rings* trilogy. Lewis wrote a series of theological books (such as *Mere Christianity* as well as *The Narnia Chronicles*). While each is recognized as a genius, what many people do not know is that the two men were close friends, deeply involved in each other's work, and greatly influenced by each other's thought and writing.

The answer to how these disparate individuals became such close friends may be found in a group known as "The Inklings" (which means "hints, suggestions, or vague ideas"). The Inklings met twice a week. One of the members would produce a manuscript (a poem, story, or chapter) and begin to read it aloud. Other members' criticism and support would follow. Then there might be more reading before the proceedings drifted into a general discussion and often heated debate on almost any subject that happened to arise. This process created a number of important outcomes.

The *first* outcome was encouragement. In C. S. Lewis, for example, Tolkien found an appreciative and sympathetic audience. "The unpayable debt that I owe to him," Tolkien wrote of Lewis years later, "was not 'influence' as it is ordinarily understood, but sheer encouragement."

The *second* outcome was motivation. Tolkien told Walter Hooper, "I wrote the *Lord of the Rings* to make Lewis a story out of *The Silmarillion*." The meetings of the Inklings represented a network of minds energizing each other into creativity.

The *third* outcome was pressure to work. In the beginning of 1944 Tolkien had done no work on *The Lord of the Rings* for several months. Lewis, noticing his friend's lack of progress, urged him to resume work. "I needed some pressure," wrote Tolkien in a letter, "and shall probably respond." By April he was writing again.

The *fourth* outcome was the cross-fertilization of ideas. Through presenting their writings and having them criticized, all members were exposed to each other's ideas and styles of expressing those ideas. Lewis's "Narnia Stories," for example, were deeply influenced by Tolkien's writings.

Intellectual conflict was central to the interaction among the Inklings. Toward the end of the war, for example, in November 1944, Tolkien wrote of a meeting with Lewis and Williams, stating that he could "recollect little of the feat of reason and flow of soul, partly because we all agree so." Later in the same month, in a letter to his son Christopher, Tolkien wrote of "a great event: An evening 'Inklings.' In this meeting, Owen Barfield tackled C. S. Lewis, making him define everything and interrupting his most dogmatic pronouncements with subtle distinguo's. The result was a most amusing and highly contentious evening, on which (had an outsider eavesdropped) he would have thought it a meeting of fell enemies hurling deadly insults before drawing their guns."

When the process of constructive controversy is followed, many positive outcomes result. These outcomes are reviewed in this chapter.

OUTCOMES

General characteristics of controversy research

Theory, however, tends to be of limited value unless it adequately subsumes the existing research into a meaningful conceptual framework and generates further research that validates or disconfirms the theory and establishes the conditions under which the hypothesized relationships occur. Constructive controversy theory has done both. The relationship between theory and research, however, is not unidirectional (Merton, 1957). Empirical research can shape the development of theory through the discovery of valid results that are unanticipated, the accumulation of research findings that the theory does not adequately explain, the clarification of the nature of theoretical concepts, and the demonstration of the relationship between the theory and new dependent variables. In this section, the number and characteristics of the research studies focusing on social interdependence are described, their results are presented, and the variables mediating the relationship between social interdependence and its outcomes are discussed.

The research on constructive controversy has been conducted by many different researchers in a variety of settings using many different participant populations and many different tasks within an experimental and field-experimental format. For a detailed listing of all the supporting studies, see Johnson and Johnson (2009b). All studies randomly assigned participants to conditions. The studies have all been published in journals (except for one dissertation), have high internal validity, and have taken from 1 to 60 hours to conduct. The studies have been conducted on elementary, intermediate, and university students. The studies have lasted from 1 to over 30 hours. Taken together, their results have considerable validity and generalizability. A series of meta-analyses were conducted on the available research to provide the data to validate or disconfirm the theory (Johnson & Johnson, 1979, 1989, 2003, 2007, 2009b). Numerous outcomes of controversy have been documented by the research.

Quality of decision making and problem solving, achievement, and retention

Controversy tends to result in greater mastery and retention of the material and skills being learned than does concurrence seeking (effect size = 0.70), debate (effect size = 0.62), or individualistic learning (effect size = 0.76) (Johnson & Johnson, 2009b). Constructive controversy tends to result in higher-quality decisions (including decisions that involve ethical dilemmas) and higher-quality solutions to complex problems for which different viewpoints can plausibly be developed (Boulding, 1964; Glidewell, 1953; Hall & Williams, 1966, 1970;

Hoffman, Harburg, & Maier, 1962; Hoffman & Maier, 1961; Maier & Hoffman, 1964; Maier & Solem, 1952). Participation in a constructive controversy tends to result in (a) significantly greater ability to recall the information and reasoning contained in one's own and others' positions, (b) more skillfully transferring this learning to new situations, and (c) greater generalization of principles learned to a wider variety of situations than do concurrence seeking, debate, or individualistic efforts. Disagreeing for mutual benefit also tends to result in integrated, high-quality solutions to problems (Lovelace, Shapiro, & Weingart, 2001; Nauta, De Dreu, & Van Der Vaart, 2002). Concurrence seeking, by complying to the conclusion of an expert source, has also been shown to decrease the future use of a diagnostic strategy (Butera, Mugny, & Tomei, 2000, Study 1), thus concurrence seeking may reduce transfer of learning to new situations.

Academic learning

Engaging in constructive controversy increases learning in subject areas such as science (Driver, Newton, & Osborne, 2000), mathematics (Lampert, Rittenhouse, & Crumbaugh, 1996), reading (Anderson, Nguyen-Jahiel, McNurlen, Archodidou, Kim, Reznitskaya, Tillmanns, & Gilbert, 2001), and comprehension of issues in history and social studies (De La Paz, 2005). Stavy and Berkovits (1980) found that teaching by creating conceptual conflict (compared to traditional teaching) significantly increased children's understanding of the concept of temperature. Ma-Naim, Bar, and Zinn (2002) compared conceptual conflict with traditional teaching and found that conceptual conflict significantly improved adult students' understanding of the concepts involved in thermodynamics. Finally, there is evidence that the resolution of differences is not essential for learning (Howe, 2006; Howe, Rogers, & Tolmie, 1990; Howe, Tolmie, & Rogers, 1992; Howe, Tolmie, Thurston, Topping, Christie, Livingston, Jessiman, & Donaldson, 2007). Group members who do not resolve their differences have been found to learn more than members of groups that do resolve their differences. It seems that it is not the resolution of differences in reasoning and conclusions that is important, but rather it is going through the process of trying to achieve the resolution.

Constructive controversy stimulates a higher degree of learning in individuals through deeper problem exploration (Tjosvold, 1982; Tjosvold & Deemer, 1980) and increases teams' learning from mistakes (Tjosvold, Yu, & Hui, 2004) and managers learning to do a better job (Tjosvold & Halco, 1992). Zohar and Nemet (2002) conducted a quasi-experiment with nine intact ninth-grade classes. The experimental group was taught how to engage in effective arguments (e.g., relevancy, soundness, consideration of counterarguments). They discussed two dilemmas on human genetics using what they were taught about arguing. The control classes simply solved standard human genetics problems. The experimental classrooms performed higher on a test of human genetics knowledge than did the control classrooms. Asterhan and Schwarz (2007) conducted two experiments in which the control group was instructed to reach the best solution together, and the experimental group was instructed to have a critical discussion by arguing for and against different solutions. Students in the experimental condition maintained gains from a pretest to a one-week delayed post-test on an individually administered test of conceptual understanding, while students in the control condition showed gains on an immediate post-test but did not preserve their gains. In the second experiment a student confederate was used in each dyad in the experimental condition to ask the partner questions that made critical discussions much more likely in the experimental group. The students who were prompted to engage in critical argumentation performed significantly higher on both the immediate and delayed post-tests of conceptual understanding. Howe, Tolmie, Thurston, Topping, Christie, Livingston, Jessiman, and Donaldson (2007) have recorded the dialogue of primary school children aged 10–12 years, while the children worked for 3+ weeks through extended assignments on evaporation and condensation, and force and motion. The expression of contrasting opinions in learning groups was the single most important predictor of learning gain. The learning gain was found not simply between pretests and post-tests a few weeks apart, but also was found to be sustained after an 18-month interval (Howe, Tolmie, Thurston, Topping, Christie, Livingston, Jessiman, & Donaldson, 2007).

Two of the explanations for the long-term retention found in controversy conditions are as follows. One is that engaging in arguments strengthens the neural links representing these relationships and forges additional links, including links with prior knowledge, which makes it easier for students to recall and reconstruct their knowledge at a later point in time. Another explanation is that controversy may lead to joint representations, such as a diagram or text that participants construct and revise together. Schwartz (1995) found that dyads, working on science problems, were more likely to construct abstract visualizations than individuals working alone. They did so to create a common representation that everyone in the group could refer to. In other words, the presence of more than one person requires communication that changes the ways in which individuals conceptualize the phenomena they are thinking about. In addition, there is evidence that concurrence seeking may reduce transfer of learning to new situations. Butera et al. (2000, Study 1) found that concurrence seeking, by complying by adopting the conclusion of an expert source, has been shown to decrease the future use of a diagnostic strategy.

Decision making

An *effective group decision* fully utilizes the resources of group members, uses time well, makes a correct or high-quality decision, implements the decision fully (by all the required group members), and improves (or at least not lessens) the problem-solving ability of the group (Johnson & F. Johnson, 2013) (see Table 5.1). An important influence on effective decision making is intellectual disagreement and challenge (i.e., constructive controversy). All decision making involves a choice among alternative courses of action and, thereby, involves controversy. Controversy is structured within problem-

Table 5.1 *Meta-analysis of controversy studies: average effect sizes*

Dependent variable	Mean	*Article I.sd*	*Article II.n*
Quality of Decision Making/Achievement			
Controversy/concurrence seeking	0.68	0.41	15
Controversy/debate	0.40	0.43	6
Controversy/individualistic efforts	0.87	0.47	19
Cognitive Reasoning			
Controversy/concurrence seeking	0.62	0.44	2
Controversy/debate	1.35	0.00	1
Controversy/individualistic efforts	0.90	0.48	15
Perspective Taking			
Controversy/concurrence seeking	0.91	0.28	9
Controversy/debate	0.22	0.42	2
Controversy/individualistic efforts	0.86	0.00	1
Motivation			
Controversy/concurrence seeking	0.75	0.46	12
Controversy/debate	0.45	0.44	5
Controversy/individualistic efforts	0.71	0.21	4
Attitudes			
Controversy/concurrence seeking	0.58	0.29	5
Controversy/debate	0.81	0.00	1
Controversy/individualistic efforts	0.64	0.00	1
Interpersonal Attraction			
Controversy/concurrence seeking	0.24	0.44	8
Controversy/debate	0.72	0.25	6

Table 5.1 (*cont.*)

Dependent variable	Mean	*Article I.sd*	*Article II.n*
Controversy/individualistic efforts	0.81	0.11	3
Debate/individualistic efforts	0.46	0.13	2
Social Support			
Controversy/concurrence seeking	0.32	0.44	8
Controversy/debate	0.92	0.42	6
Controversy/individualistic efforts	1.52	0.29	3
Debate/individualistic efforts	0.85	0.01	2
Self-esteem			
Controversy/concurrence seeking	0.39	0.15	4
Controversy/debate	0.51	0.09	2
Controversy/individualistic efforts	0.85	0.04	3
Debate/individualistic efforts	0.45	0.17	2

solving groups through the use of advocacy subgroups. In order to participate competently in the decision-making process, group members must be able to prepare a position, advocate it, defend it from criticism, critically evaluate the alternative positions, be able to view the problem from all perspectives, and be able to synthesize and integrate the best parts of all solutions.

In other words, effective decision making depends on the occurrence of constructive controversy. The evidence indicates that compared to decision making without controversy decision making with controversy leads to more integrative and complex decisions (Smith, Petersen, Johnson, & Johnson, 1986; Tjosvold, 1982; Tjosvold & Deemer, 1980), especially when it occurs in a cooperative context where decision-makers express warm versus cold nonverbal behavior (Tjosvold & Sun, 2003), confirm each other's social face (Tjosvold,

Hui, & Sun, 2004), express shared responsibility for a solution (Tjosvold, 1988), and use persuasive rather than coercive behavior (Tjosvold & Sun, 2001). Group members who view the decision as a challenge versus a threat are inclined to be open-minded toward opposing positions and seek to integrate the best ideas from both positions, making complex decisions by incorporating arguments and information from other members (Tjosvold, 1984). Constructive controversy has a significantly higher predictability of decision quality than the results achieved by decision making without controversy (Tjosvold, Wedley, & Field, 1986). Finally, Kirchmeyer and Cohen (1992) report that constructive controversy tends to lead partially to better decision quality within a multicultural group with an ethnic minority.

Productivity

A number of studies focusing on the outcomes of constructive controversy assess aspects of productivity, such as performance (Hui, Wong, & Tjosvold, 2007; Tjosvold & Halco, 1992), efficiency (Tjosvold, Meredith, & Wong, 1998), effectiveness (Alper, Tjosvold, & Law, 1998; Tjosvold, Law, & Sun, 2003), and productivity (Etherington & Tjosvold, 1998; Tjosvold, 1998b; 2002; Tjosvold, Hui, & Law, 1998; Tjosvold et al., 2004; Tjosvold & Poon, 1998). These authors assess task progress, goal attainment, progress in solving a problem, and how people work together efficiently and effectively. Given these different operationalizations, constructive controversy is found to increase productivity between employees (Tjosvold, 1998b, 2002; Tjosvold & De Dreu, 1997), between managers (Etherington & Tjosvold, 1998; Tjosvold & Halco, 1992; Tjosvold et al., 1998; Tjosvold & Poon, 1998), and between subordinates and superiors (Hui, Wong, & Tjosvold, 2007; Tjosvold et al., 1998; Tjosvold et al., 2004). In addition to these studies at the individual level, there are studies that indicate there is a positive relationship between constructive controversy and productivity at the team level (Alper, Tjosvold, & Law, 1998; Tjosvold, Law, & Sun, 2003).

Cognitive and moral reasoning

Cognitive developmental theorists such as Piaget (1950), Kohlberg (1969), and Flavell (1963) have posited that it is repeated interpersonal controversies in which individuals are forced again and again to take cognizance of the perspective of others that promote cognitive and moral development, the ability to think logically, and the reduction of egocentric reasoning. Such interpersonal controversies are posited to create a breakdown in equilibrium by creating an internal conflict as to the correct answer to a problem. The internal conflict results in a re-equilibration process through which individuals reach a new and higher level of equilibrium. While a single individual can create his or her own disequilibrium, working with others facilitates the experience of disequilibrium. The disequilibrium within individuals' cognitive structures motivates a search for a more adequate and mature process of reasoning. Their reasoning follows from Darwin's (1874) position that ethical reasoning, once begun, pushes against initially limited ethical frameworks, always leading individuals toward a more universal point of view. The impact of controversy on cognitive and moral reasoning has been found in varied size groups and among markedly diverse student populations (Johnson & Johnson, 2007).

Individuals who participate in constructive controversies end up using more higher-level reasoning and metacognitive thought more frequently than individuals participating in concurrence seeking (effect size = 0.84), debate (effect size = 1.38), or individualistic efforts (effect size = 1.10) (Johnson & Johnson, 2009b). There are several studies that demonstrated that pairing a conserver with a nonconserver, and giving the pair conservation problems to solve and instructing them to argue until there is agreement or stalemate, resulted in the conserver's answer prevailing on the great majority of conservation trials and in the nonconserver learning how to conserve. Change tended to be unidirectional and nonreversible. Walker (1983) found that students progressed in their stage of reasoning when confronted with reasons that opposed their own views and were one stage above their way of reasoning. Students also developed cognitively when confronted with counterarguments at the same stage of reasoning. Children who understood conservation did not adopt erroneous strategies while nonconservers tended to advance toward a greater understanding of conservation. Even two immature children who argued erroneous positions about the answer tended to make modest but significant gains toward an understanding of conservation. The discussion of the task per se did not produce the effects. There had to be conflict among individuals' explanations for the effects to appear. It seems like social interaction only increases learning and cognitive development when divergent points of view are actually presented and argued (Mugny, Doise, & Perret-Clermont, 1975–1976; Mugny, Giroud, & Doise, 1978–1979).

More specifically, Murray (1972, 1982) composed dyads of a conserver and a nonconserver to make a conservation judgment cooperatively, and found that substantial gains in conservation resulted on a post-test given one week after the cooperative experience. It was the conflict between the two points of view that seemed to generate the advancement in cognitive reasoning. Glachan and Light (1982), in a view of the research on conservation and spatial manipulation tasks, concluded that cognitive growth is most pronounced when the conserver gives arguments in support of her or his position and counterarguments against the partner.

Roy and Howe (1990) found similar results in a series of studies on moral reasoning, finding that the exchange of contrasting conclusions resulted in progress in moral reasoning, and Damon and Killen (1982) found that when contrasting conclusions led to personal hostility, the benefits on cognitive and moral development were lost. Studies with secondary- and tertiary-level students (as well as primary students) have shown that groups comprised of members who differed in their conclusions about the solution to problems, compared with students in groups where all members had the same opinion, advanced to significantly higher levels of cognitive and moral reasoning (Blaye,

1990; Damon & Phelps, 1988; Howe, Tolmie, & Mackenzie, 1995a; Howe, Tolmie, Anderson, & Mackenzie, 1992; Miell & MacDonald, 2000; Pontecorvo, Paoletti, & Orsolini, 1989; Schwarz, Neuman, & Biezuner, 2000). Snell, Tjosvold, and Su (2006) provide evidence that constructive controversy enhances international justice and the dealing with ethical dilemma of high moral intensity between managers and employees. Tichy, Johnson, Johnson, and Roseth (2010) examined the impact of controversy compared with individualistic learning on the four components of moral development (Narvaez & Rest, 1995). Although they did not find a consistent effect on moral sensitivity, controversy tended to result in significantly higher levels of moral motivation, moral judgment, and moral character.

Patterns of verbal interaction
There are a number of researchers who have analyzed student verbal interactions trying to identify the patterns of exchange in arguments that promote higher-level reasoning. Those patterns of interaction include exploratory talk, collaborative reasoning, and operational transacts. Barnes and Todd (1977, 1995) identified a form of dialogue that they termed *exploratory talk*. Its key features are effective sharing of information, the clear explanation of opinions, and the critical examination of explanations. Not only is it a kind of thinking aloud that precipitates ideas and creative thinking, but it is inherently a collaborative activity involving partners in a purposeful, critical, and constructive engagement with each other's ideas (Mercer & Littleton, 2007). Students offer statements and suggestions for joint consideration that other students challenge and counterchallenge based on evidence and alternative hypotheses, and then decisions are jointly made. In exploratory talk, argumentation is aimed at accomplishing mutual goals. There is also evidence showing that exploratory talk regarding the best way to solve Raven Progressive Matrices resulted in greater individual performance than did conflictual or agreement-oriented discourse (Wegerif, Mercer, & Dawes, 1999).

Researchers (Anderson, Chinn, Waggoner, & Nguyen, 1998; Chinn & Anderson, 1998; Kim, Anderson, Nguyen-Jahiel, & Archodidou, 2007) have identified a pattern of verbal interaction they call *collaborative reasoning*, in which children actively work cooperatively to construct arguments consisting of complex networks of reasons and supporting evidence. They found that in jointly constructing arguments, the quality of students' individual reasoning is much higher than in usual classroom discussions.

Another form of dialogue that has been highlighted is *operational transacts* (Berkowitz & Gibbs, 1983; Berkowitz, Gibbs, & Broughton, 1980). Operational transacts take reasoning and transform it in some way, as, for example, with "I think the box will float because it's wood" followed by "But it's half full of water and that will make it sink." The transformation can involve a justification for disagreement as in the example, but it can also involve a clarification or an elaboration. Operational transacts were shown by Berkowitz and Gibbs (and later Kruger, 1992, 1993; Roy & Howe, 1990) to promote understanding of moral and legal issues, and by Miell and MacDonald (2000) to support children's collaborative compositions in music.

In all three of these patterns of interaction, individuals share knowledge, challenge ideas, evaluate evidence, and consider options in a reasoned and equitable fashion. Individuals present their ideas as clearly and as explicitly as necessary for the ideas to become shared, jointly analyzed, and critically evaluated.

Two wrong answers inducing a right answer

An interesting question concerning controversy and problem solving is, "What happens when erroneous information is presented by participants?" Simply, can the advocacy of two conflicting but wrong solutions to a problem result in participants discovering the correct one? In most of the studies conducted, two conflicting but legitimate alternative solutions were advocated by members of problem-solving groups. There are, however, creative contributions that may be made by opposing positions, even when they are wrong. The value of the controversy process lies in the attention and thought processes it induces, not so much in the correctness of an opposing position. More cognitive processing may take place when individuals are exposed to more than one point of view, even if the point of view is incorrect. Nemeth and Wachtler (1983) found that subjects exposed to a credible minority view generated more solutions to a problem and more correct solutions than did subjects exposed to a consistent single view, even if the minority view was correct. A number of studies on cognitive reasoning have focused on the ways in which nonconserving, cognitively immature children can be influenced to gain the critical insights into conservation. Presenting children with erroneous information that conflicts with their initial position has been found to promote some cognitive growth (even when the disagreement comes from a child at a lower level of cognitive reasoning), although not as much growth as when they received correct information (Cook & Murray, 1973; Doise & Mugny, 1979; Doise, Mugny, & Perret-Clermont, 1975, 1976; Mugny, Giroud, & Doise, 1978–1979, Study 2; Mugny, Levy, & Doise, 1978; Murray, 1972). On subsequent post-tests taken individually after the controversy, significant gains in performance were found. Glachan and Light (1982) argue that the children involved in the "two wrongs make a right" phenomenon often make cognitive strategies that they would not normally make, thus discovering that their original strategies were ineffective. Their conclusion was further confirmed by Schwarz et al. (2000), with low-achieving Israeli high school students solving decimal fraction problems. They concluded that the effect worked because dyad partners who had different conceptual strategies tended to use hypothesis testing to resolve their disagreements more than dyads where one student used the correct strategy. In the latter case, the "right" student tended to be less engaged and not operating under a condition of uncertainty, therefore the disagreement and hypothesis testing tended to be less effective. Ames and Murray (1982) compared the impact of controversy, modeling, and nonsocial presentation of information on the performance of nonconserving, cognitively immature children on conservation tasks. The immature children were presented with erroneous information that conflicted with their initial position. They found modest but significant gains in conservation performance. Three children with scores of 0 out of 18 scored between 16 and 18 out of 18 on the posttest, and 11 children with initial scores of 0 scored between 5 and 15. They conclude that conflict *qua* conflict is not only cognitively motivating, but that the resolution of the conflict is likely to be in the direction of correct performance. In this limited way, two wrongs came to make a right.

Exchange of expertise

Compared with concurrence seeking, debate, and individualistic efforts, controversy tends to result in greater exchange of expertise (Johnson & Johnson, 1989, 2007, 2009b). Students often know different information and theories, make different assumptions, and have different opinions. Within any cooperative learning group, naturally occurring controversies become inevitable as students with a wide variety of expertise and perspectives work together to maximize each member's learning, and students who study different parts of an assignment are expected to share their expertise with the other members of their group. Knowing the procedures for exchanging information and perspectives and how to engage in intellectual controversies are essential competencies for maximizing one's learning and growth.

Perspective taking

Understanding and considering all perspectives is helpful in discussing difficult issues, making joint reasoned judgments, and increasing commitment to implement a decision. In most situations, group members are often unaware of their groupmates' alternative perspectives and frames of reference, and of the potential effects of their alternative perspectives on the accumulation and understanding of information and knowledge (Tversky & Kahneman, 1981). Two group members interpreting information using different perspectives can draw directly opposing conclusions without recognizing the limitations of their thinking. Group members at times do not see the *whole picture*. They see only what their perspective allows them to see, and they tend to overestimate the validity of their conclusions. In addition, group members are apt to process information in a biased manner, accepting confirming evidence at face value and subjecting disconfirming evidence to highly critical evaluation (Lord, Ross, & Lepper, 1979). To make reasoned judgments, group members need to be able to view the issue from all relevant perspectives.

Constructive controversy tends to promote more accurate and complete understanding of opposing perspectives than do concurrence seeking (effect size = 0.97), debate (effect size = 0.20), and individualistic efforts (effect size = 0.59) (Johnson & Johnson, 2009b). Engaging in controversy tends to result in greater understanding of another person's cognitive perspective than the absence of controversy, and individuals engaged in a controversy tend to be better able subsequently to predict what line of reasoning their opponent would use in solving a future problem than are individuals who interact without any controversy. Increased understanding of opposing perspectives tends to result from engaging in controversy (as opposed to engaging in concurrence-seeking discussions or individualistic efforts), regardless of whether one is a high-, medium-, or low-achieving student. This is important because increased perspective taking tends to enhance individuals' ability to discover beneficial agreements in conflicts (Galinsky, Maddux, Gilin, & White, 2008). Finally, when group members make comments that transform, extend, or summarize the reasoning of another person, more effective moral discussions tend to occur (Berkowitz & Gibbs, 1983; Berkowitz et al., 1980).

Creativity

Controversy tends to promote creative insight by influencing individuals to (a) view problems from different perspectives and (b) reformulate problems in ways that allow the emergence of new orientations to a solution (Johnson, 1979; Johnson & Johnson, 1989, 2007, 2009b).

Controversy increases the number of ideas, quality of ideas, feelings of stimulation and enjoyment, and originality of expression in creative problem solving (Bahn, 1964; Bolen & Torrance, 1976; Dunnette, Campbell, & Jaastad, 1963; Falk & Johnson, 1977; Peters & Torrance, 1972; Torrance, 1970, 1971, 1973; Triandis, Bass, Ewen, & Midesele, 1963). Being confronted with credible alternative views has resulted in the generation of more novel solutions (Nemeth & Wachtler, 1983), varied strategies (Nemeth & Kwan, 1987), and original ideas (Nemeth & Kwan, 1985). And there is also evidence that controversy resulted in more creative problem solutions, with more member satisfaction, compared to group efforts that did not include controversy (Glidewell, 1953; Hall & Williams, 1966, 1970; Hoffman et al., 1962; Maier & Hoffman, 1964; Rogers, 1970). These studies further demonstrated that controversy encouraged group members to dig into a problem, raise issues, and settle them in ways that showed the benefits of a wide range of ideas being used, as well as resulting in a high degree of emotional involvement in and commitment to solving problems. In addition, being confronted with credible alternative views has resulted in the generation of more novel solutions (Nemeth & Wachtler, 1983), varied strategies (Nemeth & Kwan, 1987), and original ideas (Nemeth & Kwan, 1985). E. Paul Torrance (1957); Levi, Torrance, & Pletts (1955) concluded from a series of experiments with US Air Force personnel that the most important factor affecting creativity in a group was the willingness to tolerate disagreement, which resulted in better decisions, increased creativity, and better combat performance. He confirmed these findings with a series of studies on elementary students from grades three to five (Torrance, 1963, 1965). Finally, closely related to creativity is innovation. Constructive controversy leads to increased individual innovativeness (Chen & Tjosvold, 2002; Chen, Liu, & Tjosvold, 2005) and team innovativeness (Tjosvold & Yu, 2007).

Open-mindedness

Open-minded consideration of all points of view is critical for deriving well-reasoned decisions that integrate the best information and thought from a variety of positions. Individuals participating in controversies in a cooperative context tend to be more open-minded than do individuals participating in controversies in a competitive context (Tjosvold & Johnson, 1978). In deciding how to resolve a moral dilemma, when the context was cooperative, there was more open-minded listening to the opposing position. Whereas when the context was competitive, there was a closed-minded orientation, in which participants comparatively felt unwilling to make concessions to the opponent's viewpoint and closed-mindedly refused to incorporate any of it into their own position. Within a competitive context the opportunity for increased understanding resulting from controversy tended to be ignored for a defensive adherence to one's own position.

More generally, within a cooperative context, controversy tends to induce an open-minded listening to the opposing positions, motivation to hear more about the opponent's arguments, and more accurate understanding of the opponent's position (Johnson, 1971, 1975a, 1975b; Tjosvold, 1995, 1998a). Conversely, controversy within a competitive context tends to result in closed-minded disinterest and rejection of the opponent's ideas and information, a refusal to incorporate any of the opponent's viewpoints into one's own position, and a defensive and rigid adherence to one's own position. In a competitive context, people often sacrifice open-mindedness for advocacy when they construct arguments (Baron, 1995; Perkins, Farady, & Bushey, 1991; Voss & Means, 1991).

Motivation to improve understanding

Continuing motivation to learn about an issue is critical for such things as quality of long-term learning, decision making, creativity, and political discourse. Participants in a constructive controversy tend to have more continuing motivation to learn about the issue and come to the best reasoned judgment possible than do participants in concurrence seeking (effect size = 68), debate (effect size = 0.73), and individualistic efforts (effect size = 0.65) (Johnson & Johnson, 2009b). Participants in a controversy tend to search for (a) more information and new experiences and (b) a more adequate cognitive perspective and reasoning process in hopes of resolving the uncertainty. There is also an active interest in learning others' positions and developing an understanding and appreciation of them. Lowry and Johnson (1981), for example, found that students involved in a controversy, compared with students involved in concurrence seeking, read more library materials, reviewed more classroom materials, more frequently watched an optional movie shown during recess, and more frequently requested information from others. Thus, continuing motivation to improve one's understanding of the issue being discussed tends to be promoted more by controversy than by other methods of decision making.

Attitude change about the issue and task

Participating in a controversy tends to result in attitude and position change (Johnson & Johnson, 1989, 2007, 2009b). Participants in a controversy tend to reevaluate their attitudes about the issue and incorporate opponents' arguments into their own attitudes. Participating in a controversy tends to result in attitude change beyond that which occurs when individuals read about the issue, and these attitude changes tend to be relatively stable over time. In addition, individuals who engaged in controversies tended to like the task better than did individuals who engaged in concurrence-seeking discussions (effect size = 0.35), debate (effect size = 0.84), or individualistic efforts (effect size = 0.72) (Johnson & Johnson, 2009b).

Attitudes toward the controversy procedure and decision making

If participants are to be committed to implement the decision and participate in future decision making, they must decide that the decision is worth making. Individuals who engaged in controversies tended to like the decision-making task better than did individuals who engaged in concurrence-seeking discussions (effect size = 0.63) (Johnson & Johnson, 2009b). Individuals participating in a controversy liked the procedure better than did individuals working individualistic-ally, and participating in a controversy always promoted more positive attitudes toward the experience than did participating in a debate, concurrence-seeking discussions, or individualistic efforts (Johnson & Johnson, 1985; Johnson, Johnson, Pierson, & Lyons, 1985; Johnson, Johnson, & Tiffany, 1984; R. Johnson, Brooker, Stutzman, Hultman, & Johnson, 1985; Lowry & Johnson, 1981; Smith, Johnson, & Johnson, 1981, 1984). Controversy experiences promoted stronger beliefs that controversy is valid and valuable.

Commitment

Constructive controversy tends to increase different forms of commit-ment at the individual, team, and organizational levels. Constructive controversy utilized in discussions with managers tends to increase employees' commitment to their job (Chen, Tjosvold, & Su, 2005; Chen, Tjosvold, & Wu, 2008). Constructive controversy positively impacts employees' commitment to the team (Tjosvold, 2002). Tjosvold (1998b) also found that employees tend to have a higher commitment to common tasks when discussions utilized constructive controversy. Finally, organizational commitment tends to be related to constructive controversy (Cosier & Dalton, 1990; Dalton & Cosier, 1989). Tjosvold et al. (1998) showed that constructive controversy is a predictor of the empowerment of the relationship between managers and employees and a democratic leadership style.

Interpersonal attraction among participants

Within controversy there is disagreement, argumentation, and rebut-tal that could create difficulties in establishing good relationships. Constructive controversy, however, has been found to promote greater liking among participants than did concurrence seeking (effect size = 0.32), debate (effect size = 0.67), or individualistic efforts (effect size = 0.80) (Johnson & Johnson, 2009b). Debate tended to promote greater interpersonal attraction among participants than did individualistic efforts (effect size = 0.46). Thus, certain types of conflict (i.e., constructive controversy) can significantly improve the quality of relationships among participants.

Within organizations, research studies have focused on relationships between employees, between employees and superiors, or between managers. Constructive controversy increases the quality of interpersonal relationships between subordinates and superiors even across cultural boundaries (Chen & Tjosvold, 2006; Tjosvold et al., 1998). Constructive controversy fosters positive interpersonal relationships among employees in conflict situations (Tjosvold & De Dreu, 1997), in cost reduction discussions between employees (Tjosvold, 1998b), and in anger management situations among employees (Tjosvold, 2002; Tjosvold & Su, 2007). The relationships between subordinates and superiors are perceived as stronger (and more cooperative) when they take place within a cooperative context (Tjosvold & Sun, 2003), group members engage in warm rather than cold behavior (Tjosvold & Sun, 2003), discussions are held in a persuasive rather than coercive manner (Tjosvold & Sun, 2001), the approach to the problem is choosing versus blaming (Tjosvold et al., 2004), and the discussion allows the confirming of each other's social face (Tjosvold, Hui, & Law, 1998). Finally, constructive controversy increases positive relationships between line managers and managers of accountants (Tjosvold & Poon, 1998) and between managers of different departments (Etherington & Tjosvold, 1998; Tjosvold et al., 1998).

Social support

Constructive controversy tends to promote greater social support among participants than does concurrence seeking (effect size = 0.50), debate (effect size = 0.80), or individualistic efforts (effect size = 2.18) (Johnson & Johnson, 2009b). Debate tended to promote greater social support among participants than did individualistic efforts (effect size = 0.85). Constructive controversy has been found to be significantly correlated with both task support and personal support (Tjosvold, XueHuang, Johnson, & Johnson, 2008).

Psychological health

Predisposition to engage in constructive controversy has been found to be significantly positively correlated with life satisfaction and optimistic life orientation (Tjosvold et al., 2008). In addition, controversy was significantly related to a sense of empowerment and egalitarianism/open-mindedness values. These findings provide evidence that constructive controversy enhances participants' psychological health. Two other indices of psychological health are self-esteem and values.

Self-esteem

Constructive controversy tends to promote higher self-esteem than does concurrence seeking (effect size = 0.56), debate (effect size = 0.58), or individualistic efforts (effect size = 0.85) (Johnson & Johnson, 2009b). Debate tends to promote higher self-esteem than does individualistic efforts (effect size = 0.45). Constructive controversy has been found to be significantly correlated with task self-esteem (Tjosvold et al., 2008). In addition, the threat of losing an argument in win–lose conditions can damage the image that students project to others and to themselves (Chiu, 2008; Lampert et al., 1996).

Values

The methods we use to make decisions and teach leave an imprint on participants (of course, other influences do also). From the way individuals act at the beginning of making a decision or a learning experience, we can tell a great deal about their previous managers and instructors. If constructive controversy is frequently used, participants are imprinted with a pattern of open-minded inquiry that includes building coherent intellectual arguments, giving persuasive presentations, critically analyzing and challenging others' positions, rebutting others' challenges, seeing issues from a variety of perspectives, and seeking reasoned judgments. Participants learn that the purpose of advocacy and criticism is not to win, but rather to clarify the strengths and weaknesses of various courses of action so that a joint agreement may be reached as to what represents the best reasoned judgment.

In other words, engaging in the constructive controversy procedure implicitly teaches values. The process itself, regardless of the outcomes, teaches that (a) individuals have both the right and the responsibility to advocate for their conclusions, theories, and beliefs; (b) insight and understanding come from a *disputed passage* where ideas and conclusions are advocated and subjected to intellectual challenge; (c) truth is derived from the clash of opposing ideas and positions; (d) issues must be viewed from all perspectives; and (e) it is desirable to seek a synthesis that subsumes seemingly opposed positions (Johnson & Johnson, 2007). In addition, participating in the controversy process teaches hope and optimism about the future and provides a sense of empowerment (Tjosvold et al., 2008). Finally, it teaches a belief in the importance of egalitarianism, of keeping an open mind, of mutual respect and support, and of respect for organizational superiors.

SUMMARY

The outcomes generated by the process of controversy (compared to concurrence seeking, debate, and individualistic efforts) are (a) higher quality of decision making, problem solving, achievement, and retention; (b) higher cognitive and moral reasoning; (c) greater exchange of expertise; (d) more frequent and accurate perspective taking; (e) greater creativity; (f) greater open–mindedness; (g) greater motivation to improve understanding; (h) greater attitude change about the issue and task; (i) more positive attitudes toward the controversy procedure and decision making; (j) greater commitment to process and outcomes; (k) greater interpersonal attraction and support among participants; (l) greater social support; (m) higher self-esteem; and (n) more democratic values. These outcomes, however, may only be achieved under a certain set of conditions. That is the focus of the next chapter.

6 Conditions mediating the effects of constructive controversy

INTRODUCTION

Ignac Semmelweiss, in 1847, very forcefully told his fellow physicians to wash their hands before delivering babies. Although he did not know why, he had concluded that more babies and mothers would survive if the attending physicians' hands were clean. He tried to explain that from treating people with various diseases and doing autopsies on women who had died of childbed fever, a "morbid poison" was somehow on physicians' hands, which was then transferred to the women in labor. Therefore, Semmelweiss ordered his own medical staff and students to wash their hands with a chlorine antiseptic solution before treating a patient. The death rates from childbed fever dropped radically thereafter. But when he argued that his colleagues were murdering their patients through dirty hands, his colleagues became defensive and refused to change their behavior. No one knows how many women died because Semmelweiss's arguments created defensiveness and closed-minded rejection of his thesis rather than acceptance and appreciation. Semmelweiss did not create the conditions under which his thesis and supporting arguments would be listened to. Those conditions are discussed in this chapter.

CONDITIONS MEDIATING THE EFFECTS OF CONTROVERSY

Although controversies can operate in a beneficial way, they will not do so under all conditions. As with all types of conflicts, the potential for either constructive or destructive outcomes is present in a controversy. Whether there are positive or negative consequences depends on the conditions under which controversy occurs and the way in which it is managed. These conditions and procedures include (a) the social context within which the controversy occurs, the heterogeneity of participants, the amount of relevant information distributed among participants, and the social skills of participants (Johnson & Johnson, 1989, 2007, 2009b).

Cooperative context

The context in which conflicts occur has important effects on whether the conflict turns out to be constructive or destructive (Deutsch, 1973). There are two possible contexts for controversy: cooperative and competitive (Johnson & Johnson, 1979). A cooperative context tends to facilitate constructive controversy and a competitive context tends to promote destructive controversy. Controversy tends to be more constructive when

1. Information and ideas are communicated accurately. Communication of information is far more complete, accurate, encouraged, and utilized in a cooperative context than in a competitive context (Johnson, 1974).
2. A supportive climate exists in which group members feel safe enough to challenge each other's ideas. Cooperation provides a far more supportive climate than competition (Johnson & Johnson, 1991).
3. Controversy is valued. Cooperative experiences promote stronger beliefs that controversy is valid and valuable (Johnson, Johnson, & Scott, 1978; Lowry & Johnson, 1981; Smith, Johnson, & Johnson, 1981).
4. Feelings are dealt with as well as ideas and information. Cooperativeness is positively related and competitiveness is negatively related to the ability to understand what others are feeling and why they are feeling that way (Johnson, 1971, 1975a, 1975b).
5. Controversies are defined as problems to be solved in a cooperative context. Within a competitive context controversies tend to be defined as "win-lose" situations (Deutsch, 1973).
6. Similarities are recognized among positions as well as differences. Group members participating in a controversy within a cooperative context identify more of the similarities between their positions than do members participating in a controversy within a competitive context (Judd, 1978).

7. There is an open-minded consideration of all points of view. Within a cooperative context, controversy tends to induce an open-minded listening to the opposing positions, motivation to hear more about the opponent's arguments, and more accurate understanding of the opponent's position (Johnson, 1971, 1975a, 1975b; Tjosvold, 1995, 1998a). Conversely, controversy within a competitive context tends to result in closed-minded disinterest and rejection of the opponent's ideas and information, a refusal to incorporate any of the opponents' viewpoints into one's own position, and a defensive and rigid adherence to one's own position. In a competitive context, people often sacrifice open-mindedness for advocacy when they construct arguments (Baron, 1995; Perkins, Farady, & Bushey, 1991; Voss & Means, 1991).

8. Distributed knowledge and different perspectives tend to be viewed as complementary and interdependent. In a cooperative context, differences in information and perspectives are seen as resources to help solve the problem and focus participants' attention on coordinating the different points of view to enhance the cooperative effort which leads to increased learning and productivity (Butera, Huguet, Mugny, & Prez, 1994; Butera, Mugny, & Buchs, 2001; Gruber, 2006). In a competitive context, differences in information and perspectives are seen as threats to one's chances of "winning" and, therefore, tend to be rejected and ignored.

The evidence indicates that a cooperative context increases the effectiveness of constructive controversy. There tends to be a significant positive correlation between positive goal interdependence and constructive controversy (Snell, Tjosvold, & Su, 2006; Tjosvold, 1998b; Tjosvold & De Dreu, 1997). The perception that the situation is competitive undermines learning (Buchs & Butera, 2004; Doise & Mugny, 1984). A cooperative context also tends to increase participants' interest in disconfirming information, reduce competence threat, decrease downward social comparison, decrease perceiving disputants as biased, and increase perceived aspects of leadership.

Interest in disconfirming information
Within a cooperative context, controversy tends to induce feelings of comfort, pleasure, and helpfulness in discussing opposing positions

and the reaching of more integrated positions where both one's own and one's opponent's conclusions and reasoning are synthesized into a final position (Tjosvold, 1995, 1998a). Within a competitive context, Lowin (1969) and Kleinhesselink and Edwards (1975) found that when individuals were unsure of the correctness of their position, they selected to be exposed to disconfirming information when it could easily be refuted, presumably because such refutation could affirm their own beliefs. Avoidance of controversy resulted in little interest in or little actual knowledge of opposing ideas and information and the making of a decision that reflected one's own views only.

Competence threat

A competitive context for a controversy tends to induce competence threat. *Competence threat* is the aversive feeling that results when one is afraid that one's competence will be judged to be lower than the competence of the other individuals involved. Feeling incompetent can affect a person's perception of self-worth (Covington, 1984, 1992; Steele, 1988; Tesser, 1988). The person may then react by defending and protecting one's own competence, for example, by demonstrating that one is right and that the other person is wrong, which is referred to as *relational conflict regulation* (Doise & Mugny, 1984). When a competitive social comparison of competencies occurs, participants tend to deny the other's competence and try to confirm their own point of view instead of solving the task (Butera & Mugny, 1995). This happens because in a competitive situation, the other's competence threatens self-competence and, therefore, individuals tend not to recognize the other's competence (e.g., Butera & Mugny, 2001; Mugny, Butera, Quiamzade, Dragulescu, & Tomei, 2003). This is not the case in a noncompetitive situation, in which another's competence is unrelated to one's own and thus can be accepted (Butera & Mugny, 1995). Additionally, the more competitive the situation is, the larger the difference is between reported self-competence (which tends to be presented as higher than it actually is) and the other's competence (which tends to be presented as lower than it actually is) (Butera & Mugny, 1995; Butera, Mugny, & Tomei, 2000, Study 3).

Downward social comparison

Related to competence threat is downward social comparison (Wills, 1981). *Downward comparison* is the social comparison of oneself with another individual or group one considers to be worse off than oneself. Doing so tends to make a person feel better about oneself or one's personal situation. Social comparison with others who are better off or superior can lower self-regard, whereas downward comparisons can elevate self-regard (Gibbons, 1986; Tesser, Millar, & Moore, 1988; Wills, 1981). Thus, in a competitive context, engaging in a controversy with someone who has more expertise tends to be threatening, as adopting the expert's conclusions implies acknowledging one's own incompetence (Butera & Mugny, 2001). In situations where the other's superior expertise has to be recognized, being obligated to recognize one's inferior competence tends to lead to rejection of the expert's information (Mugny, Tafani, Falomir, & Layat, 2000).

Perceived bias

In a competitive context, people generally perceive their opponent as being biased, and this perception motivates them to act in competitive, aggressive, and conflict-escalating ways (Kennedy & Pronin, 2008). Butera and Mugny (1995) found that a cooperative context resulted in cognitive advancement from conflict, while a competitive context resulted in self-serving, defensive protection of participants' competence without any cognitive advancement.

Leadership

Aspects of leadership may be antecedents of constructive controversy. Examples are leader–member exchange (Chen & Tjosvold, 2006, 2007) and positive affectivity (Hui, Wong, & Tjosvold, 2007).

Heterogeneity among members

Differences among individuals in personality, gender, attitudes, background, social class, reasoning strategies, cognitive perspectives, information, ability levels, and skills lead to diverse perspectives, processing of information, and experiences (Johnson & F. Johnson, 2013; Johnson & R. T. Johnson, 2007). When group members have diverse views, they tend to create more ideas, representations, justifications, and proposed solutions, especially when they value each other's diverse contributions (Johnson & F. Johnson, 2013; Larson, 2007; Paulus & Brown, 2003; Stasson & Bradshaw, 1995; Swann, Kwan, Polzer, & Milton, 2003). Heterogeneity among individuals leads to more diverse interaction patterns and resources for achievement and problem solving. It may also promote higher achievement and productivity than that found in homogeneous groups (Johnson & Johnson, 1989, 2007, 2009b). The diverse views of group members tend to help them justify the validity of an idea, identify flawed reasoning and information, and revise their views to create new ideas (De Lisi & Goldbeck, 1999; Orlitzky & Hirokawa, 2001). Paulus and Brown (2003) note that group members with diverse views can build on one another's ideas through processes such as sparked ideas, jigsaw pieces, and creative misinterpretations. A key word or comment by one group member may spark another member to think of a new idea (Nijstad, Diehl, & Stroebe, 2003). Like fitting jigsaw pieces together, group members may also put other members' ideas together to create a new idea (Milliken, Bartel, & Kurtzberg, 2003). Even a group member misinterpreting another member's idea may result in the member creating a new idea (Chiu, 1997). Thus, even wrong ideas can be the inspiration for new ideas. In addition, ethnic and cultural diversity often increases the number of perspectives, number of ideas, and quality of ideas (McLeod, Lobel, & Cox, 1996; Johnson & Johnson, 2002). The differences among group members can create naturally occurring controversies. The greater the heterogeneity among individuals, the greater the amount of time spent in argumentation (Nijhof & Kommers, 1982).

Distribution of information

The more information individuals have about an issue, the greater their achievement and successful problem solving tends to be (Johnson & Johnson, 1989, 2007, 2009b). Having relevant information available, however, does not mean that it will be utilized. Individuals need the interpersonal and group skills necessary to ensure that all individuals involved contribute their relevant information and that the information is synthesized effectively (Hall & Williams, 1966; Johnson, 1977). Buchs, Butera, and Mugny (2004) found that group members become more competitive when both the pro and con sides have the same information compared to groups in which members have different information.

Skilled disagreement

In order for controversies to be managed constructively, individuals need two types of collaborative and conflict management skills (Johnson, 2014; Johnson & F. Johnson, 2013; Johnson, Johnson, & Holubec, 2013. The first set of skills involves persuading others to change their minds and agree with one's position and conclusions. Relevant skills for this involve construction and exposition of one's own arguments. Recent research indicates that younger and less skilled disputants focus on arguments that support their own position, paying relatively little attention to the claims and arguments of the other disputants (Felton, 2004; Felton & Kuhn, 2001; Kuhn & Udell, 2003). They tend to see the objective of controversy as presenting the most compelling case possible as to the merits of their own position in which case the opposing positions will fade away without needing to be addressed.

The second set of skills involves undermining the other disputants' positions by identifying and challenging weaknesses in their arguments. One of the most important of these is to challenge each other's ideas while confirming each other's personal competence (Tjosvold, 1998a). Disagreeing with others, and at the same time imputing that the other disputants are incompetent, tends to increase the other disputants' commitment to their own ideas and the other disputants' rejection of one's information and reasoning (Tjosvold, 1974). Tjosvold, Johnson, and Fabrey (1980) and Tjosvold, Johnson, and Lerner (1981) found that when individuals involved in a controversy had their personal competence disconfirmed by their opponent, a closed-minded rejection of the opponent's position, information, and reasoning resulted. The amount of defensiveness generated influenced the degree to which individuals incorporated the opponent's information and reasoning into their position, even when they understood accurately their opponent's position. Disagreeing with others' ideas while simultaneously confirming their personal competence, however, results in being better liked by the opponents and in the opponents being less critical of one's ideas, more interested in learning more about one's ideas, and more willing to incorporate one's information and reasoning into their own analysis of the problem. Similarly, Monteil and Chambres (1990) found that disagreement associated with expressions of liking resulted in more learning than did disagreement associated with expressions of dislike. Chiu (2008) and Hagler and Brem (2008), on the other hand, found that rudeness, that is, disagreeing with others in a direct and confrontational way, is less effective in generating new ideas and coordinating efforts to achieve than polite disagreement. Competitive goals may be reflected in the lack of politeness and skill with which members disagree with each other (Chiu & Khoo, 2003). Impolite disagreeing has pronounced negative influences on relationships, achievement, and group success. Keefer, Zeitz, and Resnick (2000) found that when engaging in small-group discussions of literary texts, collaborative argumentation resulted in deeper arguments and better understanding of literary themes than did adversarial argumentation.

Another important set of skills for exchanging information and opinions within a controversy is *perspective taking* (Johnson, 1971; Johnson & Johnson, 1989). More information, both personal and impersonal, is disclosed when one is interacting with a person engaging in perspective-taking behaviors such as paraphrasing to demonstrate understanding and communicating the desire to understand accurately (Colson, 1968; Johnson, 1971; Noonan-Wagner, 1975; Sermat & Smyth, 1973; Taylor, Altman, & Sorrentino, 1969). Perspective-taking ability increases one's capacity to phrase messages so that they are easily understood by others and to comprehend accurately the messages of others (Feffer & Suchotliff, 1966; Flavell, 1968; Hogan & Henley, 1970). Engaging in perspective taking in conflict situations tends to increase understanding and retention of the opponent's information and perspective; facilitate the achievement of creative, high-quality problem solving; and promote more positive perceptions of the information-exchange process, fellow group members, and the group's work (Falk & Johnson, 1977; Johnson, 1971, 1977). The greater the clarity of group members' understanding of all sides of the issues and the more accurate the assessment of their validity and relative merits, the more creative the synthesis of all positions in a controversy tends to be (Johnson, 1971).

Rational argument

Arguments are goal directed, aimed at finding the "truth" or making a good decision (Johnson & Johnson, 2007). Rational argumentation includes generating ideas, collecting and organizing relevant information, using inductive and deductive logic, and making tentative conclusions based on current understanding. It also requires that participants keep an open mind, changing their conclusions and positions when others are persuasive and convincing in their presentation of rationale, proof, and logical reasoning. The abilities to gather, organize, and present information, to challenge and disagree, and to engage in reason logically are essential for the constructive management of controversies. Skillfully engaging in rational arguments is central to critical thinking and skilled decision making (Byrnes, 1998; Klaczynski, 2004).

While there has been no direct evidence gathered comparing rational and irrational argumentation in controversies, it is assumed that during a controversy individuals need to follow the canons of rational argumentation (Johnson & Johnson, 2007). Rational argumentation begins with each side constructing their pro and con arguments. Constructing an argument includes generating ideas, collecting relevant information, organizing it using inductive and deductive logic, and making tentative conclusions based on current understanding. One's position (i.e., conclusion and the information and logic that support it) is then presented to a person holding the opposite point of view. Within a controversy, participants present their position and its supporting rationale while asking other participants to do the same. A dialogue subsequently takes place. Engaging in intellectual arguments is like dancing with the opponent. Each move creates a countermove. Person 1 can make an assertion or claim, and Person 2 can respond with a concession, request for justification (i.e., the reasons why the assertion or claim is true), or refutation (i.e., a challenge to the validity of the information and/or logic contained in the assertion). If asked for justification, Person 1 responds with empirical evidence or an explanation. Empirical evidence tends to be the strongest form of justification because it ties the assertion to actual events. Plausible explanations of how a cause is connected to an effect are useful when empirical evidence is lacking (explanations are often stories or examples about how a cause and effect are linked). If confronted with a refutation, Person 1 can respond with a rebuttal delineating the validity of his or her information and logic and the flaws in Person 2's refutation. Rational argumentation requires that participants keep an open mind, changing their conclusions and positions when others are persuasive and convincing in their presentation of rationale, evidence, and logical reasoning.

The absence of rational argumentation usually results in negative outcomes in constructive controversy. Controversy does not result in beneficial outcomes when one or more persons impose his or her view on the other without explanation (Mugny & Doise, 1978), due to unilateral decision making (Carugati, De Paolis, & Mugny, 1980–1981, Study 2; Mugny, De Paolis, & Carugati, 1984), asymmetrical power or authority (a child works with an adult or a leader is appointed) (Carugati et al., 1980–1981, Study 1; Mugny, Giroud, & Doise,

1978–1979, Study 1), or when communication is not possible (Doise & Mugny, 1975).

SUMMARY

The conditions mediating the effects of the controversy process include (a) a cooperative context, which includes interest in disconfirming (as well as confirming) information, decrease in competence threat, decrease in downward social comparison, decreased perceived bias, and greater leadership; (b) heterogeneity among members; (c) distribution of information; (d) skilled disagreement; and (e) rational argument. The constructive controversy procedure has been applied in numerous practical situations. Four of the most important are decision making, education, creativity, and political discourse. They will be discussed in the next four chapters.

7 Constructive controversy and decision making

INTRODUCTION

Theory may inform, but practice convinces.

George Bain (1881–1968), Scottish artist

A large pharmaceutical company faced the decision of whether to buy or build a chemical plant (*The Wall Street Journal*, October 22, 1975). To maximize the likelihood that the best decision was made, the president established two advocacy teams to ensure that both the "buy" and the "build" alternatives received a fair and complete hearing. An advocacy team is a subgroup that prepares and presents a particular policy alternative to the decision-making group. The "buy" team was instructed to prepare and present the best case for purchasing a chemical plant, and the "build" team was told to prepare and present the best case for constructing a new chemical plant near the company's national headquarters. The "buy" team identified over 100 existing plants that would meet the company's needs, narrowed the field down to 20, further narrowed the field down to 3, and then selected 1 plant as the ideal plant to buy. The "build" team contacted dozens of engineering firms and, after four months of consideration, selected a design for the ideal plant to build. Nine months after they were established, the two teams, armed with all the details about cost, (a) presented their best case and (b) challenged each other's information, reasoning, and conclusions. From the spirited discussion, it became apparent that the two options would cost about the same amount of money. The group, therefore, chose the "build" option because it allowed the plant to be conveniently located near company headquarters. This procedure represents the structured use of constructive controversy to ensure high-quality decision making.

In this chapter the application of constructive controversy in decision-making situations is explored. Decision making will first be defined, the constructive controversy procedure for decision making is then described, and the relevance of constructive controversy for thoughtful and considered decision making will then be described.

DECISION MAKING

> The best way ever devised for seeking the truth in any given situation is advocacy: presenting the pros and cons from different, informed points of view and digging down deep into the facts.
>
> *Harold S. Geneer, Former CEO IT&T*

The purpose of group decision making is to decide upon well-considered, well-understood, realistic action toward goals every member wishes to achieve (Johnson & F. Johnson, 2013). A *group decision* implies that some agreement prevails among group members as to which of several courses of action is most desirable for achieving the group's goals. Typically, groups try to make their decisions as effective as possible. There are five major characteristics of an effective group decision (Johnson & F. Johnson, 2013):

1. The resources of group members are fully utilized.
2. Time is well used.
3. The decision is correct, or of high quality.
4. The decision is implemented fully by all the required group members.
5. The problem-solving ability of the group is improved, or at least not lessened.

A decision is effective to the extent that these five criteria are met; if all five are not met, the decision has not been made effectively.

CONSTRUCTIVE CONTROVERSY PROCEDURE
IN DECISION MAKING

To structure a constructive controversy in a decision-making situation, group members are instructed to do the following:

1. **Propose several courses of action that will solve the problem under consideration.**

2. **Form advocacy teams**: To ensure that each course of action receives a fair and complete hearing, assign several (at least two) group members to be an advocacy team to present the best case possible for the assigned position. *Positive interdependence* is structured by highlighting the cooperative goal of making the best decision possible (goal interdependence) and noting that a high-quality decision cannot be made without considering the information that is being organized by the other advocacy teams (resource interdependence). *Individual accountability* is structured by ensuring that each member participates in preparing and presenting the assigned position. Any information discovered that supports the other alternatives is given to the appropriate advocacy pair.

3. **Engage in the constructive controversy procedure:**

   a. *Each advocacy team researches its position and prepares a persuasive presentation to be given to the entire group to ensure their position gets a fair and complete hearing.* The goal is to convince the members of the other advocacy teams of the validity of the team's position. If there are three advocacy teams (Team A, B, and C), for example, Team A prepares the best case possible for its position and makes a persuasive presentation to Teams B and C, trying to convince the members of Teams B and C that the position of Team A is the most valid. The advocacy teams are given the time needed to research their assigned alternative course of action and find all the supporting evidence available. They organize what is known into a coherent and reasoned position. They plan how to present their case so that all members of the group understand thoroughly the advocacy team's position, give it a fair and complete hearing, and are convinced of its soundness.

   b. *Each advocacy team presents without being interrupted the best case possible for its assigned alternative course of action to the entire group.* Other advocacy teams listen carefully, take notes, and strive to learn the information provided.

   c. *There is an open discussion characterized by advocacy, refutation, and rebuttal.* The advocacy teams give opposing positions a "trial by fire" by seeking to refute them by challenging the validity of their information and logic. Members of Team A, for example, try to find every flaw in information and reasoning in the positions of Teams B and C. Members of each team defend their position while continuing to attempt to persuade other group members of its validity. For higher-level reasoning and critical thinking to occur, it is necessary to probe and push each other's conclusions. Members ask for data to support each other's statements, clarify rationales, and show why their position is the most valid and rational. Members of Team A, for example, try to rebut the criticisms of their position being made by the members of Teams B and C, and continue to point out the inadequacies of the positions of Teams B and C. They take careful notes on and thoroughly learn the alternative positions. Members follow the specific rules for constructive controversy. Sometimes a "time-out" period needs to be provided so that advocacy teams can caucus and prepare new arguments. Members should encourage spirited arguing and playing devil's advocate. Members are instructed to argue forcefully and persuasively for their position, present as many facts as they can to support their point of view listen critically to the opposing teams' positions, ask them for the facts that support their viewpoint, and then present counterarguments. They are to remember the issue is complex and they need to know all sides to make a good decision.

d. *Advocacy teams reverse perspectives and positions by presenting the best case possible for one or more of the opposing positions as sincerely and forcefully as team members can.* Members may be told to present an opposing position as if it were theirs. They are to be sincere and forceful. They are to add any new facts they know. They are to elaborate their position by relating it to previously learned information. They are to strive to see the issue from all perspectives simultaneously.

e. *All group members drop their advocacy and reach a decision by consensus.* Members are no longer advocating for their assigned position; they are trying to make the best reasoned judgment they are capable of. Often the final decision is different from and more rational than the original alternatives considered. Members may be instructed to summarize and synthesize the best arguments for *all* points of view. Members try to reach a decision by consensus, changing their mind only when the facts and the rationale clearly indicate that they should do so. They then write a report with the supporting evidence and rationale for their synthesis and sign it.

f. *Group members process how well the group functioned* and how their performance may be improved during the next decision in which they use advocacy teams.

4. **Implement decision**: Once the decision is made, all members commit themselves to implement it regardless of whether they initially favored it or not.

CONSTRUCTIVE CONTROVERSY AND CONSIDERED AND THOUGHTFUL DECISION MAKING

> When two men in business always agree, one of them is unnecessary.
>
> *William Wrigley, Jr.*

Making a considered and thoughtful decision that everyone is committed to implementing is difficult (Johnson & F. Johnson, 2013). It may be impossible to do without the use of constructive controversy. In fact, decisions by their very nature involve controversy, as alternative solutions are suggested and considered before agreement is reached. The controversy procedure, therefore, is the heart of effective decision making.

Decision making occurs within the context of problem solving. In order to consider the steps involved in making considered and thoughtful decisions, the problem-solving procedure must be discussed (Johnson & F. Johnson, 2013; Johnson & R. T. Johnson, 1989). Decision making is part of the larger problem-solving process of (a) identifying and defining the issue being considered, (b) formulating and considering alternative courses of action to solve the problem, (c) deciding on which course of action to adopt, and (d) evaluating the success of the course of action in solving the problem.

Identifying and defining the problem or issue

The first step a decision-making group needs to take is to identify and define the problem (Johnson & F. Johnson, 2013). A *problem* is a discrepancy or difference between an actual state of affairs and a desired state of affairs. Problem solving requires both an idea about where the group should be and valid information about where it is now. The more clear and accurate the definition of the problem, the easier it is to complete the other steps in the problem-solving processes. There are three steps in defining the problem:

1. Reaching agreement on what the desired state of affairs is (that is, the group's purposes, goals, and objectives).
2. Obtaining valid, reliable, directly verifiable, descriptive (not inferential or evaluative), and correct information about the existing state of affairs.
3. Discussing thoroughly the difference between the desired and actual state of affairs; awareness of this discrepancy creates the commitment and motivation to solve the problem.

Because problem-solving groups often progress too quickly toward a solution to the problem without first getting a clear, consensual definition of the problem itself, members of the group should see to it that everyone understands what the problem is before trying to assess its magnitude. Valid information about the problem must be gathered. Then the information must be thoroughly discussed and analyzed to ensure that all group members understand it. Actual frequency of occurrence of the problem needs to be documented. It is important that each participant understand the nature and extent of the problem so that he or she can think of effective courses of action to take to solve the problem. The less the problem is understood, the fewer the alternative courses of action that will be proposed and given serious consideration. When information is minimal, the definition of the problem will be inadequate, fewer alternative strategies for the solution will be generated, and potential consequences of those alternatives will not be properly explored. Not getting the needed information about the nature and extent of the problem results in relatively inadequate solutions. Asking each member to summarize the problem in his or her own words may be the easiest way to assess how well understood the problem is.

Besides ensuring that all participants understand the problem, all participants should be involved in the definition of the group's decision making. Being involved increases the quality of the decision by making more resources available and more fully utilizing the resources of each participant. The members responsible for implementing the decision, furthermore, should be especially knowledgeable about the nature of the problem, and that knowledge is best obtained through being involved in defining the problem.

Formulating alternative solutions

The second step in problem solving is identifying and analyzing alternative ways to solve the problem. Identifying and analyzing alternative ways to solve the problem require creative, divergent, and inventive reasoning. Such "higher-level" thinking and analysis come primarily from intellectual disagreement and challenge (i.e., constructive controversy). Failure to formulate alternative courses of action to solve the problem limits the quality of the resulting decision. If a course of action is not identified, it cannot be considered and evaluated.

Considering and evaluating the alternative solutions

By definition, all decisions involve controversy, as decision making is a choice among alternative courses of action. Groups often make poor decisions because (a) they generate too few alternative courses of action to consider, (b) they do not give every alternative a fair and complete hearing, (c) they do not critically analyze the pros and cons of each of the proposed alternatives (i.e., they do not give each one a "trial by fire"), and (d) they choose an alternative course of action to implement on criteria other than its promise for solving the problem (i.e., the boss likes it best, and the majority puts on pressure to conform to their opinion). Systematically analyzing the advantages and disadvantages of each alternative before making a final decision may be the most important factor in effective decision making. To reduce the likelihood that an alternative is overlooked or rationalized away, an explicit and systematic evaluation process should be used.

A barrier to effective decision making is the premature elimination of courses of action without proper analysis and evaluation, or uninformed and premature choice. Groups often make poor decisions, not because they did not think of the proper alternatives, but because they do a poor job of evaluating and choosing among the alternatives they considered (Maier & Thurber, 1969). For most people, ideas are fragile creations, easily blighted by a chilly or even indifferent reception. As groups proceed in their problem-solving activities, they must avoid all tendencies to squelch each idea as it comes along; instead, they should create an atmosphere that supports the presentation and the pooling of a wide assortment of ideas. All alternative solutions should receive a fair hearing. Only then can the group avoid becoming fixated on the first reasonable solution suggested and critically evaluate the worth of all alternatives. Another contribution of constructive controversy in decision making is the motivation it supplies for (a) increased information, (b) critical analysis of the information and logic being presented to support each alternative course of action, and (c) different perspectives from which to view the issue.

Deciding on a solution

> Gentlemen, I take it we are all in complete agreement on the decision here ... Then I propose we postpone further discussion until our next meeting to give ourselves time to develop disagreement and perhaps gain some understanding of what the decision is all about.
>
> *Alfred Sloan, Chairman of General Motors*

Once all the possible solutions have been identified and formulated in specific terms, the group needs to select the solution to implement (Johnson & F. Johnson, 2013). Making a decision involves considering possible alternatives and choosing one. The purpose of group decision making is to decide on well-considered, well-understood, realistic action toward goals every member wishes to achieve. Controversy is structured within problem-solving groups through the use of advocacy subgroups. Each advocacy subgroup prepares a position, advocates it, defends it from criticism, critically evaluates the alternative positions, views the problem from all perspectives, and synthesizes and integrates the best parts of all solutions. Whenever possible, decisions should be made by consensus. Consensus is not easy to achieve, as it is characterized by more conflict among members, more shifts of opinion, and a longer time to reach a decision. It is, however, worth the time and trouble, and it leads to group members' increased confidence in the correctness of their decision.

Even when decisions are made by consensus, there are times when members fixate on an alternative without thinking through all its consequences. One procedure for ensuring that a decision is not made too hastily is *second-chance meetings*. After a preliminary consensus on the best alternative, a *second-chance meeting* can be held in which all members are encouraged to express any remaining doubts and criticisms. Second-chance meetings help prevent premature consensus and concurrence seeking. There are a number of societies that have assumed that under the influence of alcohol there would be fewer inhibitions against expressing residual doubts about a preliminary decision made when everyone was sober. According to Herodotus, the ancient Persians would make important decisions twice – first sober and then drunk. According to Tacitus, the Germans in Roman times also followed this practice. In Japan, where an emphasis is placed on harmony and politeness, a decision is frequently reconsidered after work in a bar. "Sake talk" takes place after each person has had a couple of cups of sake and, therefore, is no longer required to be polite. How group members really feel about the decision is then revealed. Although it is not necessary to bring alcohol into the decision-making process, groups should consider second-chance meetings as opportunities to make sure people are expressing themselves fully and truthfully. For example, a group may decide to meet a week after the decision initially is made for another, more casual follow-up discussion.

When a decision is made, the constructive controversy ends and participants commit themselves to a common course of action. Many poor decisions are made not because of the absence of or a complexity in the information but rather because individuals did not apprise themselves of the information that was readily available (Janis, 1982). To make high-quality decisions, individuals need to search actively for relevant information in an unbiased way, to process that information centrally or systematically, and to consider the issue from multiple perspectives (Hackman, Brousseau, & Weiss, 1976; Janis & Mann, 1977; Johnson & F. Johnson, 2013; Johnson & R. T. Johnson, 1989; Nemeth, 1995). The constructive controversy procedure ensures that all of these activities take place.

Evaluating extent and success of implementation

The responsibilities of the group members do not end when the group makes a decision. The decision has to be implemented (Johnson & F. Johnson, 2013). *Decision implementation* is a process of taking the necessary actions that result in the execution of the decision. Decision implementation requires internal commitment by relevant group members to the decisions made. No decision is worthwhile unless it is implemented. A major reason to ensure that all participants are involved in the decision-making and constructive-controversy processes is that such involvement increases participants' commitment to implement the decision. Involvement in decision making tends to increase members' allegiance to the group and commitment to seeing the decision through to fruition.

To evaluate the success of the solution the group has decided to implement, members must determine whether the solution was successfully implemented and what the effects were. The first activity is *process evaluation* because it deals with the process of implementing a course of action. The second is *outcome evaluation* because it involves assessing or judging the consequences of implementing the course of action. The major criterion for assessing the outcome of an implemented course of action is whether the actual state of affairs is closer to the desired state of affairs than it was before the course of action was carried out.

SUMMARY

There are businesses and industrial organizations all over the world that have applied the constructive controversy process in their decision making. This may be especially true in China and in engineering schools. To engage in considered and thoughtful decision making, individuals identify and define the problem, gather the information needed to diagnose it, formulate alternative solutions, decide on the solution to implement, and evaluate the success of the implementation to determine if the problem has been solved. An essential aspect of decision making is deciding among alternative courses of action. To do so effectively, conflict among members' preferences, analyses, conclusions, and theories must be encouraged and resolved constructively. Constructive controversy provides a cooperative context in which ideas can be freely expressed and participants can formulate creative decisions that lead to innovations. Constructive controversy is the heart of effective decision making. In order to make good decisions that are fully implemented, each alternative course of action must be given (a) a fair and complete hearing and (b) a "trial by fire" in which it is critically analyzed in order to clarify its strengths and weaknesses. Another contribution of constructive controversy to decision making is the motivation it supplies for (a) increased information, (b) critical analysis of the information and logic being presented to support each alternative course of action, and (c) different perspectives from which to view the issue. A second application of constructive controversy is in education, which is discussed in the next chapter.

8 Constructive controversy in education

Around 1200 a city that we call Mesa Verde was built on a cliff on the Colorado Plateau by the Anasazi. Mesa Verde is a remarkably beautiful city consisting of both single- and multistoried pueblo dwellings. Even today, it is one of the most impressive sights in North America. Around 1295, after the Anasazi lived in it for almost a hundred years, the city was abruptly abandoned. In a three- to four-year period, the Anasazi walked away and never came back. Why? No one knows. Many classes are to students what Mesa Verde was to the Anasazi. Students enroll in a course, pay the tuition, and spend considerable time attending class sessions, completing assignments, and passing tests, but when the course is over, so is their interest. They walk away and intellectually, never to come back.

Wouldn't it be nice if students got so involved in the subject being taught that they sparkled with energy, were deeply involved in the topics being discussed, rushed to the library to get more information and resources, continued discussing the topics over lunch and at night, sought out experts in the field to consult, and impatiently waited for the next class session to begin. Wouldn't it be nice if students stayed fascinated by the subject the rest of their lives, gathering new information about the subject whenever they could. How do students get that interested in what is being taught? An essential and often overlooked part of the answer is, "Stir up intellectual conflict."

INSTRUCTOR'S ROLE IN ACADEMIC CONTROVERSIES

> Conflict is the gadfly of thought. It stirs us to observation and memory. It instigates invention. It shocks us out of sheep-like

passivity, and sets us at noting and contriving. Not that it always effects this result, but conflict is a "sine qua non" of reflection and ingenuity.

John Dewey, Human Nature and Conduct: Morals Are Human.
Dewey Middle Works, *Vol. 14, p. 207*

Are wolves a national treasure that should be allowed to roam freely while being protected from hunting and trapping? Or are wolves a renewable resource that should be managed for sport and revenue? Ecologists say that wolves should be a protected species. But many farmers, ranchers, and sportspersons believe that wolves should be managed.

Peggy Tiffany, a fourth-grade instructor in Wilmington, Vermont, asked her class to take a stand on the wolf. "You," she says to her class, "must write a report in which you explain what should happen to the wolf in the continental United States and why! To ensure that the reports represent your best thinking, you will write it cooperatively with several of your classmates!" She then randomly assigns students to groups of four, ensuring that both male and female and high-, medium-, and low-achieving students are all in the same group. She then divides each group into two pairs. One pair is assigned the position that wolves should be a protected species. The other pair is assigned the position that wolves should be a managed species. Each pair is given a packet of materials relevant to their position.

Ms. Tiffany has prepared the way for structuring an academic controversy by: (a) choosing a topic that has content manageable by the students and on which at least two well-documented positions (pro and con) can be prepared and (b) structuring cooperative learning by assigning students to learning groups of four, creating resource interdependence by giving each pair half of the materials, and highlighting the cooperative goals of reaching a consensus on the issue, writing a group report on which all members will be evaluated, and preparing each member to take a test on the information studied. She is now ready to conduct the controversy, which involves a structured, but complex, process. The instructor's role in conducting a controversy is an extension of the instructor's role in structuring cooperative learning. To conduct a controversy, instructors (Johnson & Johnson, 1979, 1989, 2007):

1. specify the objectives for the lesson;
2. make a number of preinstructional decisions;
3. clearly explain the task, the positive interdependence, and the controversy procedure to the students;
4. monitor the effectiveness of cooperative learning groups and intervene to provide assistance in (a) completing the task, (b) following the controversy procedure, or (c) using the required interpersonal and group skills; and
5. evaluate students' achievement and help students process how well they functioned as a group.

PREINSTRUCTIONAL DECISIONS AND PREPARATIONS

Objectives and topic

There are two types of objectives that an instructor needs to specify before the lesson begins. The *academic objective* needs to be specified at the correct level for the students and matched to the right level of instruction according to a conceptual or task analysis. The *social skills objective* details what interpersonal and small-group skills are going to be emphasized during the lesson. A common error many instructors make is to specify only academic objectives and ignore the social skills needed to train students to cooperate and disagree constructively with each other.

In specifying the objectives, you, the instructor, must choose a topic for the controversy. Criteria for the selection include that at least two well-documented positions can be prepared and that the content be manageable by the students. Almost any issue being studied can be turned into a controversy. Most environmental, energy, public policy, social studies, literature, and scientific issues are appropriate. It should also be noted that whenever students work together in cooperative learning groups, natural controversies will arise in their decision-making and problem-solving activities. By participating in structured academic controversies, students will learn the procedures and skills to use when unplanned, natural controversies suddenly arise.

Deciding on the size of the group

Unless you plan to use an observer, cooperative learning groups of four should be used for structured controversies. Each position usually has two students assigned to work as a team in preparing to advocate it. While some issues may lend themselves to three positions (and thus to groups of six), the complexity of synthesizing three positions and managing the interaction among six students is such that groups are typically limited to four. The more inexperienced students are in working cooperatively and engaging in controversy, the shorter the class period; and the more limited the materials, the more the size of the group should definitely be limited to four.

Assigning students to groups

In order to increase the potential for controversy, the heterogeneity of students within each learning group should be maximized so that students of different achievement levels in math, ethnic backgrounds, sexes, and social classes work together. The heterogeneity among group members increases the likelihood that different perspectives and viewpoints will naturally occur. In addition, heterogeneity among students typically increases performance in problem-solving and conceptual-learning tasks. When a student is isolated from his or her classmates, either because of shyness or because of being stigmatized as having a special learning problem or being from a minority group, instructors will want to plan carefully to ensure that the student is placed with outgoing, friendly, and accepting peers. When in doubt as to how to maximize heterogeneity, however, randomly assign students to groups.

Arranging the room

Members of a learning group should sit close enough to each other that they can share materials, talk to each other quietly, and maintain eye contact with all group members. Circles are usually best. The instructor should have clear access lanes to every group. Students will have to move into pairs and then back into groups of four.

Planning instructional materials to promote interdependence and controversy

Within controversies, materials are divided into pro and con so that each pair of students has part of the materials needed to complete the task. The following materials are typically prepared for each position:

1. a clear description of the group's task,
2. a description of the phases of the controversy procedure and the collaborative skills to be utilized during each phase,
3. a definition of the position to be advocated with a summary of the key arguments supporting the position, and
4. a set of resource materials (including a bibliography) to provide evidence for and elaboration of the arguments supporting the position to be advocated.

A balanced presentation should be given for all sides of the controversy and the materials should be separated into packets containing articles, reports, or summaries supporting each position on the issue.

Assigning roles

Inherent in the controversy procedure is assigning students to a pro or con advocacy pair. In effect, this is assigning students complementary roles that signal their positive interdependence within the controversy process. In addition, instructors may wish to assign students other roles related to working together cooperatively and engaging in intellectual arguments.

EXPLAINING AND ORCHESTRATING THE ACADEMIC TASK, COOPERATIVE GOAL STRUCTURE, AND CONTROVERSY PROCEDURE

Have you learned lessons only of
those who admired you, and were tender
with you, and stood aside for you?

Have you not learned great lessons
from those who braced themselves
against you, and disputed the passage
with you?

Walt Whitman, 1860

Explaining the academic task

Instructors explain the academic task so that students are clear about the assignment and understand the objectives of the lesson. Direct teaching of concepts, principles, and strategies may take place at this point. Instructors may wish to answer any questions students have about the concepts or facts they are to learn or apply in the lesson. The task must be structured so that there are at least two well-documented positions (e.g., pro and con). The choice of topic depends on the interests of the instructor and the purposes of the course.

Structuring positive interdependence

Instructors communicate to students that they have a group goal and must work cooperatively. There are two group goals in a controversy:

1. The group is told to produce a single report and arrive at consensus concerning what decision should be made. Students are responsible for ensuring that all group members participate in writing a quality group report and making a presentation to the class.
2. Students are informed that they are responsible for ensuring that all group members master all the information relevant to both sides of the issue (measured by a test that each student takes individually).

To supplement the effects of positive goal interdependence, the materials are jigsawed within the group (*resource interdependence*) and bonus points may be given if all group members score above a preset criterion on the test (*reward interdependence*).

Structuring the controversy

The constructive controversy procedure consists of the instructor assigning students to groups of four members, dividing each group into two pairs, and assigning the task of writing a group report and/or passing a test (given to each member) on the topic being studied (Johnson & Johnson, 1979, 1989, 2007). The cooperative goal is for students to reach their "best reasoned judgment" on the issue. The assignment for one pair is to develop and advocate the best case possible for the pro position, and the assignment for the other pair is to develop and advocate the best case possible for the con position. The instructor then supervises the controversy procedure. Constructive controversy may be used in all subject areas. Any topic can be presented as a controversy as long as at least two sides can be identified.

An example of a controversy may help in explaining its educational use. A US history instructor is presenting a unit on the nature of democracy. The instructor notes that in numerous instances individuals democratically elected to office wish to hold on to their power indefinitely. Thus, they undermine the democratic process in order to stay in office. In other cases, people in power peacefully turn over power to those who have been elected to replace them. The central question is, "Is democracy a viable form of government in today's world?" In today's world, will democratically elected officials (such as members of congress) undermine the democratic process to stay in power or will they promote democracy and live with the consequences? Students are placed in groups of four members and given the assignments of writing a report and passing a test (that each student takes individually on his or her own) on whether democracy is viable. Each group is divided into two pairs. One pair is assigned the task of developing and advocating the best case possible for the viability of democracy, and the other pair is given the assignment of developing and advocating the best case possible for the nonviability of democracy. The overall group goal is for students to reach consensus as to the viability of the democratic form of government. The students are to learn the information relevant to the issue being studied and ensure that all other group members learn the information. All members should then be able to (a) help their group write a high-quality report on the issue and (b) achieve high scores on a test on both sides of the issue.

Students proceed through the steps of constructive controversy (Johnson & Johnson, 1979, 1989, 2007). In Step 1, each pair prepares the best case possible for its assigned position by (a) researching the assigned position and learning all relevant information, (b) organizing the information into a persuasive argument that contains a thesis, assertion, or claim ("Democracy is a viable form of government in today's world"), the asserting the rationale supporting the thesis ("The following points provide proof that democracy is viable"), providing a logical conclusion that is the same as the thesis ("Therefore, democracy is a viable form of government in today's world"), and (c) planning how to advocate the assigned position effectively to ensure it receives a fair and complete hearing.

In Step 2, students present the best case for their assigned position to ensure it gets a fair and complete hearing. They strive to be forceful, persuasive, and convince advocates in being so, ideally using more than one medium. They listen carefully to and learn the opposing position, clarifying anything they do not understand.

In Step 3, students engage in an open discussion of the issue. Students freely exchange information and ideas while arguing forcefully and persuasively for their position (presenting as many facts as they can to support their point of view) and engaging in spirited disagreement. They critically analyze the opposing position (its evidence and reasoning), ask for data to support assertions, and refute the opposing position by pointing out the inadequacies in the information and reasoning. While doing so students thoroughly learn the opposing position and criticize its information and reasoning while following the rules for constructive controversy. Finally, students rebut attacks on their position. The instructor may take sides to encourage more spirited arguing, play devil's advocate, ask one group to observe another group engaging in a spirited argument, and generally stir up the discussion.

In Step 4, students reverse perspectives and present the best case possible for the opposing position. In presenting the opposing position sincerely and forcefully, students may use their notes and add new facts. Students should strive to see the issue from both perspectives.

In Step 5, students drop all advocacy and strive to find a synthesis to which they can all agree. Students summarize the best evidence and reasoning from both sides and integrate it into a joint position that is new and unique. Students write a group report on the synthesis including the supporting evidence and rationale, individually take a test on both positions, process how well the group functioned, and celebrate the group's success and the hard work of each member.

The rules for engaging in constructive controversy are as follows:

1. I am critical of ideas, not people. I challenge and refute the ideas of the opposing pair, but I do not indicate that I personally reject them.
2. Remember, we are all in this together, sink or swim. I focus on coming to the best decision possible, not on winning.
3. I encourage everyone to participate and to master all the relevant information.
4. I listen to everyone's ideas, even if I don't agree.
5. I restate what someone has said if it is not clear.
6. I first bring out all ideas and facts supporting both sides, and then I try to put them together in a way that makes sense.
7. I try to understand both sides of the issue.
8. I change my mind when the evidence clearly indicates that I should do so.

In addition, participating in academic controversies teaches students essential problem-solving skills they will use for the rest of their lives. Students learn how to research and formulate the "best case" for a position, present a persuasive and convincing case for it, critically analyze and refute opposing positions while rebutting attacks on their own position, see the issues from both perspectives, and synthesize the best reasoning from both sides in order to reach a group consensus on the best reasoned judgment possible. It is important for students to understand that the purpose of advocacy and criticism is not to win, but rather to clarify the strengths and weaknesses of various courses of action so that a joint agreement may be reached as to what represents the best reasoned judgment that can be made at this time.

In addition to explaining the procedure, the instructor may wish to help the students "get in role" by presenting the issue to be decided in as interesting and dramatic a way as possible.

Structuring individual accountability

The purpose of the controversy is to make each member a stronger individual. The level of each student's learning, therefore, needs to be assessed. Individual accountability is structured by individually testing each student on the material studied and/or randomly choosing one member of each group to present their group's decision and its rationale to the class as a whole. Students should also be observed to ensure that each participates in each step of the controversy procedure.

Explaining criteria for success

Evaluations within cooperatively structured lessons (and controversies are no exception) need to be criteria-referenced. At the beginning of the lesson, instructors need to explain clearly the criteria by which students' work will be evaluated.

Specifying desired behaviors

No matter how carefully instructors structure controversies, if students do not have the interpersonal and small-group skills to manage conflicts constructively the controversy does not produce its potential effects. The *social skills* emphasized are those involved in systematically advocating an intellectual position and evaluating and criticizing the position advocated by others, as well as the skills involved in synthesis and consensual decision making. Students should be taught the following skills.

1. Emphasize the mutuality of the situation and avoid win–lose dynamics. Focus on coming to the best decision possible, not on winning.
2. Confirm others' competence while disagreeing with their positions and challenging their reasoning. Be critical of ideas, not people. Challenge and refute the ideas of the members of the opposing pair, but do not reject them personally.
3. Separate your personal worth from criticism of your ideas.
4. Listen to everyone's ideas, even if you do not agree with them.
5. First bring out all the ideas and facts supporting both sides and then try to put them together in a way that makes sense. Be able to differentiate the differences between positions before attempting to integrate ideas.
6. Be able to take the opposing perspective in order to understand the opposing position. Try to understand both sides of the issue.
7. Change your mind when the evidence clearly indicates that you should.
8. Paraphrase what someone has said if it is not clear.
9. Emphasize rationality in seeking the best possible answer, given the available data.
10. Follow the golden rule of conflict. The golden rule is, act toward your opponents as you would have them act toward you. If you want people to listen to you, then listen to them. If you want others to include your ideas in their thinking, then include their ideas in your thinking. If you want others to take your perspective, then take their perspective.

Structuring intergroup cooperation

When preparing their positions, students can check with classmates in other groups who are also preparing the same position. Ideas as to how best to present and advocate the position can be shared. If one pair of students finds information that supports its position, members can share that information with other pairs who have the same position. The more conferring between pairs of students, the better. The positive outcomes found with a cooperative learning group can be extended throughout a whole class by structuring intergroup cooperation. Bonus points may be given if all members of a class reach a preset criteria of excellence. When a group finishes its work, the instructor should encourage the members to go and help other groups complete the assignment.

MONITORING AND INTERVENING

Monitoring students' behavior

Instructors observe group members to see what problems they are having completing the assignment and skillfully engaging in the controversy procedure. Whenever possible, instructors should use a formal observation sheet where they count the number of times they observe appropriate behaviors being used by students. The more concrete the data, the more useful it is to the instructor and to students. Instructors should not try to count too many different behaviors at one time, especially when they first start formal observation. At first they may just want to keep track of who talks in each group to get a participation pattern for the groups. We have a chapter describing systematic observation of cooperative groups in *Learning Together and Alone* (1999) and our current list of behaviors (though rather long) includes: contributing ideas, asking questions, expressing feelings, active listening, expressing support and acceptance (toward ideas), expressing warmth and liking (toward group members and group), encouraging all members to participate, summarizing, checking for understanding, relieving tension by joking, and giving direction to group's work. All the behaviors we look for are positive behaviors that are to be praised when they are appropriately present and are a cause for discussion when they are missing. It is also a good idea for the instructor to collect notes on specific student behaviors so that the frequency data is extended. Especially useful are skillful interchanges that can be shared with students later as objective praise and perhaps with parents in conferences or telephone conversations.

Providing academic assistance

In monitoring the learning groups as they work, instructors will wish to clarify instructions, review important concepts and strategies, answer questions, and teach academic skills as necessary. Students may need assistance at any stage of the controversy procedure, whether it is researching their position, advocating it, refuting the opposing position, defending their position from attack, reversing perspectives, or creatively synthesizing.

Intervening to teach cooperative skills

While monitoring the learning groups, instructors will often find (a) students who do not have the necessary conflict skills and (b) groups where members are having problems in disagreeing effectively. In these cases, instructors intervene to suggest more effective procedures for working together and more effective behaviors. Basic interpersonal and small-group skills may be directly taught (Johnson, 1991, 2014; Johnson & F. Johnson, 2013). Instructors may also wish to intervene and reinforce particularly effective and skillful behaviors that they notice. At times the instructor becomes a consultant to a group in order to help it function more effectively.

The best time to teach conflict skills is when the students need them. Intervening should leave a cooperative learning group with new skills that will be useful in the future. At a minimum,

1. Students need to recognize the need for the skill.
2. The skill must be defined clearly and specifically including what students should say when engaging in the skill.
3. The practice of the skill must be encouraged. Sometimes just the instructor standing there with a clipboard and pencil will be enough to promote student enactment of the skill.
4. Students should have the time and procedures for discussing how well they are using the skills. Students should persevere in the practice until the skill is appropriately internalized. We never drop a skill; we only add on.

EVALUATING AND PROCESSING

Providing closure to lesson

At the end of each instructional unit, students should be able to summarize what they have learned. You may wish to summarize the major points in the lesson, ask students to recall ideas or give examples, and answer any final questions students have.

Assessing and evaluating students' learning

Students' work is evaluated, their learning is assessed, and feedback is given as to how their work compares with the criteria of excellence. Qualitative as well as quantitative aspects of performance should be addressed. Students receive a group grade on the quality of their final report and receive an individual grade on their performance on the test covering both sides of the issue.

Processing how well the group functioned

Some time should be spent talking about how well the groups functioned today, what things were done well, and what things could be improved. Discussing group functioning is essential. Students do not learn from experiences that they do not reflect on. If the learning groups are to function better tomorrow than they did today, members must receive feedback, reflect on how their actions may be more effective, and plan how to be even more skillful during the next group session.

Every small group has two primary goals: (1) to accomplish the task successfully, and (2) to build and maintain constructive relationships in good working order for the next task. Learning groups are often exclusively task-oriented and ignore the importance of maintaining effective working relationships among members. Group sessions should be enjoyable, lively, and pleasant experiences. If no one is having fun, something is wrong. Problems in cooperating and engaging in controversy should be brought up and solved, and there should be a continuing emphasis on improving the effectiveness of the group members in collaborating with each other.

Often during the "working" part of the class period, students will be very task-oriented, and the "maintenance" of the relationships among group members may suffer. During the processing time, however, the emphasis is on maintenance of the group. When groups "process," they discuss any member actions that need to be improved in order for everyone's learning to be maximized. Instructors often have students turn in a "process sheet" along with the paper from the task assignment.

Online use of constructive controversy

Cary Roseth and his colleagues (Roseth, Saltarelli, & Glass, 2011; Saltarelli & Roseth, 2014) have conducted two studies examining the use of online constructive controversies. Roseth et al. (2011) compared face-to-face and computer-mediated versions of constructive controversy. They included three conditions: face-to-face versus computer-mediated controversy, three mediums (video, audio, text), and synchronous versus asynchronous communication. Only 62 percent of asynchronous online students completed the procedure compared to 100 percent of face-to-face and synchronous online students. Face-to-face and synchronous communication increased cooperative perceptions and individualistic perceptions decreased compared to asynchronous computer-mediated communication, resulting in predicted increases in motivation (e.g., relatedness, interest, value) and academic achievement. These results suggest that synchronicity but not medium plays an important role in computer-mediated constructive controversy.

In a second study, Saltarelli and Roseth (2014) examined whether belongingness and the synchronicity of computer-mediated communication affected the processes underlying constructive controversy. The conditions were (a) face-to-face, synchronous, and asynchronous interaction and (b) acceptance, mild rejection, and no response from the other participants. Results indicate that face-to-face and synchronous online interaction, compared with asynchronous online interaction, increased motivation and cooperative perceptions and decreased relational regulation. In terms of achievement, 100 percent of the students in the face-to-face and synchronous online interaction conditions completed the controversy, while only 55 percent of the students in the asynchronous condition did so. Belongingness and synchronicity tend to have additive effects on constructive controversy, and that acceptance buffers but does not offset the effects of asynchronous computer-mediated communication.

IMPLEMENTATION

While most of the implementations of constructive controversy have occurred in elementary and secondary schools, there has been widespread application in some university settings, such as engineering schools. Constructive controversy is a featured pedagogy in the Purdue University Engineering Education PhD program (Smith, Matusovich, Meyers, & Mann, 2011). Under the guidance of Karl Smith (1984), Neil Mickleborough, Tracy Zou, and other colleagues in the Center for Engineering Education Innovation at Hong Kong University of Science and Technology implemented constructive controversy in a course on engineering grand challenges (Zou, Mickleborough, & Leung, 2012). Constructive controversy has been used in Azerbaijan, the Czech Republic, Lithuania, and the United States by secondary school instructors as part of the "Deliberating in a Democracy Project" to teach students how to be citizens in a democracy (Avery, Freeman, Greenwalt, & Trout, 2006). A related procedure, cooperative learning, has been used to teach elementary and secondary students in Armenia how to be citizens in a democracy (Hovhannisyan, Varrella, Johnson, & Johnson, 2005). Thus, in both mature and developing democracies, constructive controversy has been used to socialize citizens into the understandings, attitudes, and competencies they need to participate effectively in political discourse and be citizens in a democracy. Overall, constructive controversy is being used in many different countries around the world in almost every subject area and grade level.

EXAMPLE OF ACADEMIC CONTROVERSY

The instructional use of constructive controversy can be illustrated by the following example. While the example focuses on the wolf, any endangered species could be the subject of the lesson. What follows is a briefing sheet and then a list of possible arguments for the pro position and another list for the con position. These suggested points are only to prime the students to find more information and formulate their own arguments.

The wolf situation

Minnesota contains the last large stand of wolves in the continental United States. There are two major views toward the wolf. One is that wolves are a national treasure and should be a protected species and left to roam freely through Northern Minnesota. The other is that wolves are (a) a varmint that threatens domestic livestock and (b) a renewable resource to be managed for sport and revenue. Wolves should, therefore, be hunted and trapped to keep their numbers small and then confined to small areas that do not contain livestock and farms.

In 1973 the eastern timber wolf was classified as endangered in all of the lower 48 states, protecting it from all hunting and trapping. Minnesota boasts the only viable population of wolves at a stable 1,200 animals. Small populations also exist in Wisconsin (20–25) and on Isle Royal, Michigan (23). In 1978 ranchers and sportspersons were successful in persuading government officials to reclassify the wolf as "threatened" in Minnesota, which allowed government killing of wolves suspected of livestock predation. An effective predator control program in northern Minnesota has been in effect since then.

You are a committee in the Minnesota Department of Natural Resources (DNR) who have been asked to make a recommendation as to the future classification of the gray wolf. The US Fish and Wildlife Service (FWS) has been asked to approve a sport season for hunting wolves in Minnesota and to give the state of Minnesota full control over the wolf. In the past it has denied such requests on the basis that the wolf is protected under the Endangered Species Act. It has asked, however, for a full report and a recommendation from your committee. Two of you are from ecological groups that are deeply concerned with preserving the wolf and, therefore, wish the wolf to be classified as an "endangered species." Two of you are from farmer and rancher organizations who wish the control of the wolf to be given to the state of Minnesota so that wolves may be hunted and trapped. As a group you must make a plan for the future of the wolf that all four members can agree to. Share your position and its rationale with the group. Stick to your guns unless logically persuaded otherwise. At the same time, help your group achieve consensus on the issue.

PRESERVE THE WOLF

Your position is to preserve the wolf. You believe that it is time to dispel the myth of "the big bad wolf" and recognize that the wolf has a valuable role to play in the ecosystem and that we humans can adapt a little and compromise a little to share our space with this magnificent animal.

Whether or not you agree with this position, argue for it as strongly as you can. Take the preservation viewpoint honestly, using arguments that make sense and are rational. Be creative and invent new supporting arguments. Seek out information; ask members of other groups who may know. Remember to learn the rationale for both your position and the "manage" position. Challenge the "manage" position. Think of loopholes in the evidence and logic. Demand facts and information to back up their arguments.

You are members of a group at the University of Minnesota in Duluth. Your group works to promote preservation of the wolf by conducting awareness campaigns, lobbying at the state capitol, and conducting expeditions into the wilderness to track and observe wolves. You are adamantly opposed to the management efforts of the State Department of Natural Resources and fear the extinction of the wolf and its natural habitat.

1. The gray wolf represents a national treasure that is one of the last remnants of true wilderness left in the United States. Wolves have disappeared from 99 percent of their original range. Minnesota is one of the last states in America where wolves live. The wolf should be protected in this last 1 percent of their original habitat.

2. In the Endangered Species Act, Congress mandated that the regulated killing of a member of a threatened species is prohibited except in the "extraordinary case where population pressures within a given ecosystem cannot otherwise be relieved." This is clearly not the case with Minnesota's wolf population, which remains well within its biological carrying capacity.

3. Wolf depredation on Minnesota livestock is minor. Only 0.1 percent of livestock within wolf range and 0.3 percent of all Northern Minnesota farms have been affected. Wolves often eat some farm animals, but it is because farmers fail to remove the carcasses of dead animals that wolves are attracted to the area. Farmers are only serving to entice the wolves.

4. According to government studies published in 1982, many cases of livestock depredation by wolves can be attributed to poor animal husbandry practices. Cattle are allowed to roam in forested areas or in remote open pastures where wolf encounters are more likely. Dead livestock are dumped in or near pastures, attracting wolves and giving them a taste for livestock. Proper disposal methods and better pasturing techniques would prevent many of the depredation problems.

5. Any farmer or rancher who suffers losses, verified as wolf kills, receives compensation through the Minnesota livestock compensation program. Domestic livestock does not need protection because owners will not lose financially from any killing of livestock by wolves.

6. A successful federal predator control program, under the direction of Dr. L. David Mech and Dr. Steven Fritts, has been operative since 1978. Under this program government trappers took 29 wolves in 1981 and 20 wolves in 1982. It is estimated that only 30–35 Minnesota wolves prey on livestock. The focus of the program has been to locate and trap only those wolves causing damage.

7. If control of the wolf is given over to the state of Minnesota, any and all wolves within a one-half mile radius of farms reported to have had depredation problems can be trapped. There will be no criteria for selecting trappers or for verifying wolf kills. No limit to the length of time that trapping may be carried out will be given. The result will be indiscriminate killing of wolves.

8. Up to 400 wolves are killed illegally in Minnesota each year. A sport trapping season will officially sanction the public killing of wolves and an increase in illegal kills will occur.

9. Years of concerted effort on the part of environmental groups and millions of concerned citizens have gone into the creation of the Endangered Species Act. The classification needs to be changed back immediately or else all of this money and effort will be wasted.
10. There has been a drop in the deer population in Minnesota due to having seven severe winters in a row.
11. There is a natural balance between the wolf and the deer. By killing the weak and sick deer, more food is left for the healthy deer. If humans kill wolves, they upset this natural balance.

MANAGE THE WOLF

Your position is that control over the gray wolf should be turned over to the state of Minnesota and a sport hunting and trapping season established. You believe that it is time to face the reality that wolves are dangerous animals running rampant in northern Minnesota and are threatening the economic survival of many farmers. Wolves must be trapped and shot to keep their population within reasonable limits.

Whether or not you agree with this position, argue for it as strongly as you can. Take the management viewpoint honestly, using arguments that make sense and are rational. Be creative and invent new supporting arguments. Seek out information; ask members of other groups who may know. Remember to learn the rationale for both your position and the "preserve" position. Challenge the "manage" position. Think of loopholes in the evidence and logic. Demand facts and information to back up their arguments.

You represent farmers and ranchers in northern Minnesota. They believe that to let the wolves roam free is nothing but a dream of some environmentalists who are not faced with the reality of the situation. To observe wolves is one thing, but to live with the threats they pose is quite another.

1. The gray wolf is a varmint that threatens domestic livestock and a renewable resource to be managed for sport and revenue.
2. A sport trapping season will reduce public antagonism toward wolves and, therefore, reduce the number of illegal kills.

3. The Minnesota Department of Natural Resources (DNR) has maintained for a long time that the Minnesota population of wolves is neither endangered nor threatened. Further, the DNR has maintained that the wolf must be actively managed to ensure its survival.

4. The DNR has a history of fighting for the wolf. In 1965 the DNR attempted to have the Minnesota state legislature eliminate the antiquated bounty system on wolves. In the early 1970s, the DNR attempted to have the legislature elevate the timber wolf from an unprotected species to that of a game animal. Their recommendations, therefore, should be taken seriously.

5. Controlled hunting will protect the wolf and ensure its survival by lessening some of the rage against wolves by people who would exterminate this animal if given the opportunity. Unless a hunting season is established, illegal killing will grow.

6. A balance must be established between people and a great predator. Compromise and balance is the approach we should take. In some areas we can maintain a viable wolf population where wolves do not compete directly with humans. In other areas, the wolf must be managed and controlled if we are to avert wholesale destruction of the animal.

7. *The Federal Register* (vol. 48, no. 155, page 36256) of August 10, 1983, has this sentence included as a part of its statement relating to wolf predation on livestock – sheep, poultry, and cattle: "In areas where recurrent depredation appears, the Service is of the view that it would be consistent with sound conservation of the wolf to authorize a limited public trapping season for wolves, provided the wolf population density in the affected zones not fall below the level recommended by the Wolf Recovery Team."

8. The DNR plan providing a mechanism to control wolf encroachment into areas of human habitation is essential if illegal killing is to be eliminated. If the wolf is to remain a part of our priceless wildlife heritage, we believe the DNR plan must be supported.

9. Farmers and ranchers believe that wolves are reproducing rapidly, the number of deer (their natural prey) is going down, and, therefore, wolves have taken to eating farm animals, including pet dogs. In 1965 we had 700,000 deer in Minnesota. Now we have only 200,000.

SUMMARY

How you ride a horse leaves an imprint that can be detected by a skilled trainer. Some indicators are fairly obvious. If the horse has well-developed muscles underneath its neck, then the rider has habitually been pulling back on the reins. If the horse has well-developed muscles on the top of its neck, then the rider has held the reins loosely and moved the horse forward with his or her seat and legs. More subtle imprints can be detected only when the trainer rides the horse. By the way the horse moves, the trainer can tell who was the last person to ride it.

The methods we use to teach leave an imprint on students. From the way students act at the beginning of a class, we can tell a great deal about the professors who have taught them previously. If students sit passively and are interested primarily in what will be on the test, or if students volunteer their conclusions and engage in spirited disagreement, you know a great deal about their previous instructors. How instructors teach leaves an imprint. If they frequently use recitation, students are imprinted with a pattern of listening carefully, waiting to be called on, and giving factual answers that the instructor likes. If they frequently use group discussion, students are imprinted with a pattern of active participation, jointly considering higher-level questions, exchanging ideas, and utilizing each other's thinking. If they frequently use constructive controversy, students are imprinted with a pattern of intellectual inquiry that includes building coherent intellectual arguments, giving persuasive presentations, critically analyzing and challenging others' positions, rebutting others' challenges, seeing issues from a variety of perspectives, and seeking reasoned judgments. Students learn that the purpose of advocacy and criticism is not to win, but rather to clarify the strengths and weaknesses of various courses of action so that a joint agreement may be reached as to what represents the best reasoned judgment.

The instructor's role in implementing structured academic controversies is an extension of the instructor's role in using cooperative

learning. It consists of specifying the learning and social skills objectives, making a number of preinstructional decisions, explaining and
orchestrating the academic task and the controversy procedure, monitoring and intervening, and evaluating and processing. Academic controversies may be used in any subject area with students of any age.
Yet implementing structured academic controversies is not easy. It
can take years to become an expert. Instructors may wish to start
small by taking one subject area or one class and using controversy
procedures until they feel comfortable, and then expand into other
subject areas or other classes. Instructors are well advised to pick out
topics for which they are pretty sure a controversy will work, plan
carefully, and do not rush the process. In order to implement academic
controversies successfully, instructors will need to teach students the
interpersonal and small-group skills required to cooperate, engage in
intellectual inquiry, intellectually challenge each other, see a situation from several perspectives simultaneously, and synthesize a variety of positions into a new and creative decision. Implementing
academic controversies in your classroom is not easy, but it is worth
the effort.

9 Constructive controversy and political discourse in democracies

In 1859 Horace Greeley and Henry David Thoreau were having a discussion about John Brown's exploits at Harper's Ferry. "No matter how well intended John Brown was," Horace said, "his methods were completely unacceptable. The man broke the law! Terrorism for a good cause is still terrorism. It does not follow that because slavery is wrong, John Brown's actions were right. No matter how opposed to slavery one is, one cannot condone what John Brown did." "Now Horace," Henry replied, "you are missing the whole point. It does not matter whether John Brown broke the law or not. It only matters what he symbolizes. And he symbolizes eternal justice, glory, and devotion to principle. We should pay homage to the ideals John Brown represents, not get caught in a mundane discussion of legalities."

Thomas Jefferson, James Madison, and the other founders of the United States would have applauded Greeley and Thoreau's discussion. They believed that free and open discussion should serve as the basis of influence within society (not the social rank within which a person was born). This free and open discussion was to be characterized by conflict among ideas and opinions, open-minded consideration of all points of view, and changing one's mind in order to find the best action to take for the good of the country as a whole. Jefferson had a deep faith in the value and productiveness of conflict. Thomas Jefferson noted, "Differences of opinion lead to inquiry, and inquiry to truth." James Madison described political discourse as (a) including open-minded consideration of other points of view ("much is gained by a yielding and accommodating spirit") and (b) keeping conclusions tentative by realizing that one's current knowledge is not the whole

153

truth (no citizen is "obligated to retain his opinions any longer than he is satisfied of their propriety and truth"). Citizens in our democracy are expected to advocate conflicting positions while keeping an open mind and keeping conclusions tentative. Each alternative course of action is expected to (a) receive a complete and fair hearing and (b) be critically analyzed to reveal its strengths and weakness, so that the best reasoned judgment can be made about the course of action the country should take. Thus, citizens are expected to research their positions, advocate them, critically analyze and challenge opposing positions, step back and see the issue from all perspectives simultaneously, and help find a synthesis that utilizes the best information and reasoning from all sides. It is citizens' ability to make thoughtful, reasoned judgments that makes a democracy viable.

In the United States, Thomas Jefferson and the other founders of the American Republic considered conflict among positions and the resulting political discourse to be the heart of democracy. They believed that instead of the social rank in which a person was born (i.e., the higher your social rank, the more influence you had on social policy and decision making), the basis of influence within society should be discourse in a free and open discussion characterized by conflict among ideas and opinions (i.e., whoever had the most compelling arguments supported by accurate information and logic has the most influence on social policy and decision making). The views of political discourse of Jefferson, Madison, and their contemporaries were grounded in the philosophy and thought of the 1700s. The philosopher Edmund Burke (1790), for example, recommended conflict among ideas by stating that our skills are sharpened, and our nerves are strengthened, by those who wrestle with us (not by those who give in to our will). Jefferson (1815) noted that inquiry results from differences of opinion, and then reveals the truth. James Madison described political discourse as (a) including open-minded consideration of other points of view and (b) keeping conclusions tentative by realizing that one's current knowledge is not the whole truth.

Two of the major purposes of political discourse are involving all citizens in the making of decisions and building a moral bond among all citizens of the society. Each of these is discussed below. First, however, the way in which constructive controversy is used in political discourse is discussed.

PROCEDURE FOR POSITIVE POLITICAL DISCOURSE

The constructive engagement in positive political discourse is dependent on having an effective normative procedure. Positive political discourse may be seen as a six-step procedure (Johnson & Johnson, 2014).

First, citizens need the freedom and opportunity to propose courses of action that they believe will solve the problem under consideration. In the United States such freedom of information and speech is guaranteed by the First Amendment to the Constitution or more universally by Article 19 of the Universal Declaration of Human Rights and the International Covenant on Civil and Political Rights. Free expression of one's views inherently involves conflict among ideas (i.e., controversy) as not everyone will have the same view of any issue.

Second, individuals or small groups of citizens initially decide on what course of action is needed to solve a societal problem. They come to an initial conclusion. They organize what they know into a coherent and reasoned position. They research their position and prepare persuasive presentations to convince others of their position's validity. They plan how to advocate their position so that all citizens understand it thoroughly, give it a fair and complete hearing, and are convinced of its soundness.

Third, citizens present the best case possible for their position and listen carefully to the opposing presentations. Their advocacy takes place within the cooperative framework of making the best decision possible (i.e., goal interdependence) and believing that a high-quality decision cannot be made without considering the information organized by advocates of opposing positions (i.e., resource interdependence). They strive to gain insights into opposing positions' strengths and weaknesses by learning the information provided in the opposing presentations and understanding the reasoning underlying the opposing positions.

Fourth, citizens engage in an open discussion characterized by advocacy, refutation, and rebuttal. The advocacy groups give opposing positions a "trial by fire" by attempting to refute them by challenging the validity of their information and logic. They probe and push each other's conclusions. They rebut attacks on their own position while continuing to attempt to persuade other citizens of its validity. Citizens continue to attempt to learn thoroughly the opposing positions to gain insights into their weaknesses and flaws. An important skill in doing so is "confirming the other person's competence while criticizing their ideas." The goal of persuading others to agree with one's position is never forgotten.

Fifth, citizens strive to see the issue from all perspectives simultaneously and demonstrate their understanding by summarizing the opposing positions accurately and completely. This ensures that the advocates of the opposing positions believe they have been heard and understood. Citizens are expected to be able to step back and objectively view the issue from all sides. This prevents advocacy leading to selective perception and bias in viewing the issue.

Finally, citizens strive to create a synthesis that subsumes the various positions being advocated, or at the very least integrates the best information and reasoning from all points of view. A vote is taken in which the majority rules. The political minority helps implement the decision because they know (a) they had a fair chance to influence others' opinions, (b) they will have another chance to advocate their position in a set number of years, and (c) their rights will be protected in the meantime. Protection of rights of minority opinion groups is critical for positive political discourse to occur.

This procedure does not automatically appear when decisions need to be made. It must be learned and perfected. Schools are the most logical place to teach such a procedure as it is there that citizens are growing up and developing.

COLLECTIVE DECISION MAKING

In a democratic society, each generation has to learn how to participate in the democratic process. To be good citizens, individuals need
to learn how to engage in collective decision making about community and societal issues (Dalton, 2007). Collective decision making
involves political discourse. While the word "discourse" has been
defined in many different ways by linguists and others (Fairclough,
1995; Foucault, 1970; Jaworski & Coupland, 1999), according to
Webster's dictionary, the concept *discourse* has two major meanings:
(a) formal communication of thoughts about a serious subject through
words (spoken or written) and (b) rationality or the ability to reason.
Political discourse is the formal exchange of reasoned views as to which
of several alternative courses of action should be taken to solve a societal
problem. Political discourse is intended to involve all citizens in the
making of a decision – participants attempt to persuade each other
(through valid information and logic) and clarify what course of action
would be most effective in solving the societal problem. Political discourse is in turn closely related to *deliberation*, a public discussion
aimed at reaching a justifiable decision to solve a societal problem or,
if a decision cannot be made, live respectfully with the reasonable disagreements that remain unresolvable (Guttman, 2000).

In political discourse there is an emphasis first on dissensus and
conflict among positions (Mouffe, 2000; Ranciere, 1995) and then as the
decision is made, consensus and agreement among advocates of the
opposing and differing positions is sought. Mouffe (2000) especially
emphasizes that there are emotional and nonrational aspects to holding
and advocating positions and that true consensus may be rare. What
may be more common is that a temporary decision is made by majority
vote that leaves minority opinions unsatisfied. The holders of minority
positions will support the majority out of respect and concern for the
majority (and the majority will protect the rights of the holders of the
minority positions out of the same respect and concern) until the next
election occurs, and the underlying disagreements surface and are

argued again. While the conflict among positions may never be fully resolved, it is the moral bond created by mutual commitment to the common good and the society's values (e.g., equality, liberty, justice) that holds the society together.

Political discourse is a method of decision making in a democracy intended to involve all citizens. Rule by the people means rule by all the people. Citizen involvement is characterized by presenting positions, attempting to persuade others (through valid information and logic), listening to others, gathering new information and subsequently adjusting positions, clarifying what course of action would be most effective in solving the societal problem, and voting for the candidates who will implement that course of action. Effective democratic decisions are supposed to be of high quality, reflecting the best reasoned judgment of the citizens. The process of making the decision at its best increases the commitment of citizens to (a) implementing the decision (whether they agree with it or not) and (b) having democracy as their form of government. The political discourse process also tends to increase the cohesiveness of the society. The process ensures that the rights of the political minority (those who disagree with the decision) are protected until the issue is reopened in the next election. Finally, the decision making should ensure that the capabilities of the citizens to engage in political discourse are enhanced, or at least not lessened.

DEVELOPMENT OF A MORAL BOND AMONG CITIZENS

Among the most important effects of political discourse is its impact on the cohesiveness of the society and the moral bonds among citizens. In 1748 Baron Charles de Montesquieu published *The Spirit of Laws*, in which he explored the relationship between people and different forms of government. He concluded that while dictatorship survives by the fear of the people and monarchy survives by the loyalty of the people, a free republic (the most fragile of the three political systems) survives on the virtue of the people. Virtue is reflected in the way a person balances his or her own needs with the needs of the society as a whole. Motivation to be virtuous comes from "a sense of belonging, a concern for the whole, a moral bond with the community whose life is at stake." This moral bond is cultivated by "deliberating with fellow citizens about the common good and helping shape the destiny of the political community."

Establishing such a moral bond (to act in the service of the common good and shape the destiny of their society) requires (a) citizen participation in their own governance and (b) a common set of values. Participation involves both actively engaging in political discourse and seeking out and valuing the participation of all other citizens, especially when their views conflict with one's own. In the United States, the values underlying such participation were primarily spelled out in the Declaration of Independence and the Constitution (e.g., equality, liberty, justice). De Tocqueville (1945), in the mid-nineteenth century, concluded that of the principal factors maintaining democracy in the United States (situation and context, law, and manners/customs of the people), the most important were the general principles about citizenship that Americans held in common. He called these manners and customs "habits of the heart" and defined them as including taking responsibility for the common good, trusting others to do the same, being honest, having self-discipline, and reciprocating good deeds. Much later, a panel of distinguished political theorists in the 1950s concluded that for democracy to exist, citizens must (a) be committed to fundamental values such as liberty and equality and (b) be in consensus on the procedural norms by which substantive decisions are made (Griffith, Plamenatz, & Pennock, 1956).

Jefferson, Madison, Adams, and the other founders of the American Republic assumed that political discourse would be positive. In actual practice, however, instead of resulting in a consensual decision and building a common moral bond, political discourse can result in divisiveness and dislike.

ABILITY TO ENGAGE IN POLITICAL DISCOURSE

Dewey (1916) stated that the capacity to communicate about controversial issues is central to participation in democratic decision making. Dalton (2007) echoed those sentiments by stating that for individuals to be "good" citizens, they need to learn how to engage in collective decision making about community and societal issues. Such collective decision making is known as political discourse (Johnson & Johnson, 2000b). Thomas Jefferson, James Madison, and the other founders of the American Republic considered political discourse to be the heart of democracy. The clash of opposing positions was expected to increase citizens' understanding of the issue and the quality of decision making, given that citizens would keep an open mind and change their opinion when logically persuaded to do so. The presence of diverse political viewpoints stimulates more thorough information searches and more careful scrutiny of alternatives (Delli Carpini, Cook, & Jacobs, 2004; Mendelberg, 2002; Nemeth, 1986; Nemeth & Rogers, 1996). Exposure to other perspectives also increases familiarity with the rationales that motivate opposing views, which can in turn foster political tolerance (Mutz, 2002; Price, Cappella, & Nir, 2002). Conversely, if individuals effectively avoid viewpoint-challenging information, the society to which they belong is likely to become more politically fragmented (Sunstein, 2002). When contact with other viewpoints is absent, groups of citizens may become more polarized, and their ability to find common ground and to reach political agreement may decrease.

Generally, political education in US schools is considered to be unremarkable (Parker, 2006). In order to be active citizens, students need to be educated for a "culture of argument" (Walzer, 2004, p. 107). When students master the constructive controversy procedure, therefore, they are also mastering the procedures necessary to be a citizen in a democracy.

NEGATIVE POLITICAL PERSUASION

There are dangers when political discussion becomes destructive rather than illuminating. *Destructive political persuasion* exists when misleading, superficial, or irrelevant information is presented in ways that decrease citizens' understanding of the issue, result in an absence of thoughtful consideration of the issue, divide citizens into warring camps who dislike each other, and decrease citizen participation in the political process. Discourse may be replaced by other means of persuasion, such as using deceit through misinformation, de-emphasizing and ignoring important issues, positioning, pandering to voters, and argumentum ad hominem. *Argumentum ad hominem* consists of directing arguments at the opponent rather than at his or her ideas and proposals (Johnson & Johnson, 2007). Ad-hominem arguments can involve questioning the motives of the opponent, accusing the opponent of acting on personal interest, accusing the opponent of inconsistency, or accusing the opponent of past misconduct. In essence, ad-hominem arguments communicate that the opponent is "bad," and therefore must be wrong. By focusing attention on the candidates rather than the issues, such persuasive procedures may be markedly unhelpful in clarifying which course of action should be adopted. In addition, ad-hominem arguments weaken the moral bond underlying the democratic process, discourage others from presenting opposing positions, undermine trust in the political system and each other, and undermine the overall positive interdependence that holds society together. Negative persuasive tactics may discredit political discourse and disillusion citizens about the political process. Political discourse may then be ignored or rejected.

The power of the personal attack rather than discourse in campaigning is illustrated by the negativity effect. The *negativity effect* exists when a negative trait affects an impression more than a positive trait, everything else being equal (Vonk, 1993). There is evidence that individuals tend to pay special attention to negative information (Fiske, 1980; Pratto & John, 1991) and weigh negative information more heavily than positive information (Coovert & Reeder, 1990; Taylor, 1991), especially in regard to moral traits. In a wide variety of studies, ranging from forming impressions about other people to evaluating positive and negative information to reach a decision or judgment, negative information figured more prominently than positive information (Taylor, 1991). Capitalizing on the power of negativity, however, may be inherently dangerous to the health of a democracy. Adlai Stevenson (1952), for example, noted that it is the American "tradition of critical inquiry and discussion that informs our entire civilization" but critical inquiry only advances the general welfare when its purpose is honest. He notes that "criticism, not as an instrument of inquiry and reform, but as an instrument of power, quickly degenerates into the techniques of deceit and smear."

What Stevenson and others point out is that when negative personal attacks are used as an instrument of power, they tend to (a) increase intolerance aimed at the other person and the views he or she represents (which is directly opposite to the values of democracy, which emphasize tolerance of others even if they are promoting unpopular views), (b) undermine trust and other influences on political participation, and (c) undermine the overall positive interdependence and moral bonds that hold society together. The more widespread the use of negative personal attacks, the greater tends to be the disillusionment of citizens about the political process. Disillusionment may result in decreased participation, as well as resentment and a refusal to help implement the will of the winners.

NEED FOR CITIZEN SOCIALIZATION

In a democracy, each generation has to be socialized into the procedures, competencies, attitudes, and values needed to engage in positive political discourse. The health of the democracy depends upon the effectiveness of this socialization process. In order to do so, there are two things that are essential. The first is a basic social science theory that organizes what is known about positive political discourse and leads to a program of research aimed at improving our understanding of political discourse and the conditions under which it is constructive. The research validates the theory. The second is a procedure for socializing children and young adults into the nature of positive discourse. A normative procedure for this socialization has been extrapolated from the theory (validated by research) so that (a) citizens know the steps needed to engage in constructive political discourse and

(b) the procedure may be used to teach each successive generation how to engage in positive political discourse and thereby participate in the political process.

SUMMARY

In the 1700s there was a widespread belief in Europe and America that the "truth" was discovered primarily through the collision of differing opinions. Many philosophers and politicians had a deep faith in the value and productiveness of conflict. Thomas Jefferson, James Madison, and the other founders of the United States believed that free and open discussion should serve as the basis of influence within society (not the social rank within which a person was born). This free and open discussion was to be characterized by conflict among ideas and opinions, open-minded consideration of all points of view, and changing one's mind in order to find the best action to take for the good of the country as a whole.

In a democracy, individuals or small groups of citizens initially decide on what course of action is needed to solve a societal problem. They organize what they know into a coherent and reasoned position. Next, citizens present the best case possible for their position and listen carefully to the opposing presentations. Third, citizens engage in an open discussion characterized by advocacy, refutation, and rebuttal. Fourth, citizens strive to see the issue from all perspectives simultaneously. Finally, citizens strive to create a synthesis that subsumes the various positions being advocated or, at the very least, integrates the best information and reasoning from all points of view. A vote is taken in which the majority rules. The political minority helps implement the decision because they know (a) they had a fair chance to influence others' opinions, (b) they will have another chance to advocate their position in a set number of years, and (c) their rights will be protected in the meantime. Protection of rights of minority opinion groups is critical for positive political discourse to occur.

Collective decision making in a society involves political discourse. The concept *discourse* has two major meanings: (a) formal communication of thoughts about a serious subject through words (spoken or written) and (b) rationality or the ability to reason. *Political discourse* is the formal exchange of reasoned views as to which of several alternative courses of action should be taken to solve a societal problem. Political discourse is a method of decision making in a democracy intended to involve all citizens. Among the most important effects of political discourse is its impact on the cohesiveness of the society and the moral bonds among citizens.

Learning how to engage in constructive political discourse is the responsibility of every citizen. As they are growing toward full citizenship, children and adolescents need to learn how to engage in constructive political discourse. They need to learn from different points of view being expressed in a public discussion and to become competent in the constructive controversy procedure and the related skills needed to make it work.

10 Constructive controversy, creativity, and innovation

INTRODUCTION

Many countries around the world are becoming more diverse. There are a few countries, such as the United States, Canada, and, more recently, Australia, that have encouraged the emigration of diverse populations and pride themselves for their diverse citizenry. Imagine yourself as part of a committee of government officials who are trying to decide whether diversity of emigration should be encouraged or discouraged. To ensure that both sides get a complete and fair hearing, you have divided your committee into two groups to present the best case possible for each side of the issue. You assign Group A the position that diversity is a resource that has many beneficial influences. You assign Group B the position that diversity is a problem that has many harmful influences. The overall goal is for the entire committee to write a report giving their best reasoned judgment about what the emigration policy should be regarding diversity. Ideally, all members will agree. The steps of constructive controversy are then followed to ensure that the resulting interaction will enhance creative problem solving.

"We should encourage the emigration of diverse populations to our country," stated a member of Group A. "Not only will it increase our productivity as a country, but it will decrease the stereotyping and prejudice in our country and result in positive relationships. Opposites attract, you know."

"Nonsense," said a member of Group B. "We have to stop any emigration of diverse populations to our country. Not only will it decrease our productivity by causing so many interpersonal problems on the job, it will increase anxiety and tension and strain in interacting with store clerks, colleagues, and neighbors. Forced friendliness actually is not easy. That strain cannot be good for people. Since people tend to like people they think are similar to themselves, there is going to be a lot of negativity and dislike among citizens. Stereotyping and prejudice is bound to get worse."

"Look," said a member of Group A. "Diversity is the future. It is going to come whether we like it or not. We might as well control it and make sure it has positive rather than negative outcomes."

"You have it exactly wrong," said a member of Group B. "Let other countries make the mistake of welcoming diversity. They will soon be head over heels in problems. We need to be smarter than they are and avoid the problems by not allowing diverse immigrants in."

"Tell me why these other countries will have problems," said a member of Group A. "What problems do you mean? How widespread will they be? Will they be short-term or long-term problems? Of course there will be initial problems as the members of our society get used to the diversity, but in the long run we all benefit."

The reason for structuring a constructive controversy to aid in the committee's decision making is to increase the creativity of the course of action they will recommend. Creativity and innovation are built on the foundation of cooperating to achieve mutual goals and constructive controversy over the most desirable means of doing so. Constructive controversy is an important tool to increase creativity, open-mindedness, and innovation (Johnson & Johnson, 2007). It is through constructively managed disagreement and argument that creative ideas are discovered and new innovations are put in place.

There are two views of creativity. One is that creativity is a personality trait that is genetically determined. Some people are creative, while some are not. The second is that creativity results from a social process. All people have the potential to be creative if they are in a situation that promotes it. While historically the individual creative person view has dominated the thinking about creativity, there have always been some social psychologists who have maintained that creativity is a social process. Each view has research and theory to support it. This latter position is the point of view presented in this chapter. In this chapter, the impact of constructive controversy on creativity and innovation will be discussed. This involves discussing three major topics: understanding the social nature of the creative process, viewing issues with an open mind, and innovating in organizations.

THE SOCIAL NATURE OF CREATIVITY

> Every man works better when he has companions working in the same line, and yielding to the stimulus of suggestion, comparison, emulation. Great things have been done by solitary workers, but they have usually been done with double the pains they would have cost if they had been produced in more genial circumstances.
>
> *Henry James (1843–1916)*

Creativity is the process of bringing something new into existence (Johnson & F. Johnson, 2013). It involves transcending traditional or commonly accepted ideas, patterns, relationships, and so forth and formulating something new, original, imaginative, valuable, and meaningful. A creative idea is most often defined as one that is both novel and useful (Amabile, 1983). It is novel because it diverges from existing solutions and useful in that it presents a potentially viable solution to a problem. Creativity is focused on the development and generation of new and useful ideas (Amabile, 1996). Creativity can be distinguished from innovation. *Innovation* refers to the process through which they are successfully implemented at the organization level.

Creativity as an individual trait

There is a view that creativity is something magical that appears in certain individuals when it is needed. Certain individuals become inspired almost as if angels reached down from heaven to touch them. The result is a creative person who has inherited certain genes and has the "creativity" trait. Western society has long had a belief that creativity is an individual trait (Johnson & F. Johnson, 2013).

Certain lone creative geniuses strolled through our history, leaving dramatic works in their wake. Creative heroes, such as Michelangelo, Picasso, Victor Hugo, Charles Dickens, and Walt Disney, are viewed as extraordinary individuals who, essentially working alone, created great works of art. In Western culture, furthermore, creativity was originally seen as resulting from divine inspiration. The Greeks saw creativity as being inspired by Muses who were sent by the Gods. Judeo-Christian tradition viewed creativity as resulting from an expression of God's inspiration. The view of creativity changed in the eighteenth century (the Age of Enlightenment), as creativity became linked with imagination. Thomas Hobbes saw imagination as the key element of human thought. Some people were blessed with more imagination than others. Early research on creativity was conducted primarily at the individual level, especially on the traits that distinguish highly creative individuals from their peers (Helson, 1996). This large body of research on personality traits supports the widespread position that creative insights are most likely to emerge from the mind of a lone genius working in isolation (Perry-Smith & Shalley, 2003). While it has various forms, Western culture has long promoted "The Great Person" theory of creativity.

Creativity as a social process

The creation of new and wonderful things is also seen as resulting from interaction among individuals. Creativity comes alive in the interaction among individuals striving to achieve a mutual goal. Creativity is a social endeavor. Individuals are creative or noncreative primarily in interaction with other individuals. The social environment is responsible for either enhancing or diminishing one's creativity. Groups can be potentially creative by encouraging members to generate, build upon, combine, and improve each other's ideas. In the past 30 years or so, research on creativity has increasingly focused on social situations (Amabile, 1996) and groups of people who collaborate to generate creative ideas (Bennis & Biederman, 1996; Paulus & Nijstad, 2003; Perry-Smith, 2006).

A social view of creativity is that it is primarily a social process derived from the way in which individuals interact as they make decisions and solve problems. James Watson, for example, who won a Nobel Prize as the codiscoverer of the double helix DNA molecule, stated, "Nothing new that is really interesting comes without collaboration." The creative genius is seen as the product of cooperative efforts in which conflict over ideas takes place. The interaction pattern that results in creative ideas and insights involves diverse positions being seriously considered, argumentation that includes critically examining the benefits and costs of each position, viewing the issue from all perspectives, and seeking a synthesis that includes the best reasoning from all sides. These all are elements of constructive controversy. Creativity is also stimulated by the free expression of dissenting opinions because, even when they are wrong, they cause group members to think and solve problems more creatively (Gruenfeld, 1995; Nemeth, 1986).

Decision making, constructive controversy, creativity, and innovation are, therefore, interrelated (Vollmer, Dick, & Wehner, 2014). Constructive controversy provides a cooperative context in which ideas can be freely expressed and participants can strive to help the group come up with creative decisions that lead to innovations. The free expression of dissenting positions promotes creativity. Even when dissenting positions are wrong, they cause group members to think and solve problems more creatively.

THE CREATIVE PROCESS AND CONSTRUCTIVE CONTROVERSY

Creativity is commonly a process that involves two or more people. The creative process consists of a sequence of overlapping phases involving controversy during problem solving (Johnson, 1979).

First, group members must recognize that a meaningful goal exists that is challenging enough to motivate them to solve it. It is a mutual goal that establishes positive interdependence among the individuals involved. For the possibility of creativity to exist, group members need to be aroused to a level of motivation sufficient to sustain problem-solving efforts despite frustrations and dead-ends (Deutsch, 1969). This level of motivation, however, cannot be so intense that it overwhelms members or keeps them too close to the problem (Johnson, 1979). Intrinsic motivation has been considered to be a driver of creativity (Amabile, 1996). When individuals enjoy working on the group's task, they tend to process information flexibly, experience positive affect, take more risks, and be more persistent in their efforts to achieve (Elsbach & Hargadon, 2006; Shalley, Zhou, & Oldham, 2004). The motivation to persist is increased by both controversy and a group tradition supporting the view that with time and effort constructive solutions can be discovered or invented for seemingly insoluble problems.

Second, group members must gather the necessary knowledge and resources and plan an intense, long-term effort to solve the problem. The more members are immersed in and focused on the problem and the relevant information and circumstances, the greater the likelihood they will achieve a creative insight.

Third, a cooperative context must be highlighted in order for the necessary level of social support to be achieved within the group. Members must not feel threatened or under too much pressure (Deutsch, 1969; Rokeach, 1960; Stein, 1968). Feeling threatened prompts defensiveness in group members and reduces their tolerance of ambiguity and receptiveness to new and unfamiliar ideas. Too much tension leads to stereotyping of thought processes. Feeling threatened and under pressure prevents group members from becoming sufficiently detached from their original viewpoint to be able to see the problem from new perspectives.

Fourth, one's initial ideas and conclusions need to be challenged and disputed by other group members with different perspectives and conclusions. The intellectually disputed passage results in uncertainty and leads to a search for more information, a new perspective, and insights into the problem being solved. Creative insight usually depends on (a) the availability of diverse information and viewpoints and (b) group members disagreeing and challenging one another's reasoning and perspectives. The more varied and diverse the members of a group, the more likely the group will arrive at a creative solution. Members with diverging ideas and perspectives must disagree and challenge one another's reasoning and perspectives in order to understand each other's positions, ensure the positions are valid, and put the ideas and perspectives together into new and varied patterns. Disagreements, arguments, debates, and diverse information and ideas are all important aspects of gaining creative insight. Controversy among group members tends to spark new ideas and approaches, broaden the range of available solutions, and produce moments of insight or inspiration by one or more group members. Creative insight is often accompanied by intense emotional experiences of illumination and excitement and leads to the formulation of a tentative solution.

Fifth, group members need to seek out different perspectives and different ways of viewing the problem so they can reformulate it in a way that lets new orientations to a solution emerge. Creativity is derived from divergent rather than convergent thinking (Guilford, 1950). *Divergent thinking* involves creative generation of multiple answers to a problem. *Convergent thinking* involves aiming for a single, correct solution to a problem. To generate useful and novel ideas, and to think divergently, it is necessary to take others' perspectives. The desire to take the perspective of others comes from prosocial motivation, that is, the desire to benefit others (De Dreu & Nauta, 2009; De Dreu, Weingart, & Kwon, 2000). The combination of intrinsic and prosocial motivation tends to generate the most perspective taking (Grant & Berry, 2011). It often takes an outside person to help one realize the limitations of one's analyses, lines of thoughts, and conclusions and an intellectual challenge to motivate one to reconsider one's conclusions and reopen one's perspective.

Sixth, group members need to experience an incubation period during which they feel frustration, tension, and discomfort due to their failure to produce an adequate solution to the problem and temporarily withdraw from the issue. In order for group members to derive creative answers to problems they are working on, they must be allowed time to reflect. Instant answers should not be demanded. Creative thinking "is commonly typified by periods of intense application and periods of inactivity" (Treffinger, Speedie, & Brunner, 1974, p. 21). After all sides of a controversy have been presented, group members should be allowed to think about solutions for a day or so before trying to put things together in new and varied patterns.

Seventh, group members formulate a new and unique solution to the problem, work out the details of implementing it, and test it against reality. After group members have had time to reflect on the alternatives, they need to come back together and decide on a final solution. The decision then needs to be implemented in a real-world environment to see if it does indeed solve the problem. If the implementation is successful, group members then give the validated solution to relevant audiences.

Open versus closed belief systems

For controversy to result in creativity, group members must be open-minded (Johnson & F. Johnson, 2013). Group members are *open-minded* when they are willing to attend to, comprehend, and gain insight into information, ideas, perspectives, assumptions, beliefs, conclusions, and opinions different from their own. Open-minded groups (a) seek out opposing and differing beliefs, (b) discover new beliefs, (c) remember and consider information that disagrees with currently held beliefs, and (d) organize new beliefs to solve the problem. When group members resist such opportunities, they are *closed-minded*. Closed-minded groups (a) emphasize the differences between what they believe and what they do not believe, (b) deny information that is contrary to what they believe, (c) have contradictory beliefs that go unquestioned, (d) discard as irrelevant similarities between what they believe and what they reject, (e) avoid exploring and considering differences in beliefs, and (f) distort information that does not fit their beliefs. The extent to which a group member can receive, evaluate, and act on relevant information on its own merits – as opposed to viewing it only from his or her own perspective – defines the extent to which the member is open-minded (Rokeach, 1960). Without seeing the problem from a variety of perspectives, members are not able to analyze it fully and synthesize various positions to produce creative solutions. Thus, controversy is an essential ingredient in discovering new perspectives on the problem being solved.

Rokeach (1954, 1960) has developed the concept of dogmatism to categorize people in terms of the openness or closedness of their belief systems. *Dogmatism* is a relatively closed organization of beliefs and disbeliefs about reality that is organized around a central set of beliefs about absolute authority that, in turn, provides a framework for intolerance toward others. *Closed-minded people*, compared with open-minded individuals (Ehrlich & Lee, 1969; Vacchiano, Strauss, & Hochman, 1969),

1. are less able to learn new beliefs and to change old beliefs
2. are less able to organize new beliefs and integrate them into their existing cognitive systems during problem solving, and thus take longer to solve problems involving new beliefs
3. are less accepting of belief-discrepant information
4. are more resistant to changing their beliefs
5. more frequently reject information potentially threatening to their perceptual and attitudinal organization
6. have less recall of information inconsistent with their beliefs
7. evaluate information consistent with their beliefs more positively
8. have more difficulty in discriminating between the information received and its source, so that the status of an authority is confused with the validity of what the authority is stating; in other words, dogmatic persons tend to accept what authorities say as the truth and discount what low-status individuals say as invalid
9. resolve fewer issues in conflict situations, are more resistant to compromise, and are more likely to view compromise as defeat.

The creative solution of problems requires open-mindedness. In being open-minded, group members must be willing to give up their current beliefs about the situation and adopt new ones. The new beliefs help them synthesize an unforeseen but effective solution. The replacement of old beliefs with new beliefs is called the *analytic phase* of the problem-solving process. Once new beliefs have superseded the old ones, group members must organize their new beliefs in a way that leads them to the solution of the problem. This organizational step is called the *synthesizing phase* of the problem-solving process.

The replacement of old beliefs that limit a group's thinking with new beliefs that enable whole new orientations and perspectives depends on the old beliefs being challenged and disconfirmed. It is conflict that sparks the cognitive changes that enable creative insight. If group members are to engage in creative problem solving, they must be open-minded and be challenged with opposing positions, which results in seeing the issue from a variety of perspectives, and this leads to developing a creative synthesis that solves the problem.

INNOVATION AND CONSTRUCTIVE CONTROVERSY

If organizations are to survive and flourish, their members must generate new ideas that suggest productive and profitable new directions and procedures. Organizations need to deemphasize "The Great Person" theory of creativity and promote "The Great Process" theory of creativity. Organizations, therefore, employ a variety of strategies to promote creative idea generation that can be turned into profitable new directions and innovations. Most organizations recognize that creative ideas result from a social process; that is, they result from interaction among members. The social process is based on encouraging dissent and independence of thought. Organizational members are creative through generating, building upon, combining, and improving each member's ideas and conclusions; in order words, they generate creative solutions to problems and issues through the constructive controversy process.

Enemies of innovation

Three of the enemies of innovation within organizations are the following (Johnson & F. Johnson, 2013). The *first enemy* is the view that creativity is a trait or characteristic of certain individuals; that is, some individuals tend to be creative and some do not. While it may be true, this view is largely unproductive because it makes the organization focus on hiring creative individuals rather than on creating an environment in which all members may become creative. The accomplishment of important goals, furthermore, requires the coordinated contributions of many talented people. Most problems facing individuals, groups, and societies are just too large. One person cannot create a global business or map the mysteries of the human brain, no matter how intelligent or creative he or she is. Creativity comes alive and flourishes when the "Great Process" dominates organizational thought and practice.

Many organizations give lip service to and may even desire creativity, but reward conformity and commitment to the status quo (Nemeth, 1997). The *second enemy* of innovation is pressure to conform to majority positions. Conformity pressures tend to be a significant barrier to creativity and innovation (Nemeth, 1977). Many organizations desire creativity but reward conformity, cohesion, and commitment to the status quo. Creativity should increase if conformity pressures are reduced or eliminated (Nemeth, 1977). New ideas may at first seem strange, or even offensive. Many potentially creative ideas are rejected outright because they are either too risky or they threaten business as usual (Staw, 1995). Pressure to conform can discourage people from diverging from their group to suggest a new idea others may at first find strange, or even offensive (Moscovici, 1985a). Many new ideas are initially expressed as a minority viewpoint. Novel ideas are most likely to prevail when they are expressed in the face of considerable opposition (Nemeth & Wachtler, 1983). While conformity tends to induce closed-minded rejection of minority ideas, open-minded consideration of different ideas, conflicting opinions, and opposing beliefs tends to generate creative solutions. Conformity to the majority position directly conflicts with such open-mindedness. Thus, in order to promote innovation, organizations need to ensure that pressure to conform and agree with the majority opinion is absent and that differences of opinion are encouraged and promoted.

The *third enemy* of innovation is the resistance to innovation based on fear, either because the innovation seems risky or because it threatens the status-quo. Innovation may be risky because it may involve shifts in power and in the allocation of resources. From a competitive perspective, such changes imply that there will be winners and losers as innovations are implemented. Therefore, a competitive context in which members of decision-making groups are competing for power and resources is an enemy of innovation. In order to promote innovation, organizations need to ensure that a strong cooperative context is structured for its work groups.

Innovation is best served, furthermore, when dissent is prosocial and improvement oriented (Packer, 2008; Van Dyne, Ang, & Botero, 2003), when it has constructive input about task-related issues (Van Dyne & LePine, 1998), and when errors are corrected and learning occurs (Beer & Eisenstat, 2000; Butera and Mugny, 2001). Dissent involves disagreeing with someone who has power over you, such as those who control your next pay raise or promotion (Detert & Trevino, 2010; Jetten, Hornsey, Spears, Haslam, & Cowell, 2010).

MAXIMIZING CREATIVITY AND INNOVATION

Constructive controversy provides a cooperative context in which ideas can be freely expressed and participants strive to help the group come up with needed innovations, not to "win" by proposing the best ideas. The free expression of dissenting positions promotes creativity as even when dissenting positions are wrong, they cause group members to think and solve problems more creatively. In many organizations and groups, there is considerable pressure to generate new ideas that suggest profitable new directions. Most of these organizations recognize that creative ideas result from a social process, that is, interaction among members, rather than from single/lone creative individuals. The social process is based on groups of people who cooperate to generate creative ideas by encouraging dissent and independence of thought. Groups are creative through generating, building upon, combining, and improving each member's ideas and conclusions. Creativity results when individuals advocate their current positions in a group, are confronted with opposing positions, and then engage in a conflict over ideas and conclusions in which they challenge and refute the opposing positions while rebutting attacks on their own position. This "disputed passage" results in uncertainty and a rethinking of their position and its rationale. New creative insights result that generate novel conclusions. In other words, to generate creative solutions to problems and issues, the constructive controversy procedure is needed.

The power of constructive controversy to spark creativity and innovative ideas and procedures is reflected in the research discussed in Chapter 5. Compared with concurrence seeking, debate, individualistic efforts, and majority domination, constructive controversy generates more creative ideas, more open-mindedness, greater exchange of expertise, more frequent and accurate perspective taking, more frequent higher-level cognitive and moral reasoning, and greater understanding of the issue. This leads to higher-quality decision making and problem solving, along with greater mastery and retention of the relevant information surrounding the issue being considered. Any organization interested in the creativity of its members and in innovation to stay productive and profitable should consider these results carefully.

It should be noted, furthermore, that innovations based on the creative ideas of one or two organizational members often fail, because the vast majority of the members have no commitment to making them succeed. Involvement in creating innovations is a necessity for their successful implementation (Johnson & F. Johnson, 2013). The constructive controversy procedure ensures that all members of a team are involved in creating potential innovations.

While much of the research on constructive controversy has been conducted in elementary and secondary schools, as well as universities, enough of the research has been conducted in organizations to verify the transferability of the research results. There are, however, significant differences between educational and organizational settings. In most organizations, for example, the nature of innovations has complex implications. Existing power differences may be threatened both between individuals and departments. Some individuals and departments may gain in power; others may decrease in power. Correspondingly, new innovations may result in the enhancement of the careers of some organizational members and the obstruction of the careers of others. Current reward structures may change as innovations may result in advocates receiving raises while resisters may not. Moreover, the value structure of organizations may change according to which innovations are successful and which are not. Inherently, there are values embedded in the constructive controversy procedure that are absent in many organizations, such as the valuing of argumentation, opposition, diverse viewpoints, and perspective taking. These values change the culture of an organization. In most organizations, furthermore, individuals may simultaneously have cooperative (solve the problem), competitive (get the promotion), and individualistic (get my work done) motives, and this makes conflicts more complex and difficult to manage. Creativity and innovation require the combination of cooperation and conflict that constructive controversy represents/unites. Organizations that wish to survive and flourish have no alternative but to implement constructive controversy procedures in their problem solving and decision making. Schools are an ideal setting to socialize the next generations of organizational members into the values and skills needed to engage productively in constructive controversy.

SUMMARY

Innovation depends on creativity. Ensuring that creativity is maximized within an organization requires that a strong cooperative context is structured and competition is minimized, divergent positions and perspectives are sought out and valued and that concurrence seeking is avoided, risk taking in presenting new ideas and positions is encouraged, alternative positions are given complete and fair consideration, proposed alternative positions are given a critical analysis and their validity and desirability are challenged, the issue is viewed from a variety of perspectives, and a synthesis or integration that incorporates the best ideas and reasoning from all the proposed positions is generated. Creativity depends in large part on this interaction pattern that results from constructive controversy.

11 Constructive controversy and building and maintaining peace

INTRODUCTION

The Kurds live in Turkey, Iran, and Iraq. When the boundaries of these countries were drawn, the Kurds were deliberatively divided into three different countries. What has resulted is a political tension in all three countries, as many Kurds wish to separate from the three countries and form their own state of Kurdistan. In the national discussions of Turkey, Iran, and Iraq, as well as in regional discussions, the issue of the possibility of a Kurdish state must always be addressed. Each country wishes to keep their Kurdish territory and citizens. The same may or may not be true of the Kurds. It is a difficult problem that will not go away in the near future. How may this and similar problems be discussed throughout the world? One answer is through the constructive controversy process.

In a very oversimplified way, a regional committee could be divided into two subgroups. Subgroup A could be assigned the position that the Kurds should give up their dream of a Kurdish state and identify with the country of which they are citizens. Subgroup B could be assigned the position that the Kurds should separate from the three countries and form their own state of Kurdistan. While the constructive controversy procedure is followed, the emphasis is on understanding the issue from both perspectives and coming up with a synthesis that allows both views to achieve their goals. It is not that one side should win and the other lose; rather the challenge is to find a creative way for both sides to get what they want in a way that stabilizes the region and brings lasting peace.

Thus, another important application of constructive controversy procedures is in the establishment and maintenance of world peace. In discussing the role of constructive controversy in world peace, the nature of interventions will be noted, the need for constructive controversy to manage discussions of difficult issues will be discussed, the nature of peace will be discussed, the types of peace will be noted, the nature of peace education will be discussed, the five steps of implementing a process for teaching peace education will be delineated, and the need for automaticity in implementing the constructive controversy process will be discussed.

INTERVENING TO CREATE PEACE

Intervening to create peace can involve four different levels of intervention (Duckitt, 1992; Oscamp, 2000): Interventions may focus on (a) changing human genetics and evolution, (b) instigating new laws and widespread norms through international treaties and international organizations such as the United Nations and the World Court, (c) influencing human behavior through education, mass media, work roles and group and interpersonal processes, and (d) changing personality characteristics through such processes as psychotherapy. Of these four levels, Gandhi believed that the use of Level 3 interventions such as education to influence children is the most feasible and effective approach. He is not the only one. H. G. Wells (1927), for example, in reflecting on World War I and the current state of the world, pointed out that human beings are embarked upon a race between education and catastrophe. Lorenz (1963), in reflecting on World War II and the subsequent cold war and nuclear arms race, noted that an unprejudiced observer from another planet, observing humans as with their combination of nuclear weapons and aggressiveness, would not prophesy long life for the species. He believes that humans are at a crossroads at which they either educate themselves in how to manage conflicts constructively or continue along a road leading to the extinction of the human species. He notes that from the evolutionary view, this would be about as significant as the extinction of the ichthyosaur. Many, many thoughtful people have viewed education as the hope for ending war and other forms of destructive violence, and establishing peace. They believe that education is our continual hope, as at any point in time we can change subsequent generations, hopefully toward increased humanity and peace, and improve the human condition through education.

There are two major approaches to peace education. One is teaching information about the nature of peace. Having university courses on peace and having a unit on peace in various courses are examples. The other is involving students in the process of creating and maintaining peace while they learn academic material and various skills and competencies. The day-to-day, minute-by-minute experiences in courses and activities teach students how to establish, manage, and maintain peace. The use of constructive controversy and cooperative learning are examples.

There are at least three underlying rationales for peace programs in schools and universities. One is ideological. Peace is presented as the most desirable course of action according to religious beliefs or general values. Another is that peace is a "good idea." Individual instructors can promote peace just because peace is a good, utopian idea. The third underlying rationale for peace education is theory and research. Peace can be presented as an essential outcome of applying a theory that is validated by research that indicates peace is a vital and productive state of human affairs. This is the approach taken in this chapter. We (Johnson & Johnson, 1979, 1989, 2000b, 2007, 2009b) have (a) developed a theory of constructive controversy; (b) validated it through a program of research; (c) operationalized the validated theory into practical procedures; (d) trained teachers, professors, administrators, managers, and executives throughout the world in how to implement the constructive controversy procedure; and (e) developed a series of curriculum units, academic lessons, and training exercises structured for constructive controversies.

In summary, according to Gandhi, Wells, Lorenz, and many social scientists the hope for peace lies in implementing peace education in schools and universities. The history on innovation in education, however, indicates that not every innovation is equal (Johnson & Johnson, 1999). Many new practices in schools are quickly and even widely adopted, and then dropped quickly and disappear overnight. The innovations that tend to last are characterized by being based on clear procedures that are based on a theory that has considerable validating research. The implementation of the procedures, then, reveals inadequacies in the theory, which result in revising the theory, conducting new research to validate it, and modifying the operational procedures accordingly. This interaction among theory, research, and practice is perhaps the most powerful guarantee that an innovation will be adopted in schools and universities, institutionalized, and maintained over time. Constructive controversy (Johnson & Johnson, 2007) as well as the related practices of cooperative learning (Johnson, Johnson, & Holubec, 2013) and the Teaching Students to Be Peacemakers Program (Johnson & Johnson, 2005a) procedures are derived from theory, have been validated by research, and have been implemented in schools throughout the world.

DIFFICULT DECISIONS AND CONSTRUCTIVE CONTROVERSY

Perhaps the most important aspect of establishing and maintaining peace is making decisions involving difficult issues such as ethnic differences, cultural differences, religious differences, economic interests, and political issues. Agreement may not be possible for many of these difficult issues, but some accommodation must be worked out in order for peace to be stabilized and institutionalized. When left unresolved, the difficult issues result in a renewal of war or violence. Resolving or accommodating the difficult issues is not easy, as often the discussions of the difficult issues are seen as opportunities for advocacy with little interest in learning anything about other points of view. Those who do not have direct personal experience are seen as lacking expertise and having little to contribute. In order to discuss these difficult issues, a procedure is needed that allows constructive discussions and decisions to take place. One such procedure is constructive controversy. It tends to promote the following characteristics of an effective decision.

1. The decision is of high quality, reflecting the best reasoned judgment of the participants.
2. The process of making the decision increases the commitment of all citizens to (a) implement the decision (whether they agree with it or not) and (b) the constructive controversy process.
3. The process of making the decision increases the cohesiveness of the society.
4. The rights of the political minority (those who disagree with the decision) are protected until the issue is reopened in the next election.
5. The decision-making and problem-solving capabilities of the society are enhanced, or at least not lessened.

In the decision making concerning difficult issues, it is expected that the clash of opposing positions would increase participants' understanding of the issue and the quality of their collective decision making. Each alternative course of action is expected to be strongly advocated, receive a complete and fair hearing, and be critically analyzed to reveal its strengths and weaknesses. Such political discourse requires open-minded consideration of other points of view and keeping conclusions tentative by realizing that one's current knowledge is not the whole truth.

In well-structured controversies, participants make an initial judgment, present their conclusions to other group members, are challenged with opposing views, become uncertain about the correctness of their views, actively search for new information and understanding, incorporate others' perspectives and reasoning into their thinking, and reach a new set of conclusions. This process results in significant increases in the quality of decision making and problem solving (including higher levels of cognitive and moral reasoning, perspective taking, creativity, and attitude change about the issue), motivation to learn more about the issue, positive attitudes toward the controversy and decision-making processes, the quality of relationships, and self-esteem. While the constructive controversy process can occur naturally, it may be consciously structured in decision making and learning situations. This involves dividing a cooperative group into two pairs and assigning them opposing positions. The pairs then (a) develop their position, (b) present it to the other pair and listen to the opposing position, (c) engage in a discussion in which they attempt to refute the other side and rebut attacks on their position, (d) reverse perspectives and present the other position, and (e) drop all advocacy and seek a synthesis that takes both perspectives and positions into account. Engaging in the constructive controversy procedure skillfully provides an example of how conflict creates positive outcomes.

The educational use of constructive controversy may occur in any grade level and in any subject matter. Engaging in the controversy process needs to pervade school life so that students develop considerable expertise in its use and incorporate the process into their repertoire of behavior and even their identity. Any time students participate in the constructive controversy procedure, they are getting a lesson in peace education. They are also getting a lesson in democracy. The academic controversy procedure is a Level 3 intervention aimed at creating a tipping point in which enough individuals become skillful in the constructive controversy procedure that they will use it to establish and maintain peace. The possibility of this taking place is strengthened by the foundation of theory and research on which the controversy procedure is based.

The difficulty in discussing difficult issues is illustrated in a study conducted by Trosset (1998). She conducted a study at Grinnell College (a small and somewhat isolated college in Iowa), which has in the past two decades strived to increase the diversity of its student body. Over several semesters she presented approximately 200 students with a list of sensitive diversity-related issues (such as "whether ethnicity is an important difference between people") and asked (a) whether it was possible to have a balanced discussion of the issue (involving more than one perspective, with each perspective receiving about equal support and with people being civil to each other) and (b) why they did or did not want to discuss the issue. The majority of the students believed that balanced discussion of these issues was impossible because a single viewpoint would dominate, and if anyone spoke against that perspective there would be reprisals. The students who wanted to discuss a particular topic typically held strong views on the subject and wished to convince others. In other words, their motivation was advocacy, not learning. The students who did not want to discuss an issue (a) tended not to have strong views ("I don't know much about it, so I don't want to discuss it") and (b) found the issue difficult to discuss ("I never know how to approach this subject"). Only 5 out of the 200 students stated they would like to discuss a difficult topic in order to learn more about it. While 75 percent of the students said they would discuss diversity issues with people of the same views or background as themselves, only 40 percent said they would discuss the same issues with people whose views were unknown to them. A majority said they would be unlikely to listen to someone with whom they disagreed ("I wouldn't want to participate in a conversation when other people have disagreeable views, but I would talk with people who have similar opinions."). One reason for avoiding discussions in which different opinions and conclusions were discussed was that the students believed the goal of such discussions was to reach consensus, rather than just learn from each other. From this study it may be concluded that even under ideal conditions, it is difficult for individuals to discuss major issues that affect conflict and peace among individuals.

In order to resolve these difficult issues, individuals need an effective procedure for doing so such as constructive controversy and they need to build a personal identity based on "how" they deal with difficult issues rather than "what" their position is on these issues. Thus, identity would not be based on "I am a conservative" or "I am a liberal," but rather it would be based on "I am a problem solver" and "I am a person skilled in constructive controversy" as opposed to "I am a stubborn, closed-minded person who rejects all things that contradict what I believe."

NATURE OF PEACE

In order to understand the nature of peace, it is also necessary to understand the nature of war. *War* is a state of open and declared armed combat between states or nations; *peace* is freedom from war or strife, or a state of mutual concord between governments (Johnson & Johnson, 2000b, 2003, 2010). War and peace are two ends of a single continuum. If there is war, there is no peace, and vice versa. Although there are certain types of cooperation during wars, peace exists when there is cooperation among nations and war ends when cooperation among nations is reestablished. Peace, however, is not an absence of conflict. Peace is a state in which conflicts occur frequently and are resolved constructively (war, in contrast, is a state in which conflicts are managed through the use of large-scale violence). Especially in order to create and maintain peace, conflicting ideas, conclusions, and ideologies must be discussed so that shared understandings and mutual accommodations may take place.

Peace as a dynamic, active, relationship process

In defining peace, several aspects of its nature must be taken into account. First, peace is a relationship variable, not a trait. Peace exists among individuals, groups, and nations. Peace is not an individual, group, or national trait or a predisposition. As a relationship, peace cannot be maintained by separation, isolation, or building barriers between conflicting parties, all of which may temporarily reduce violence (establishing a "cold" war). Second, peace is a dynamic, not a static, process. Peace is not a stable state. The level of peace constantly increases or decreases with the actions of each relevant party. Third, peace is not a passive state; it is an active process. Building and maintaining peace takes active involvement. Passive coexistence is not a viable path to peace. Finally, peace is hard to build and easy to destroy. It may take years to build up a stable peace, then one act can destroy it.

Structural liberty

Long-term, stable peace requires *structural liberty*, the situation in which social institutions (such as education, religion, and mass media) promote equality, justice, and the well-being of all relevant parties. Long-term, stable peace is not established by the domination of one party over another. Domination may be direct (through superior military and economic power) or indirect (through structural oppression). *Structural oppression* is the establishment of social institutions that create the social, economic, and political conditions (i.e., systematic inequality, injustice, violence, or lack of access to social services) that result in the repression, poor health, or death of certain individuals or groups in a society.

Intractable conflicts

Peace is most challenging in intractable conflicts. Examples include the conflicts in Northern Ireland, the former Yugoslavia, the Israeli–Palestinian conflict, the conflict between Turkish and Greek citizens in Cyprus, and many, many more. *Intractable conflicts* are conflicts in unavoidable relationships that are intense, ongoing, and difficult to resolve; each side tends to view their own group as righteous and their opponents as evil. Intractable conflicts tend to be intergroup conflicts with a history of severe imbalance of power between the parties characterized by domination and perceived injustice. The high-power group tends to exploit, control, and abuse the other group while promoting legitimizing myths about their superiority. Some intractable conflicts persist for centuries, being institutionalized and transferred from generation to generation. Agreements made to resolve intractable conflicts tend to be short term and temporary. The hope of resolving such intractable conflicts are more long-term interventions, such as peace education.

TYPES OF PEACE

Imposed peace

Imposed peace is based on domination, power, imposition, and enforcement. High-power groups use their military and economic power to force low-power groups to end hostilities and implement the peace

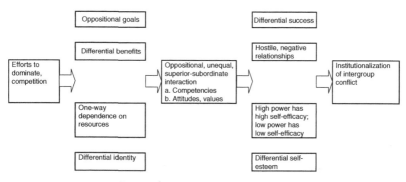

FIGURE II.I Imposed peace

accords (see Figure 11.1). There are two ways in which peace may be imposed: by the winners in a conflict or by powerful third parties such as the United Nations, NATO, or other international alliances. In both cases, military or economic power is used to ensure hostilities are ended. Imposing peace, however, suppresses the conflict, but it does not resolve underlying grievances and does not establish positive long-term relationships among disputants.

Peacekeeping: third party imposes peace
Powerful third parties may impose peace on disputants through the exercise of military or economic power. *Peacekeeping* involves suppressing violence by separating disputants and/or providing incentives for disputants to stop fighting. Examples include a police force that separates two rival street gangs to end a street war and an international military force that keeps two conflict groups separated from each other. The third party separates the disputants and ensures contact between disputants is limited and controlled. The advantage of peacekeeping is that it ends a violent, destructive behavior in a conflict. Peacekeepers are supposed to behave as a neutral third party who will not take sides. Peacekeeping does not, however, end the conflict and may in fact create a new conflict between the disputants and the peacekeepers. This is especially likely if the peacekeepers act in oppressive and abusive ways toward the disputants.

Domination: winner imposes peace

When one group wins a war or gains significant military or economic advantage over the other disputants, the high-power party may use its advantage to dominate the low-power groups and impose peace on the high-power group's terms. The goal of each group is to win, and when one wins, the other groups lose. When the "winner" imposes peace, the losing groups are often segregated or assigned specific areas in which they are to live or stay. Contact between the groups may then be limited and controlled. Long-term maintenance of peace is then attempted through structural oppression.

Negative interdependence

The imposition of peace often has destructive effects, perhaps best explained through social interdependence theory (Deutsch, 1962; Johnson & Johnson, 1989). When peace is imposed, negative interdependence exists among parties; that is, there is a negative correlation among parties' goal achievements; one party may obtain its goals if and only if the other parties involved fail to achieve their goals. In addition to oppositional goals, negative interdependence may exist through differential distribution of benefits (winners receive more benefits than losers) and a one-way dependence on resources (i.e., low-power parties are dependent on the resources of high-power parties, but not vice versa). The identities of the parties are differentiated; that is, members of the high-power group have a positive self-concept as a "winner" and members of the low-power groups have a negative identity based on being "losers." That is, the disputing groups will tend to perceive each other as unequals (i.e., winners and losers). This is based on a unidimensional view of each other taking into account only the characteristic most salient for winning or losing (such as military or economic power, history of privilege, or cultural or tribal background) (Johnson & Johnson, 1989).

Consensual peace

The consensual approach to peace is based on reaching an agreement that (a) ends violence and hostilities and (b) establishes a new

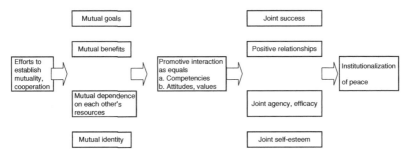

FIGURE 11.2 Consensual peace

relationship based on harmonious interaction aimed at achieving mutual goals, justly distributing mutual benefits, being mutually dependent on each other's resources, and establishing a mutual identity (see Figure 11.2). In consensual peace, all parties believe that peace is desirable, legitimate, just, and beneficial. Since all parties have a fair chance to influence the decision, their commitment to implement the decision is maximized and they are obligated to abide by the agreement and promote each other's efforts to do so (although a small minority within each party can sabotage the agreement by violating it). What tends to result is a joint success in maintaining the peace, positive relationships among the involved parties, a sense of joint agency and efficacy, and joint self-esteem.

There are two levels of consensual peace. The first level is *peacemaking*, in which the parties involved negotiate a cease-fire, an initial agreement, or a framework for resolving the conflict in the future. Peacemaking typically manages the immediate conflict but fails to deal with underlying structural issues. The second level is *peacebuilding*, in which the economic, political, and educational institutions are used to create long-term peace. Peacebuilding deals with the structural issues and is aimed at creating long-term harmonious relationships based on mutual respect and social justice. Peace education is one means of institutionalizing consensual peace. Peace education may focus on building mutuality among all citizens and teaching them the competencies, attitudes, and values needed to build and maintain cooperative systems, resolve conflicts constructively, and adopt values promotive of peace.

PEACE EDUCATION

In order to face and discuss constructively the difficult issues that are involved in establishing and maintaining peace (as opposed to war), it is necessary for individuals to have an agreed-upon procedure to use to structure the discussion and to have some expertise in using it. In addition, the use of the procedure may represent an identity based on being an educated person that supersedes identities based on group membership and certain beliefs. The procedure for decision making and problem solving that involve difficult issues is the constructive controversy procedure. The regular use of constructive controversy in schools ensures that all students get up to 12 years of practice in using the procedure before they reach adulthood.

Peace education may be defined as teaching individuals the information, attitudes, values, and behavioral competencies needed to resolve conflicts without violence and to build and maintain mutually beneficial, harmonious relationships (Johnson & Johnson, 2003, 2005b, 2005c, 2010). The ultimate goal of peace education is for individuals to be able to maintain peace among aspects of themselves (intrapersonal peace), individuals (interpersonal peace), groups (inter-group peace), and countries, societies, and cultures (international peace).

There are numerous approaches to peace education. In the Middle Ages, the Czech educator Comenius believed that peace depended on universally shared knowledge. In the twentieth century, Maria Montessori advocated teaching children to be independent decision-makers, who would not automatically follow authoritarian rulers urging them to war. Even within education, there are numerous approaches to peace education. The first academic peace studies program was probably established in 1948 at Manchester College in Indiana. Our work in peace psychology and education began in the mid-1960s and has continued to today.

The steps of institutionalizing consensual peace through education include (a) establishing public education that is compulsory and integrates the diverse members of society, (b) establishing the mutuality and positive interdependence underlying a peaceful society and teaching students the competencies and attitudes they need to establish and engage in cooperative efforts, (c) teaching students how to engage in peaceful political discourse to make difficult decisions (characterized by open-minded consideration of diverse views), (d) teaching students how to engage in integrative negotiations and mediation to resolve conflicts of interests so joint benefits are maximized, and (e) inculcating civic values.

Step 1: Establishing public education

Compulsory education

The first step in ensuring all members of a society gain experience in participating in constructive controversies is to make education compulsory, so that all children and young adults are required to attend (Johnson & Johnson, 2010). There are a number of reasons why national mandatory public education systems are needed. Schools represent a primary arena in which socialization may take place.

As part of socialization, students may be educated in the knowledge, competencies, attitudes, and values they need to build and maintain long-term consensual peace. One of the social resources needed for peace to flourish is being skilled in making difficult decisions through open-minded discussion of diverse views. Every member of the society needs to develop these social resources and, therefore, every child, adolescent, and young adult should be required to attend school. In addition, schools provide a setting in which constructive controversy may be experienced. The day-to-day fabric of school life needs to reflect the use of constructive controversy as a means for diverse students to understand issues and arrive at creative solutions to problems. Since these social resources take years to develop, their use should pervade classroom life from elementary through post-secondary education. Peace is woven into the fabric of school life primarily through instructional methods such as cooperative learning and constructive controversy. Through developing and maintaining peaceful relations with diverse schoolmates, students actually experience what they need to establish in society as a whole once they become adults. Finally, there are many economic and cultural benefits to compulsory public education.

Integrating schools

For peace to be developed, positive relations must be established among members of the formerly disputing groups. This is difficult to accomplish if schools are segregated. As long as groups are separated, long-term peace is at risk. Just seating students next to one another, however, does not in and of itself resolve the conflict. Contact is a necessary (but not sufficient) condition for decreasing prejudice, intergroup hostility, and intergroup conflict. The more different the groups in terms of culture, religion, and so forth, the greater the need for integration in school as well as at the workplace and in neighborhoods. The conditions under which contact will reduce intergroup hostilities and build positive relationships among diverse people are (a) working together cooperatively to achieve common goals, (b) interaction on a personal level where candid conversations may take place, and (c) regular use of constructive controversy (Johnson & Johnson, 2007).

Step 2: Establishing mutuality, positive interdependence

Establishing positive interdependence

In compulsory, integrated schools, three types of positive interdependence should be established: mutual goals, mutual benefits from achieving the goals (i.e., common fate), and mutual identity. Long-term peace depends on having common goals that unite all members of a society in a joint effort. The benefits received from achieving the mutual goals must be justly distributed among all relevant parties. Usually, benefits need to be equally distributed, although in some cases those with the most need may be given more than their share.

Equal benefits tend to highlight the common fate of all members of the society (Johnson & Johnson, 1989). Positive interdependence is also established through a superordinate identity that subsumes all relevant parties into one superordinate group (Johnson & Johnson, 2002). This superordinate identity is created by (a) respecting one's own cultural identity, (b) respecting others' cultural identities, (c) developing a superordinate identity that subsumes all the different cultural identities, and (d) basing the superordinate identity on a pluralistic set of values.

Using pedagogy to build a cooperative community

Peace education is concerned with fostering schools in which students work together to achieve mutual goals, distribute the benefits justly, and develop a superordinate identity that unites all students in the school. The easiest way of doing so is through the use of cooperative learning (Johnson, 2003; Johnson & Johnson, 2005b; Johnson et al., 2013). *Cooperative learning* is the instructional use of small groups so that students work together to maximize their own and each other's learning. Any assignment in any curriculum for students of any age can be done cooperatively.

Achieving mutual goals and establishing a joint identity requires that members of the diverse groups interact with each other and promote each other's success. Through promoting each other's success and building personal relationships and emotional support, students become more sophisticated about their differences and engage in candid discussions concerning their relationships, the conflict, and the peace agreement. These candid conversations involve the honest and detailed sharing of past experiences, pain, and insights involved in the healing of past traumas. Even in seemingly intractable conflicts, such candid conversations allow for reconciliation, forgiveness, and the giving up of an identity as a combatant or victim. Truth and Reconciliation Commissions are an extreme example of these candid conversations. The personal relationships and candid discussions are critical, as it takes more than superficial connections to overcome stereotyping and prejudice and to build an inclusive caring that extends to all parties relevant to the peace.

Minimizing negative interdependence

In addition to structuring positive interdependence, sources of negative interdependence and isolation should be minimized (Johnson, 2003; Johnson & Johnson, 1989, 2005b). Negative interdependence may exist through oppositional goals, differential distribution of benefits (winners receive more benefits than losers), and a one-way dependence on resources (i.e., low-power parties are dependent on the resources of high-power parties, but not vice versa). The identities of the parties are differentiated; that is, members of the high-power group have a positive self-concept as a "winner" and members of the low-power groups have a negative identity based on being "losers." Competition among disputing groups for economic resources, political power, and educational achievement will institutionalize the conflict and encourage further violence. Even isolation from each other may institutionalize the conflict.

Step 3: Teaching students how to make difficult decisions

Maintaining peace requires that difficult decisions are made through open-minded discussion of diverse views and perspectives in a way that ensures all citizens are committed to implement the decision. Peace education includes teaching students how to (a) face the difficult issues that must be discussed in order for peace to be established and maintained, (b) establish a procedure that all parties agree to use to discuss these difficult issues (i.e., constructive controversy), (c) train students how to use the procedure skillfully, and (d) incorporate the use of the procedure into students' personal identity and value system so that the procedure will be habitually used. When left unresolved, the difficult issues may result in a renewal of war or violence. In order to have constructive discussions of these difficult issues, the parties involved need an effective decision-making procedure. Any time students participate in the controversy procedure, learning how to engage in open-minded discussion of diverse views and perspectives, they are also learning how to engage in democratic political discourse.

Step 4: Teaching students how to resolve conflicts constructively

If peace is to last, individuals must learn how to resolve conflicts constructively. To build peace, all students need to know how to resolve conflicts in constructive and nonviolent ways. This means using *integrative negotiations*, where participants strive to find a resolution that maximizes the benefits for all parties. Working together cooperatively, and resolving conflicts constructively, sets the stage for reconciliation and forgiveness. In building and maintaining peace, there are usually difficult conflicts that take great skill on the part of all parties to resolve. Resolving such conflicts constructively requires the use of integrative negotiations. The conflict resolution program that most directly teaches integrative negotiations and has the most research validation is the Teaching Students to Be Peacemakers Program (Johnson & Johnson, 2005a). The Peacemaker Program has been implemented from kindergarten through high school. There are considerable benefits for students in being able to resolve conflicts integratively. Learning how to resolve conflicts constructively, and being skilled in doing so, gives students a developmental advance over those who never learned how to do so. The developmental advantage includes positive effects on actualizing one's potential, improving the quality of one's relationships, and enhancing life success. Individuals skilled in resolving conflicts constructively tend to make and keep more friends, and be more liked by and popular with peers. They tend to be more employable, be more successful in their careers, have a more fulfilling family life, be better parents, and be better able to maintain lifelong friends. Learning how to resolve conflicts integratively benefits students throughout their lives. Most of all, however, it enables individuals to build and maintain peaceful relations with others.

Step 5: Inculcating civic values

Consensual peace is maintained through the application of civic values. When parties work together to achieve mutual goals and when conflicts are managed constructively both within decision-making and conflict of interests situations, the adoption of the civic values underlying civic virtue is promoted (Johnson & Johnson, 2000a). Students need to internalize the values reflective of cooperation, controversy, and integrative negotiations, which include commitment to the common good and to the well-being of others, a sense of responsibility to contribute one's fair share of the work, respect for the efforts and viewpoints of others and for them as people, behaving with integrity, empathy with and caring for the other parties, compassion when other members are in need, equality, and appreciation of diversity. Such civic values both underlie and are promoted by the cooperation, controversy, and integrative negotiations.

Cooperation, controversy, and integrative conflicts as automatic habit patterns

Every lesson utilizing the constructive controversy procedure is also a lesson in political discourse and decision making. Constructive controversy, as well as cooperative learning and integrative negotiation, is designed to be used with all students at all grade levels. As the procedures are used in academic units, students learn to use them in nonthreatening academic situations and the procedures may be practiced several times a day year after year. It takes considerable practice to master the controversy, cooperation, and peacemaker procedures at a level in which they are automatically used without conscious thought or planning. Automaticity is not achieved in a few hours or even a few days of training. Throughout the school year, therefore, teachers should structure almost all lessons cooperatively and integrate the controversy and peacemaking procedures into academic lessons.

SUMMARY

An essential aspect of building and maintaining peace is to use the constructive controversy procedure to make difficult decisions. Education may be the primary means of training all members of a society to use the constructive controversy procedure. Constructive controversy theory focuses on the open-minded exchange of diverse views, characteristic of effective decision making and political discourse in a democracy. Participants present their conclusions, are challenged by opposing views, experience uncertainty, search for new information and a better perspective, and come to a new revised conclusion. Every time students go through the controversy process, they are receiving a lesson in political discourse and how to make difficult decisions.

Peace involves two dimensions: the absence of war and the formation of harmonious mutually beneficial relationships. Peace may be imposed by third parties (i.e., peacekeeping) or by the winner of a war or high-power group (i.e., domination). Consensual peace includes *peacemaking* (i.e., the parties involved negotiate a ceasefire, an initial agreement, or a framework for resolving the conflict in the future) and *peacebuilding* (i.e., the economic, political, and educational institutions are used to create long-term peace).

There are five essential elements in institutionalizing peace through education. First, in order for education to influence children and youth, they must attend school. Compulsory public education should, therefore, be established. Second, positive interdependence, mutuality, and an awareness of a common fate must be established so that individuals perceive that the goals of any one group can be accomplished if and only if the goals of all other groups are accomplished. Third, the children and youth in many societies have never lived in a democracy and are unfamiliar with the role of citizen in a democracy. They need to learn, therefore, how to engage in decision making involving political discourse. This may be taught through the constructive controversy procedure. Mastery of the constructive controversy procedure may be achieved through its frequent use to teach academic material. Fourth, many of the children and youth attending school may have participated in the conflict as warriors, support personnel, or victims. They need, therefore, to learn how to manage conflicts constructively. In order to teach students how to resolve conflicts of interests constructively, the Peacemaker Program (consisting of integrative negotiation and peer mediation procedures) needs to be implemented at all grade levels. Finally, the civic values necessary for consensual peace need to be inculcated, such as commitment to the common good and to the well-being of others, a sense of responsibility to contribute one's fair share of the work, equality, and compassion when other members are in need. By engaging in cooperative efforts, engaging in open-minded discussion of diverse views in order to make difficult decisions, and seeking resolutions to conflicts of interests that maximize joint benefits, students will internalize these values.

These five essential elements need to be implemented at all levels of schooling to (a) institutionalize peace education in schools, (b) ensure that students from the formerly adversarial groups experience positive interaction for years, (c) ensure the cooperative, controversy, and conflict resolution procedures become automatic habit patterns, and (d) ensure the values underlying these procedures become firmly embedded. The personal experiences resulting from learning together with diverse peers to achieve mutual goals, making informed decisions based on open-minded discussion of each other's perspectives and views, and seeking integrative agreements to resolve conflicts result in a personal understanding of the meaning and relevance of peace and justice and define a way of life.

12 Conclusions

When controversy is suppressed and concurrence seeking is emphasized, several defects in decision making and problem solving will
appear (Johnson & Johnson, 2007). When NASA, for example, decided
to launch the space shuttle *Challenger* on January 28, 1986, engineers
at the company that makes the shuttle's rocket boosters (Morton
Thiokol Company) and the company that manufactures the orbiter
(Rockwell International) had opposed the launch because of dangers
posed by the subfreezing temperatures. The Thiokol engineers feared
that the cold would make the rubber seals at the joints between the
rocket's four main segments too brittle to contain the rocket's super-
hot gases. Several months before the doomed mission, the company's
top expert had warned in a memo that it was unknown as to whether
the seal would hold, and that if it failed a catastrophe of the highest
order would result (Magnuson, 1986). The night before the launch, the
engineers argued for a delay in the launch with their managers who
were uncertain and the NASA officials who wanted to launch on
schedule. The NASA managers made a coalition with the Thiokol
managers to shut the engineers out of the decision making, giving an
illusion of unanimity. Since the engineers could not prove there was
danger, they were silenced to give an illusion of invulnerability. The
Thiokol engineers were pressured to conform. One NASA official
complained that the engineers would not want to OK a launch until
spring. Finally, to "mind-guard," the top NASA executive who made
the final decision to launch was never told about the engineers'
concerns, nor about the reservations of the Rockwell managers.
Protected from the disagreeable information, the NASA official

confidently gave the order to launch the *Challenger* on its tragic flight. The *Challenger* exploded soon after takeoff, killing everyone aboard, including a teacher who had won a national contest to be the first teacher in space.

How could such faulty decision making take place? The answer is, the lack of constructive controversy. NASA officials never gave the alternative option of delaying the launch a fair and complete hearing. Disagreement was stifled rather than utilized. Perspective taking was absent. Often in decision making, if a margin of support for one alternative develops early on in the discussion, then better ideas have little chance of being accepted. It has been reported that in mob lynchings, for example, if misgivings were not immediately expressed, they were shouted down by mob members. Group discussions can exacerbate tendencies toward overconfidence, thereby heightening an illusion of judgmental accuracy (Dunning & Ross, 1988). Minority opinions can be suppressed. When initially only one member of a six-member group knew the correct answer, in almost 75 percent of the time the single member failed to convince the others because they were not given a fair and complete hearing (Laughlin, 1980; Laughlin & Adamopoulos, 1980). Group decision making often goes wrong because alternatives are not considered carefully, minority opinions are silenced, and disagreement among members' conclusions is suppressed. It is important, therefore, that skills in implementing constructive controversy become well learned.

WHY IS INTELLECTUAL CONFLICT AVOIDED?

Conflict is to decision making, creativity, learning, and political discourse as what the internal combustion engine is to the automobile. The internal combustion engine unites the fuel and the air with a spark to create the energy for movement and acceleration. Just as the fuel and the air are inert without the spark, so are differing ideas without the spark of conflict. Conflict energizes individuals to seek out new information and work harder than ever and longer. By structuring constructive controversy, individuals can grab and hold their colleagues' attention and energize their colleagues to achieve at a level beyond what they may have originally intended. Far from being a standard practice, however, in most organizations creating intellectual conflict is the exception, not the rule. Why? There are at least six reasons. First, fear that group members might behave in uncontrolled and impulsive ways once a conflict has been initiated can stop a person from structuring a constructive controversy. Second, group members can be ignorant of how to engage in constructive controversy and, consequently, fail to do so. Third, lack of training in how to structure constructive controversy may prevent the person in charge from doing so. Fourth, the culture of the society or organization can be so anticonflict that group members do not see constructive controversy as a possibility. Fifth, specific group norms may forbid open disagreement or other aspects of engaging in constructive controversy. Sixth, with a history of avoiding conflict, inertia (the power of the status quo) may be so great that the group members just do not try anything different.

NATURE AND USE OF CONSTRUCTIVE CONTROVERSY

This book summarizes the nature of and new developments in constructive controversy theory, research, and practice. It represents nearly 50 years of work and thought about the potential positive outcomes of conflict and the specific use of constructive controversy. The nature of the book may be summarized as follows.

Foundational components of constructive controversy

Constructive controversy is based on a foundation of cooperation and conflict. These two underlying phenomena are essential to understanding its basic nature. Constructive controversy is based on participants seeking to achieve a common goal that unites them in a cooperative effort. Yet constructive controversy structures and promotes intellectual conflicts in which people with different opinions or conclusions express their opinions and challenge each other's reasoning. It is this combination of cooperation to achieve mutual goals and intellectual conflict to determine the most effective means of doing so that energizes the seeking of the "truth" through opposition and challenge.

Constructive controversies, therefore, are not only an inevitable and pervasive aspect of cooperative endeavors but also an essential aspect of their effectiveness. Wise individuals not only welcome facing others who disagree with them but will seek out people who disagree with them and even elicit disagreement when it is not occurring naturally. They know that it is only through being intellectually challenged that more effective courses of action will be revealed.

Nature of constructive controversy

Constructive controversy exists when individuals' ideas, opinions, theories, and conclusions are incompatible and the individuals seek to agree. While intellectual conflict may be an important tool for decision making, problem solving, creativity and innovation, instructional discourse, and political discourse, because of its potential constructive outcomes, conflict is rarely structured in such situations. While there have been many people in the past who have recommended intellectual conflict, such as Pericles, Socrates, Quintillan, John Milton, Samuel Johnson, Edmund Burke, and Thomas Jefferson, none of them formulated a specific theory or operational procedure to institutionalize the practice. Hopefully, this book does so.

Theory of constructive controversy

The theory underlying constructive controversy states that the way conflict is structured within the situation determines how individuals interact with each other, which in turn determines the quality of the relevant outcomes. This is historically known as S-P-O theory (Watson & Johnson, 1972). Intellectual conflict may be structured along a continuum, with constructive controversy at one end and concurrence seeking (i.e., avoidance of disagreement) at the other. An important part of the theory is the specification of the process by which constructive controversy works.

Process of constructive controversy

The process of constructive controversy consists of six steps: (a) organizing information and deriving conclusions; (b) presenting and advocating positions, including explaining; (c) being challenged by opposing views, including socio-cognitive conflict, argumentation, majority and minority influence, confirmatory bias, and myside bias; (d) conceptual conflict, disequilibrium, and uncertainty, including freedom to express independent opinions, misperceiving opposing information and reasoning, being overloaded with opposing information, perceiving usefulness of opposing position, and being challenged by valid or erroneous position; (e) epistemic curiosity and perspective taking, including search for information, seeking to understand opposing positions, perspective taking, and social projection; and (f) reconceptualization, synthesis, and integration, including incorporation of others' information and reasoning, attitude and position change, and transition from one stage of cognitive reasoning to another.

The process of concurrence seeking includes the following stages: (a) the dominant position is derived, (b) the dominant position is presented and advocated, (c) members are confronted with the demand to concur and conform, (d) there is conflict between public and private positions, (e) members seek confirming information, and (f) there is public consensus.

Outcomes of constructive controversy

The outcomes generated by the process of controversy are (a) higher quality of decision making, problem solving, achievement, and retention, (b) higher cognitive and moral reasoning, (c) greater exchange of expertise, (d) more frequent and accurate perspective taking, (e) greater creativity, (f) greater open-mindedness, (g) greater motivation to improve understanding, (h) greater attitude change about the issue and task, (i) more positive attitudes toward the controversy procedure and decision making, (j) greater commitment to process and outcomes, (k) greater interpersonal attraction and support among participants, (l) greater social support, (m) higher self-esteem, and (n) more democratic values.

Conditions mediating the effectiveness of constructive controversy

The conditions mediating the effects of the controversy process include (a) a cooperative context (which includes interest in disconfirming information, decrease in competence threat, decrease in downward social comparison, decrease in perceived bias, and greater leadership), (b) heterogeneity among members, (c) distribution of information, (d) skilled disagreement, and (e) rational argument.

Operationalization of constructive controversy procedure

The controversy procedure involves assigning one of two or more positions to two or more individuals. The individuals then (a) prepare the best case possible for its position, (b) present the best case for the position to the other pair and listen to the opposing position, (c) engage in a discussion in which the advocacy pairs attempt to refute the opposing positions and rebut attacks on their position, (d) reverse perspectives and present the best case possible for an opposing position, and (e) drop all advocacy and seek a synthesis that takes all perspectives and positions into account and group members can agree upon. This procedure may be applied in a wide variety of situations, including decision-making situations in groups and organizations, education, political discourse, and the establishment and maintenance of world peace.

RETURN TO THEORY, RESEARCH, AND PRACTICE

> Theory may inform, but practice convinces.
>
> *George Bain (1881–1968), Scottish artist*

Constructive controversy theory is an example of how psychological theorizing and research have resulted in valuable practical applications and how theory, research, and practice interact in ways that enhance all three. The relationship between theory and research has long been understood (Johnson, 2003). Theory identifies, clarifies, and defines the phenomena of interest and their relationships with each other. In the 1950s and 1960s, some research on constructive controversy was conducted, but it was disjointed, involved a variety of definitions of intellectual conflict, and provided little conceptual clarity as to the nature of constructive controversy or how it could be operationalized. In the mid-1970s (Johnson, Johnson, & Johnson, 1976) and the late 1970s (Johnson & Johnson, 1979), a more systematic theory and review of research were presented, as well as operational procedures for education and business. This work (a) brought considerable conceptual clarity to the nature of constructive controversy, (b) helped reorganize the previous studies by creating a framework from which to classify the operational definitions, and (c) helped operationalize constructive controversy in future studies (i.e., the rules of correspondence were clear). Thus, constructive controversy is a well-formulated theory that clearly defines the relevant concepts, summarizes the research, and generates new research.

Research validates or disconfirms the theory. There is sufficient research to test the theory, and the studies conducted have both high internal and high external validity. The amount, quality, and generalizability of the research provide strong confirmation of the basic propositions of the theory and the effectiveness of constructive controversy relative to concurrence seeking and individualistic efforts. In addition, these studies have demonstrated relationships between the theoretical constructs and new dependent variables and have contributed research findings about originally underdeveloped aspects of the theory.

In discussions of the relationships among theory, research, and practice, the role of practice has sometimes been neglected. Constructive controversy has been applied in many diverse areas, but the most systematic, widespread, and long-term applications have been in education and business. The implementation of constructive controversy has had profound effects on constructive controversy theory and research.

LOOKING FORWARD

Now that you have reached the end of this book, you are at a new beginning. Years of experience in using constructive controversy are needed to gain real expertise in managing intellectual conflict constructively. The more individuals engage in the controversy process, the more creative and knowledgeable they will become, the more they will like each other, and the healthier they will be psychologically. It is through constructive conflict that individuals grow, develop, learn, progress, create, and achieve. In the end you will find that constructive controversies enrich rather than disrupt your life.

References

Ackoff, R. L. (1967). Management misinformation systems. *Management Sciences, 14*(4), 147–156.

Alexander, R. J. (2006). *Towards dialogic teaching: Rethinking classroom talk.* York: Dialogos.

Allen, V. (1965). Situational factors in conformity. In L. Berkowitz (Ed.), *Advances in experimental social psychology* (Vol. 2, pp. 133–175). New York: Academic Press.

Allen, V. (1976). *Children as teachers: Theory and research on tutoring.* New York: Academic Press.

Allport, G. W., & Postman, L. J. (1945). The basic psychology of rumor. *Transactions of the New York Academy of Sciences, 8*(Series III), 61–81.

Alper, S., Tjosvold, D., & Law, K. S. (1998). Interdependence and controversy in group decision making: Antecedents to effective self-managing teams. *Organizational Behavior and Human Decision Processes, 74*(1), 33–52.

Amabile, T. M. (1983). The social psychology of creativity: A componential conceptualization. *Journal of Personality and Social Psychology, 45*(2), 357–376.

Amabile, T. M. (1996). *Creativity in context.* Boulder, CO: Westview Press.

Ames, G., & Murray, F. (1982). When two wrongs make a right: Promoting cognitive change by social conflict. *Developmental Psychology, 18*(6), 892–895.

Amigues, R. (1988). Peer interaction in solving physics problems: Sociocognitive confrontation and metacognitive aspects. *Journal of Experimental Child Psychology, 45*, 141–158.

Anderson, N., & Graesser, C. (1976). An information integration analysis of attitude change in group discussion. *Journal of Personality and Social Psychology, 34*, 210–222.

Anderson, R. C., Chinn, C., Waggoner, M., & Nguyen, K. (1998). Intellectually-stimulating story discussions. In J. Osborn & F. Lehr (Eds.), *Literacy for all: Issues in teaching and learning* (pp. 170–186). New York: Guildford Press.

Anderson, R. C., Nguyen-Jahiel, K., McNurlen, B., Archodidou, A., Kim, S., Reznitskaya, A., Tillmans, M., & Gilbert, L. (2001). The snowball phenomenon: Spread of ways of talking and ways of thinking across groups of children. *Cognition and Instruction, 19*, 1–46.

Annis, L. (1983). The processes and effects of peer tutoring. *Human Learning, 2*, 39–47.

Asch, S. (1952). *Social psychology*. Englewood Cliffs, NJ: Prentice-Hall.

Asch, S. (1956). Studies of independence and conformity: A minority of one against a unanimous majority. *Psychological Monographs, 70*(9), Whole No. 416.

Asterhan, C. S., & Schwarz, B. B. (2007). The effects of monological and dialogical argumentation on concept learning in evolutionary theory. *Journal of Educational Psychology, 99*, 626–639.

Atsumi, T., & Burnstein, E. (1992). *Is minority influence different from majority influence?* Brussels Congress, University of Michigan, Abstract number IN064.1.

Avery, P., Freeman, C., Greenwalt, K., & Trout, M. (2006). The *"deliberating in a democracy project."* Paper presented at the annual meeting of the American Educational Research Association, San Francisco, CA, April 10.

Azmitia, M., & Montgomery, R. (1993). Friendship, transactive dialogues and the development of scientific reasoning. *Social Development, 2*, 202–221.

Bahn, C. (1964). *The interaction of creativity and social facilitation in creative problem solving*. Doctoral dissertation, Columbia University. Ann Arbor, MI: University Microfilms, 65–7499.

Baker, S., & Petty, R. (1994). Majority and minority influence: Source-position imbalance as determinant of message scrutiny. *Journal of Personality and Social Psychology, 67*, 5–19.

Bandura, A. (1977). Self-efficacy: Toward a unifying theory of behavioral change. *Psychological Review, 84*(2), 191–215.

Bandura, A. (2000). Exercise of human agency through collective efficacy. *Current Directions in Psychological Science, 9*(3), 75–78.

Bargh, J. A., & Schul, Y. (1980). On the cognitive benefits of teaching. *Journal of Educational Psychology, 72*, 593–604.

Barnes, D., & Todd, F. (1977). *Communication and learning in small groups*. London: Routledge and Kegan Paul.

Barnes, D., & Todd, F. (1995). *Communication and learning revisited*. Portsmouth, NH: Boynton/Cook.

Baron, J. (1995). Myside bias in thinking about abortion. *Thinking and Reasoning, 1*, 221–235.

Baron, J. (2008). *Thinking and deciding* (4th edn.). Cambridge, MA: Cambridge University Press.

Bartlett, F. C. (1932). *Remembering: A study in experimental and social psychology*. Cambridge, UK: Cambridge University Press.

Beach, L. R. (1974). Self-directed student groups and college learning. *Higher Education, 3*, 187–200.

Beer, M., & Eisenstat, R. A. (2000). The silent killers of strategy implementation and learning. *Sloan Management Review* (Summer), 29–40.

Beilin, H. (1977). Inducing conservation through training. In G. Steiner (Ed.), *Psychology of the 20th century, Piaget and beyond* (Vol. 7, pp. 260–289). Zurich: Kindler.

Bennett, N., & Cass, A. (1989). The effects of group composition on group interactive processes and pupil understanding. *British Educational Research Journal, 15,* 119–132.

Bennis, W., & Biederman, P. W. (1996). *Organizing genius: The secrets of creative collaboration.* Cambridge, MA: Perseus Books.

Benware, C. (1975). Quantitative and qualitative learning differences as a function of learning in order to teach another. Unpublished manuscript, University of Rochester. Cited in Deci, E., *Intrinsic motivation.* New York: Plenum Press.

Bergquist, W., & Heikkinen, H. (1990). Student ideas regarding chemical equilibrium. *Journal of Chemical Education, 67,* 1000–1003.

Berkowitz, M., & Gibbs, J. (1983). Measuring the developmental features of moral discussion. *Merrill-Palmer Quarterly, 29,* 399–410.

Berkowitz, M., Gibbs, J., & Broughton, J. (1980). The relation of moral judgment stage disparity to developmental effects of peer dialogues. *Merrill-Palmer Quarterly, 26,* 341–357.

Berlyne, D. (1957). Uncertainty and conflict: A point of contact between information theory and behavior theory concepts. *Psychological Review, 64,* 329–339.

Berlyne, D. (1960). *Conflict, arousal and curiosity.* New York: McGraw-Hill.

Berlyne, D. (1965). *Structure and direction in thinking.* New York: John Wiley and Sons.

Berlyne, D. (1966). Notes on intrinsic motivation and intrinsic reward in relation to instruction. In J. Bruner (Ed.), *Learning about learning* (Cooperative Research Monograph No. 15). Washington, DC: US Department of Health, Education, and Welfare, Office of Education.

Blatchford, P., & Kutnick, P. (2003). Developing groupwork in everyday classrooms. *Special issue of the International Journal of Educational Research, 39,* 1–2.

Blatt, M. (1969). *The effects of classroom discussion upon children's level of moral judgment.* Unpublished doctoral dissertation, University of Chicago.

Blatt, M., & Kohlberg, L. (1973). The effects of classroom moral discussion upon children's level of moral judgment. In L. Kohlberg (Ed.), *Collected papers on moral development and moral education.* Harvard University: Moral Education and Research Foundation.

Blaye, A. (1990). Peer interaction in solving a binary matrix problem: Possible mechanisms causing individual progress. *Learning and Instruction, 2,* 45–56.

Bolen, L., & Torrance, E. (1976). *An experimental study of the influence of locus of control, dyadic interaction, and sex on creative thinking.* Paper presented at the American Educational Research Association, San Francisco, April.

Borys, S., & Spitz, H. (1979). Effect of peer interaction on the problem-solving behavior of mentally retarded youths. *American Journal of Mental Deficiency, 84,* 273–279.

Botvin, G., & Murray, F. (1975). The efficacy of peer modeling and social conflict in the acquisition of conversation. *Child Development, 45,* 796–799.

Boulding, E. (1964). Further reflections on conflict management. In R. Kahn & E. Boulding (Eds.), *Power and conflict in organizations* (pp. 146–150). New York: Basic Books.

Brehm, S. S., & Brehm, J. W. (1981). *Psychological reactance: A theory of freedom and control.* New York: Academic.

Brock, T. C., & Balloun, J. L. (1967). Behavioral receptivity to dissonant information. *Journal of Personality and Social Psychology, 6,* 413–428.

Brown, R. A. J., & Renshaw, O. D. (2000). Collective argumentation: A sociocultural approach to reframing classroom teaching and learning. In H. Cowie & G. van der Aalsvoort (Eds.), *Social interaction in learning and instruction: The meaning of discourse for the construction of knowledge* (pp. 52–66). New York, NY: Elsevier Science.

Bruner, J., & Minturn, A. (1955). Perceptual identification and perceptual organization. *Journal of Genetic Psychology, 53,* 21–28.

Buchs, C., & Butera, F. (2004). Socio-cognitive conflict and the role of student interaction in learning. *New Review of Social Psychology, 3,* 80–87.

Buchs, C., Butera, F., & Mugny, G. (2004). Resource interdependence, student interactions, and performance in cooperative learning. *Educational Psychology, 24*(3) 291–314.

Burdick, H., & Burnes, A. (1958). A test of "strain toward symmetry" theories. *Journal of Abnormal and Social Psychology, 57,* 367–369.

Burke, E. (1790). *Reflections on the French revolution* (p. 144). Pearson Longman, 2006.

Butera, F., & Buchs, C. (2005). Reasoning together: From focusing to decentering. In V. Girotto & P. N. Johnson-Laird (Eds.), *The shape of reason* (pp. 193–203). New York: Psychology Press.

Butera, F., Huguet, P., Mugny, G., & Prez, J. A. (1994). Socio-epistemic conflict and constructivism. *Swiss Journal of Psychology, 53,* 229–239.

Butera, F., & Mugny, G. (1992). Influence minoritaire et falsification [Minority influence and falsification]. *Revue Internationale de Psychologie Sociale, 5,* 115–132.

Butera, F., & Mugny, G. (1995). Conflict between incompetences and influence of a low-competence source in hypothesis testing. *European Journal of Social Psychology, 25,* 457–462.

Butera, F., & Mugny, G. (2001). Conflicts and social influences in hypothesis testing. In C. K. W. De Dreu & N. K. De Vries (Eds.), *Group consensus and minority influence implications for innovation* (pp. 160–192). Oxford: Blackwell.

Butera, F., Mugny, G., & Buchs, C. (2001). Representation of knowledge as a mediator of learning. In F. Butera & G. Mugny (Eds.), *Social influence in social reality* (pp. 160–182). Seattle, Bern: Hopefe & Huber.

Butera, F., Mugny, G., Legrenzi, P., & Perez, J. A. (1996). Majority and minority influence, task representation, and inductive reasoning. *British Journal of Social Psychology, 35,* 123–136.

Butera, F., Mugny, G., & Tomei, A. (2000). Incertitude et enjeux identitaires dans l'influence sociale. In J. L. Beauvois, R. V. Joule, & J. M. Moneil (Eds.), *Perspectives cognitives et conduits sociales* (Vol. 7, pp. 205–229). Rennes: Presses Universitaires.

Byrnes, D. S. (1998). *Complexity theory and the socal sciences.* London: Routledge.

Carugati, F., De Paolis, P., & Mugny, G. (1980–1981). Conflit de centrations et progr's cognitive, III: regulations cognitive et relationnelles du conflit socio-cognitif. *Bulletin de Psychologie, 34,* 843–851.

Chen, G., Liu, C. H., & Tjosvold, D. (2005). Conflict management for effective top management teams and innovation in China. *Journal of Management Studies, 42,* 277–300.

Chen, G., & Tjosvold, D. (2002). Conflict management and team effectiveness in China: The mediating role of justice. *Asia Pacific Journal of Management, 19,* 557–572.

Chen, Y. F., & Tjosvold, D. (2006). Participative leadership by American and Chinese managers in China: The role of relationships. *Journal of Management Studies, 43,* 1727–1752.

Chen, Y. F., & Tjosvold, D. (2007). Guanxi and leader member relationships between American managers and Chinese employees: Open-minded dialogue as mediator. *Asia Pacific Journal of Management, 24,* 171–189.

Chen, Y. F., Tjosvold, D., & Su, F. (2005). Goal interdependence for working across cultural boundaries: Chinese employees with foreign managers. *International Journal of Intercultural Relations, 29,* 429–447.

Chen, Y. F., Tjosvold, D., & Wu, P. G. (2008). Foreign managers' guanxi with Chinese employees: Effects of warm-heartedness and reward distribution on negotiation. *Group Decision and Negotiation, 17*, 79–96.

Chinn, C. A. (2006). Learning to argue. In A. M. O'Donnell, C. E. Hmelo-Silver, & G. Erkens (Eds.), *Collaborative learning, reasoning, and technology* (pp. 355–383). Mahwah, NJ: Erlbaum.

Chinn, C. A., & Anderson, R. C. (1998). The structure of discussions that promote reasoning. *Teachers College Record, 100*, 315–368.

Chinn, C. A., O'Donnell, A. M., & Jinks, T. S. (2000). The structure of discourse in collaborative learning. *The Journal of Experimental Education, 69*, 77–97.

Chiu, M. M. (1997). *Building on diversity* (ERIC Documentation Reproduction Service No. ED 410 325). Los Angeles: University of California, Los Angeles.

Chiu, M. M. (2008). Effects of argumentation on group micro-creativity: Statistical discourse analyses of algebra students' collaborative problem solving. *Contemporary Educational Psychology, 33*, 382–402.

Chiu, M. M., & Khoo, L. (2003). Rudeness and status effects during group problem solving. *Journal of Educational Psychology, 95*, 506–523.

Coleman, E. B., Brown, A. L., & Rivkin, I. D. (1997). The effect of instructional explanations on learning from scientific texts. *Journal of the Learning Sciences, 6*, 347–365.

Collins, J. C., & Porras, J. I. (1994). *Built to last: Successful habits of visionary companies.* New York: Harper Collins Publisher.

Colson, W. (1968). *Self-disclosure as a function of social approval.* Unpublished masters thesis. Howard University, Washington, DC.

Cook, H., & Murray, F. (1973). *Acquisition of conservation through the observation of conserving models.* Paper presented at the meetings of the American Educational Research Association, New Orleans, March.

Cooper, P. (1995). *Cubism* (p. 14). London: Phaidon.

Coovert, M. D., & Reeder, G. D. (1990). Negativity effects in impression formation: The role of unit formation and schematic expectations. *Journal of Experimental Social Psychology, 26*(1), 49–62.

Cosier, R. A., & Dalton, D. R. (1990). Positive effects of conflict: A field assessment. *International Journal of Conflict Management, 1*(1), 81–92.

Covington, M. (1984). The motive for self-worth. In R. Ames & C. Ames (Eds.), *Research on motivation in education: Vol. 1. Student motivation* (pp. 17–113). New York: Academic Press.

Covington, M. (1992). *Making the grade: A self-worth perspective on motivation and school reform.* New York: Cambridge University Press.

Crockenberg, S., & Nicolayev, J. (1977). *Stage transition on moral reasoning as related to conflict experienced in naturalistic settings.* Paper presented at the Society for Research in Child Development. New Orleans, March.

Dalton, D. R., & Cosier, R. A. (1989). Development and psychometric properties of the decision conflict and cooperation questionnaire (DCCQ). *Educational and Psychological Measurement, 49,* 697–700.

Dalton, R. (2007). *The good citizen: How a younger generation is reshaping American politics.* Washington, DC: CQ Press, A Division of SAGE Publications.

Damon, W., & Killen, M. (1982). Peer interaction and the process of change in children's moral reasoning. *Merrill-Palmer Quarterly, 28,* 347–367.

Damon, W., & Phelps, E. (1988). Strategic uses of peer learning in children's education. In T. J. Berndt & G. W. Ladd (Eds.), *Peer relations in child development* (pp. 135–157). New York: John Wiley.

Darnon, C., Doll, S., & Butera, F. (2007). Dealing with a disagreeing partner: Relational and epistemic conflict elaboration. *European Journal of Psychology of Education, 22,* 227–242.

Darwin, C. (1874). *The descent of man and selection in relation to sex.* New York: Rand, McNally.

Dearborn, C., & Simon, H. (1958). Selective perception: A note on the departmental identification of executives. *Sociometry, 23,* 667–673.

De Dreu, C. K. W., & De Vries, N. K. (Eds.). (1996). *Group consensus and minority influence: Implications for innovation* (pp. 161–182). Oxford: Blackwell.

De Dreu, C. K. W., & Nauta, A. (2009). Self-interest and other-orientation in organizational behavior: Implications for job performance, prosocial behavior, and personal initiative. *Journal of Applied Psychology, 94,* 913–926.

De Dreu, C. K. W., Weingart, L. R., & Kwon, S. (2000). Influence of social motives on integrative negotiation: A meta-analytic review and test of two theories. *Journal of Personality and Social Psychology, 76,* 889–905.

De Dreu, C. K. W., & West, M. A. (2001). Minority dissent and team innovation: The importance of participation in decision making. *Journal of Applied Psychology, 86,* 1191–1201.

Dekkers, P. J. J. M., & Thijs, G. D. (1998). Making productive use of students' initial conceptions in developing the concept of force. *Science Education, 82*(1), 31–52.

De La Paz, S. (2005). Effects of historical reasoning instruction and writing strategy mastery in culturally and academically diverse middle school classrooms. *Journal of Educational Psychology, 97,* 139–156.

Delgado, M. R., Locke, H. M., Strenger, V. A., & Fiez, J. A. (2003). Dorsal striatum responses to reward and punishment: Effects of valence and magnitude manipulations. *Cognitive, Affective, Behavioral Neuroscience, 3*(1), 27–38.

Delgado, M. R., Nystrom, L. E., Fissell, C., Noll, D. C., & Fiez, N. A. (2000). Tracking the hemodynamic responses to reward and punishment in the striatum. *Journal of Neurophysiology, 84*(6), 3072–3077.

Delgado, M. R., Schotter, A., Ozbay, E. Y., & Phelps, E. A. (2008). Understanding overbidding: Using the neural circuitry of reward to design economic auctions. *Science, 321*, 1849–1852.

De Lisi, R., & Goldbeck, S. L. (1999). Implications of Piaget's theory for peer learning. In A. M. O'Donnell & A. King (Eds.), *Cognitive perspectives on peer learning* (pp. 179–196). Mahwah, NJ: Lawrence Erlbaum.

Delli Carpini, M. X., Cook, F. L., & Jacobs, L. R. (2004). Public deliberation, discursive participation, and citizen engagement: A review of the empirical literature. *Annual Review of Political Science, 7*, 315–344.

de Montesquieu, C. (1748). *The spirit of laws*. Cambridge, UK: Cambridge University Press, 1989.

de Quervain, D. J. F., Fischbacher, U., Treyer, V., Schellhammer, M., Schnyder, U., Buck, A., & Fehr, E. (2004). The neural basis of altruistic punishment. *Science, 305*(5688), 1254–1258.

Detert, J. R., & Trevino, L. K. (2010). Speaking up to higher ups: How supervisors and skip-level leaders influence employee voice. *Organization Science, 21*(1), 249–270.

de Tocqueville, A. (1945). *Democracy in America*. New York: Knopf.

Deutsch, M. (1949). A theory of cooperation and competition. *Human Relations, 2*, 129–152.

Deutsch, M. (1962). Cooperation and trust: Some theoretical notes. In M. Jones (Ed.), *Nebraska symposium on motivation* (pp. 275–320). Lincoln, NE: University of Nebraska Press.

Deutsch, M. (1969). Conflicts: Productive and destructive. *Journal of Social Issues, 25*(1), 7–42.

Deutsch, M. (1973). *The resolution of conflict*. New Haven, CT: Yale University Press.

Deutsch, M., & Gerard, H. (1955). A study of normative and informational social influences upon individual judgment. *Journal of Abnormal and Social Psychology, 51*, 629–636.

Dewey, J. (1910). *How we think*. New York: D. C. Health & Co.

Dewey, J. (1916). *Democracy and education*. New York: Macmillan.

Diehl, M., & Stroebe, W. (1987). Productivity loss in brainstorming groups: Toward the solution of a riddle. *Journal of Personality and Social Psychology, 53*, 497–509.

Doise, W., & Mugny, G. (1975). Recherches sociogénétiques sur la coordination d'actions interdependants. *Revue Suisse de Psychologie Pure et Appliqu e, 34*, 160–174.

Doise, W., & Mugny, G. (1979). Individual and collective conflicts of centrations in cognitive development. *European Journal of Psychology, 9*, 105–198.

Doise, W., & Mugny, G. (1984). *The social development of the intellect.* Oxford, England: Pergammon.

Doise, W., Mugny, G., & Perret-Clermont, A. N. (1975). Social interaction and the development of cognitive operations. *European Journal of Social Psychology, 5*, 367–383.

Doise, W., Mugny, G., & Perret-Clermont, A. (1976). Social interaction and cognitive development: Further evidence. *European Journal of Social Psychology, 6*, 245–247.

Doise, W., Mugny, G., & Perez, J. A. (1998). The social construction of knowledge: Social marking and socio cognitive conflict. In U. Flick (Ed.), *The psychology of the social* (pp. 77–90). Cambridge, UK: Cambridge University Press.

Doise, W., & Palmonari, A. (1984). *Social interaction in individual development* (pp. 127–146). Cambridge, UK: Cambridge University Press.

Dreyfus, A., Jungwirth, E., & Eliovitch, R. (1990). Applying the "cognitive conflict" strategy for conceptual change: Some implications, difficulties, and problems. *Science Education, 74*, 555–569.

Driver, R., Newton, P., & Osborne, J. (2000). Establishing the norms of scientific argumentation in classrooms. *Science Education, 84*, 287–312.

Duckitt, J. (1992). *The social psychology of prejudice.* New York: Praeger.

Dunn, J., & Kendrick, C. (1982). *Siblings: Love, envy and understanding.* London: Grant McIntyre.

Dunnette, M., Campbell, J., & Jaastad, K. (1963). The effect of group participation on brainstorming effectiveness of two industrial samples. *Journal of Applied Psychology, 47*, 30–37.

Dunning, D., & Ross, L. (1988). *Overconfidence in individual and group prediction: Is the collective any wiser?* Unpublished manuscript, Cornell University.

Duschl, R. A. (2007). Quality argumentation and epistemic criteria. In S. Erduran & M. P. Jimenez-Aleixandre (Eds.), *Argumentation in science education: Perspectives from classroom-based research* (pp. 159–175). Dordrecht, Netherlands: Springer.

Ehrich, D., Guttman, I., Schonbach, P., & Mills, J. (1957). Post-decision exposure to relevant information. *Journal of Abnormal and Social Psychology, 54*, 98–102.

Ehrlich, H. J., & Lee, D. (1969). Dogmatism, learning, and resistance to change: A review and a new paradigm. *Psychological Bulletin, 71*, 249–260.

Eisenberg, A. R., & Garvey, C. (1981). Children's use of verbal strategies in resolving conflicts. *Discourse Processes, 4*, 149–170.

Elizabeth, L. L., & Galloway, D. (1996). Conceptual links between cognitive acceleration through science education and motivational style: A critique of Adey and Shayer. *International Journal of Science Education, 18*, 35–49.

Elsbach, K. D., & Hargadon, A. B. (2006). Enhancing creativity through "mindless" work: A framework of workday design. *Organizational Science, 17*(4), 470–483.

Ennis, R. H. (1993). Critical thinking assessment. *Theory into Practice, 32*, 179–186.

Erb, H-P., Bohner, G., Rank, S., & Einwiller, S. (2002). Processing minority and majority communications: The role of conflict with prior attitudes. *Personality and Social Psychology Bulletin, 28*, 1172–1182.

Etherington, L., & Tjosvold, D. (1998). Managing budget conflicts: Contribution of goal interdependence and interaction. *Canadian Journal of Administrative Sciences, 15*(2), 1–10.

Fairclough, N. (1995). *Critical discourse analysis.* Boston: Addison Wesley.

Falk, D., & Johnson, D. W. (1977). The effects of perspective-taking and ego-centrism on problem solving in heterogeneous and homogeneous groups. *Journal of Social Psychology, 102*, 63–72.

Feffer, M., & Suchotliff, L. (1966). Decentering implications of social interaction. *Journal of Personality and Social Psychology, 4*, 415–422.

Fehr, E., & Camerer, C. F. (2007). Social neuroeconomics: The neural circuitry of social preferences. *Trends in Cognitive Science, 11*(10), 419–427.

Felton, M. K. (2004). The development of discourse strategies in adolescent argumentation. *Cognitive Development, 19*, 35–52.

Felton, M. K., & Kuhn, D. (2001). The development of argumentative discourse skill. *Discourse Processes, 32*, 135–153.

Ferretti, R. P., Andrews-Weckerly, S., & Lewis, W. E. (2007). Improving the argumentative writing of students with learning disabilities: Descriptive and normative considerations. *Reading and Writing Quarterly, 23*, 267–285.

Ferretti, R. P., Lewis, W. E., & Andrews-Weckerly, S. (2009). Do goals affect the structure of students' argumentative writing strategies? *Journal of Educational Psychology, 101*(3), 577–589.

Festinger, L. (1957). *Cognitive dissonance.* Evanston, IL: Row, Peterson.

Festinger, L., & Maccoby, N. (1964). On resistance to persuasive communications. *Journal of Abnormal and Social Psychology, 68*, 359–366.

Fisher, E. (1993). Distinctive features of pupil–pupil talk and their relationship to learning. *Language and Education, 7*, 239–258.

Fisher, P., Jonas, E., Frey, D., & Schultz-Hardt, S. (2005). Selective exposure to information: The impact of information limits. *European Journal of Social Psychology, 35*, 469–492.

Fisher, R. (1969). An each one teach one approach to music notation. *Grade Teacher*, *86*, 120.

Fiske, S. T. (1980). Attention and weight in person perception: The impact of negative and extreme behavior. *Journal of Personality and Social Psychology*, *38*(6), 889–906.

Flavell, J. (1963). *The developmental psychology of Jean Piaget*. Princeton, NJ: Van Nostrand.

Flavell, J. (1968). *The development of role-taking and communication skills in children*. New York: Wiley.

Foley, J., & MacMillan, F. (1943). Mediated generalization and the interpretation of verbal behavior: V. Free association as related to differences in professional training. *Journal of Experimental Psychology*, *33*, 299–310.

Foucault, M. (1970). *The order of things: An archaeology of the human sciences*. New York: Pantheon Books.

Freedman, J. L., & Sears, D. O. (1963). Voters' preferences among types of information. *American Psychologist*, *18*, 375.

Freedman, J. L., & Sears, D. O. (1965). Selective exposure. In L. Berkowitz (Ed.), *Advances in experimental social psychology* (Vol. 2, pp. 57–97). New York: Academic Press.

Freedman, J. L., & Sears, D. O. (1967). Selective exposure to information: A critical review. *The Public Opinion Quarterly*, *31*(2), 194–213.

Freese, M., & Fay, D. (2001). Personal initiative (PI): An active performance concept for work in the 21st century. *Research in Organizational Behavior*, *23*, 133–187.

Freud, S. (1930). Civilization and its discontents. In J. Strachey (Ed.), *The standard edition of the complete psychological works of Sigmund Freud* (Vol. 21, pp. 86–145). London: Hogart Press, 1961.

Frey, D. (1981). Reversible and irreversible decisions: Preference for consonant information as a function of attractiveness of decision alternatives. *Personality and Social Psychology Bulletin*, *7*, 621–626.

Frey, D. (1986). Recent research on selective exposure to information. In L. Berkowitz (Ed.), *Advances in experimental social psychology* (Vol. 19, pp. 41–80). San Diego, CA: Academic Press.

Frey, D., & Rosch, M. (1984). Information seeking after decisions: The roles of novelty of information and decision reversibility. *Personality and Social Psychology Bulletin*, *10*, 91–98.

Frey, D., & Wicklund, R. A. (1978). A clarification of selective exposure: The impact of choice. *Journal of Experimental Social Psychology*, *14*, 132–139.

Galinsky, A. D., Maddux, W. W., Gilin, D., & White, J. B. (2008). Why it pays to get inside the head of your opponent: The differential effects of perspective taking and empathy in negotiations. *Psychological Science, 19*(1), 378–384.

Galton, M., Hargreaves, L., Comber, C., Wall, D., & Pell, A. (1999). *Inside the primary classroom: 20 years on.* London: Routledge.

Galton, M., Simon, B., & Croll, P. (1980). *Inside the primary classroom* (the ORACLE project). London: Routledge and Kegan Paul.

Garcia-Marques, T., & Mackie, D. (2001). The feeling of familiarity as a regulator of persuasive processing. *Social Cognition, 19,* 9–34.

Gartner, A., Kohler, M., & Reissman, F. (1971). *Children teach children: Learning by teaching.* New York: Harper & Row.

Gelman, R. (1978). Cognitive development. *Annual Review of Psychology, 29,* 297–332.

Genishi, C., & Di Paolo, M. (1982). Learning through agreement in a pre-school. In L. Wilkinson (Ed.), *Communicating in the classroom* (pp. 49–67). New York: Academic Press.

Gerard, H., & Greenbaum, C. (1962). Attitudes toward an agent of uncertainty reduction. *Journal of Personality, 30,* 485–495.

Gibbons, F. X. (1986). Social comparison and depression: Company's effect on misery. *Journal of Personality and Social Psychology, 51,* 140–148.

Gilbert, L. (1997). Why women do and do not access street-based services. *Drugs News, 17,* 30–34.

Gilly, M., & Roux, P. (1984). Efficacite compare du travail individual et du travail en interaction socio-cognitive dans l'appropriation et al mise en oeuvre de regles de resolution chez les enfants de 11–12 ans. *Cahiers de Psychologie Cognitive, 4,* 171–188.

Glachan, M., & Light, P. (1982). Peer interaction and learning: Can two wrongs make a right? In G. Butterworth & P. Light (Eds.), *Social cognition: Studies of the development of understanding* (pp. 238–262). Chicago: University of Chicago Press.

Glidewell, J. (1953). *Group emotionality and production.* Unpublished doctoral dissertation, University of Chicago.

Golanics, J. D., & Nussbaum, E. M. (2008). Enhancing collaborative online argumentation through question elaboration and goal instructions. *Journal of Computer Assisted Learning, 24,* 167–180.

Graham, D. (2006). Strategy instruction and the teaching of writing: A meta-analysis. In C. A. MacArthur, S. Graham, & J. Fitzgerald (Eds.), *Handbook of writing research* (pp. 187–207). New York: Guilford Press.

Grant, A. M., & Berry, J. W. (2011). The necessity of others is the mother of invention: Intrinsic and prosocial motivations, perspective-taking, and creativity. *Academy of Management Journal, 54*, 73–96.

Greenwald, A., & Albert, R. (1968). Acceptance and recall of improvised arguments. *Journal of Personality and Social Psychology, 8*, 31–35.

Griffith, E., Plamenatz, J., & Pennock, J. (1956). Cultural prerequisites to a successfully functioning democracy: A symposium. *American Political Science Review, 50*, 101–137.

Gruber, H. E. (2006). Creativity and conflict resolution: The role of point of view. In M. Deutsch & P. T. Coleman (Eds.), *The handbook of conflict resolution: Theory and practice* (pp. 391–401). San Francisco, CA: Jossey-Bass Inc.

Gruenfeld, D. H. (1995). Status, ideology and integrative complexity on the U.S. Supreme Court: Rethinking the politics of political decision making. *Journal of Personality and Social Psychology, 68*, 5–20.

Guilford, J. P. (1950). Creativity. *American Psychologist, 5*(9), 444–454.

Guilford, J. P. (1956). The structure of intellect. *Psychological Bulletin, 33*, 267–293.

Guttman, A. (2000). Why should schools care about civic education? In L. McDonnell, P. Timpane, & R. Benjamin (Eds.), *Rediscovering the democratic purposes of education* (pp. 73–90). Lawrence, KS: University of Kansas Press.

Hackman, J. R., Brousseau, K. R., & Weiss, J. A. (1976). The interaction of task design and group performance: Strategies in determining group effectiveness. *Organizational Behavior and Human Performance, 16*, 350–365.

Hagler, D. A., & Brem, S. K. (2008). Reaching agreement: The structure & pragmatics of critical care nurses' informal reasoning. *Contemporary Educational Psychology, 33*, 403–424.

Hall, J., & Williams, M. (1966). A comparison of decision-making performance in established ad hoc groups. *Journal of Personality and Social Psychology, 3*, 214–222.

Hall, J., & Williams, M. (1970). Group dynamics training and improved decision making. *Journal of Applied Behavioral Science, 6*, 39–68.

Hammond, K. (1965). New directions in research on conflict resolution. *Journal of Social Issues, 11*, 44–66.

Hardin, C. D., & Higgins, E. T. (1996). Shared reality: How social verification makes the subjective objective. In R. M. Sorrentino & E. T. Higgins (Eds.), *Handbook of motivation and cognition. Vol. 3. The interpersonal context* (pp. 28–84). New York: Guilford.

Hartup, W. W., French, D. C., Laursen, B., Johnston, M. K., & Ogawa, J. R. (1993). Conflict and friendship relations in middle childhood: Behaviour in a closed-field situation. *Child Development, 64*, 445–454.

Heller, P., Keith, R., & Anderson, S. (1992). Teaching problem solving through co-operative grouping. Part 1: Group versus individual problem solving. *American Journal of Physics, 60*, 627–636.

Helson, R. (1996). Arnheim Award address to division 10 of the American Psychological Association: In search of the creative personality. *Creativity Research Journal, 9*, 295–306.

Hewstone, M., & Martin, R. (2008). Social influence. In M. Hewstone, W. Stroebe, & K. Jonas (Eds.), *Introduction to social psychology* (4th edn., pp. 216–243). Malden, MA: Blackwell Publishing.

Hidi, S., Berndorff, D., & Ainley, M. (2002). Children's argument writing, interest and self-efficacy: An intervention. *Learning and Instruction, 12*, 429–446.

Hoffman, L., Harburg, E., & Maier, N. (1962). Differences in disagreements as factors in creative problem solving. *Journal of Abnormal and Social Psychology, 64*, 206–214.

Hoffman, L., & Maier, N. (1961). Sex differences, sex composition, and group problem solving. *Journal of Abnormal and Social Psychology, 63*, 453–456.

Hogan, R., & Henley, N. (1970). *A test of the empathy-effective communication hypothesis.* Baltimore, MD: Johns Hopkins University, Center for Social Organization of Schools, Report #84.

Hovey, D., Gruber, H., & Terrell, G. (1963). Effects of self-directed study on course achievement, retention, and curiosity. *The Journal of Educational Research, 56*(7), 346–351.

Hovhannisyan, A., Varrella, G., Johnson, D. W., & Johnson, R. (2005). Cooperative learning and building democracies. *The Cooperative Link, 20*(1), 1–3.

Howe, C. J. (2006). *Group interaction and conceptual understanding in science: Coconstruction, contradiction and the mechanisms of growth.* Paper presented at Annual Conference of British Psychological Society Developmental Section. Royal Holloway College, London.

Howe, C. J., & McWilliam, D. (2001). Peer argument in educational settings: Variations due to socioeconomic status, gender and activity context. *Journal of Language and Social Psychology, 20*, 61–80.

Howe, C. J., & McWilliam, D. (2006). Opposition in social interaction between children: Why intellectual benefits do not mean social costs. *Social Development, 15*(2), 205–231.

Howe, C. J., McWilliam, D., & Cross, G. (2005). Chance favours only the prepared mind: Incubation and the delayed effects of peer collaboration. *British Journal of Psychology, 96*, 67–93.

Howe, C. J., Rodgers, C., & Tolmie, A. (1990). Physics in the primary school: Peer interaction and the understanding of floating and sinking. *European Journal of Psychology of Education, V*, 459–475.

Howe, C. J., Tolmie, A., Anderson, A., & MacKenzie, M. (1992). Conceptual knowledge in physics: The role of group interaction in computer-supported teaching. *Learning and Instruction, 2*, 161–183.

Howe, C. J., Tolmie, A., Greer, K., & Mackenzie, M. (1995). Peer collaboration and conceptual growth in physics: task influences on children's understanding of heating and cooling. *Cognition and Instruction, 13*(4), 483–503.

Howe, C. J., Tolmie, A., & Mackenzie, M. (1995a). Computer support for the collaborative learning of physics concepts. In C. E. O'Malley (Ed.), *Computer supported collaborative learning* (pp. 223–243). London: Springer Verlag.

Howe, C. J., Tolmie, A., & Rogers, C. (1992). The acquisition of conceptual knowledge in science by primary school children: Group interacting and the understanding of motion down an incline. *British Journal of Developmental Psychology, 10*, 113–130.

Howe, C., Tolmie, A., Thurston, A., Topping, K., Christie, D., Livingston, K., Jessiman, E., & Donaldson, C. (2007). Group work in elementary science: Towards organisational principles for supporting pupil learning. *Learning and Instruction, 17*, 549–563.

Hui, C., Wong, A. S. H., & Tjosvold, D. (2007). Turnover intention and performance in China: The role of positive affectivity, perceived organizational support and constructive controversy. *Journal of Occupational and Organizational Psychology, 80*(4), 735–751.

Hunt, J. (1964). Introduction: Revisiting montessori. In M. Montessori (Ed.), *The Montessori method* (pp. xi–xxxv). New York: Shocken Books.

Inagaki, K. (1981). Facilitation of knowledge integration through classroom discussion. *Quarterly Newsletter of the Laboratory of Comparative Human Cognition, 3*, 26–28.

Inagaki, K., & Hatano, G. (1968). Motivational influences on epistemic observation. *Japanese Journal of Educational Psychology, 16*, 221–228.

Inagaki, K., & Hatano, G. (1977). Application of cognitive motivation and its effects on epistemic observation. *American Educational Research Journal, 14*, 485–491.

Inhelder, B., & Sinclair, H. (1969). Learning cognitive structures. In P. H. Mussen, J. Langer, & M. Covington (Eds.), *Trends and issues on developmental psychology* (pp. 2–21). New York: Holt, Rinehart & Winston.

Iverson, M. A., & Schwab, H. G. (1967). Ethnocentric dogmatism and binocular fusion of sexually and racially discrepant stimuli. *Journal of Personality and Social Psychology, 7*(1), 73–81.

Janis, I. L. (1971). Groupthink. *Psychology Today*, 5(6), 308–317.

Janis, I. L. (1972). *Victims of groupthink: A psychological study of foreign-policy decisions and fiascoes*. Oxford: Houghton Mifflin.

Janis, I. L. (1982). *Groupthink: Psychological studies of policy decisions and fiascoes*. Boston: Houghton-Mifflin.

Janis, I. L., & Mann, L. (1977). *Decision making*. New York: Free Press.

Jaworski, A., & Coupland, N. (1999). *The discourse reader*. London: Routledge.

Jefferson, T. (1815). Letter to Colonel James Monroe. In T. J. Randolph (Ed.), The papers of Thomas Jefferson. From the Memoirs, Correspondence, and Miscellanies, from the Papers of Thomas Jefferson. A Linked Index to the Project Gutenberg Editions.

Jetten, J., Hornsey, M. J., Spears, R., Haslam, S. A., & Cowell, E. (2010). Rule transgressions in groups: The conditional nature of newcomers' willingness to confront deviance. *European Journal of Social Psychology*, 40(2), 338–348.

Johnson, D. W. (1970). *Social psychology of education*. New York: Holt, Rinehart, & Winston.

Johnson, D. W. (1971). Role reversal: A summary and review of the research, *International Journal of Group Tensions*, 1, 318–334.

Johnson, D. W. (1974). Communication and the inducement of cooperative behavior in conflicts: A critical review. *Speech Monographs*, 41, 64–78.

Johnson, D. W. (1975a). Cooperativeness and social perspective taking. *Journal of Personality and Social Psychology*, 31, 241–244.

Johnson, D. W. (1975b). Affective perspective-taking and cooperative predisposition. *Developmental Psychology*, 11, 869–870.

Johnson, D. W. (1977). Distribution and exchange of information in problem-solving dyads. *Communication Research*, 4, 283–298.

Johnson, D. W. (1979). *Educational psychology*. Englewood Cliffs, NJ: Prentice-Hall.

Johnson, D. W. (1980). Group processes: Influences of student-student interaction on school outcomes. In J. McMillan (Ed.), *The social psychology of school learning* (pp. 123–168). New York: Academic Press.

Johnson, D. W. (1991). *Human relations and your career*. Englewood Cliffs, NJ: Prentice-Hall.

Johnson, D. W. (2003). Social interdependence: The interrelationships among theory, research, and practice. *American Psychologist*, 58(11), 931–945.

Johnson, D. W. (2014). *Reaching out: Interpersonal effectiveness and self-actualization* (11th edn.). Boston: Allyn & Bacon.

Johnson, D. W., & Johnson, F. (2013). *Joining together: Group theory and group skills* (11th edn.). Boston: Allyn & Bacon.

Johnson, D. W., & Johnson, R. T. (1974). Instructional goal structure: Cooperative, competitive, or individualistic. *Review of Educational Research*, 44, 213–240.

Johnson, D. W., & Johnson, R. T. (1979). Conflict in the classroom: Constructive controversy and learning. *Review of Educational Research, 49*, 51–61.

Johnson, D. W., & Johnson, R. T. (1985). Classroom conflict: Controversy versus debate in learning groups. *American Educational Research Journal, 22*, 237–256.

Johnson, D. W., & Johnson, R. T. (1989). *Cooperation and competition: Theory and research.* Edina, MN: Interaction Book Company.

Johnson, D. W., & Johnson, R. T. (1991). Critical thinking through structured controversy. In K. Cauley, F. Linder, & J. McMillan (Eds.), *Educational psychology 91/92* (pp. 126–130). Guilford, CT: The Gushkin Publishing Group.

Johnson, D. W., & Johnson, R. T. (1999). *Learning together and alone: Cooperative, competitive, and individualistic learning.* Boston: Allyn & Bacon.

Johnson, D. W., & Johnson, R. T. (2000a). Cooperative learning, values, and culturally plural classrooms. In M. Leicester, C. Modgill, & S. Modgill (Eds.), *Values, the classroom, and cultural diversity* (pp. 15–28). London: Cassell PLC.

Johnson, D. W., & Johnson, R. T. (2000b). Civil political discourse in a democracy: The contribution of psychology. *Peace and Conflict: Journal of Peace Psychology, 6*(4), 291–317.

Johnson, D. W., & Johnson, R. T. (2002). *Human relations: Valuing diversity* (2nd edn.). Edina, MN: Interaction Book Company.

Johnson, D. W., & Johnson, R. T. (2003). Controversy and peace education. *Journal of Research in Education, 13*(1), 71–91.

Johnson, D. W., & Johnson, R. T. (2005a). *Teaching students to be peacemakers* (4th edn.). Edina, MN: Interaction Book Company.

Johnson, D. W., & Johnson, R. T. (2005b). New developments in social interdependence theory. *Genetic, Social, and General Psychology Monographs, 131*(4), 285–358.

Johnson, D. W., & Johnson, R. T. (Guest Editors). (2005c). Peace education. *Theory Into Practice, 44*(4), Fall Issue.

Johnson, D. W., & Johnson, R. T. (2007). *Creative controversy: Intellectual challenge in the classroom* (4th edn.). Edina, MN: Interaction Book Company.

Johnson, D. W., & Johnson, R. T. (2009a). An educational psychology success story: Social interdependence theory and cooperative learning. *Educational Researcher, 38*(5), 365–379.

Johnson, D. W., & Johnson, R. T. (2009b). Energizing learning: The instructional power of conflict. *Educational Researcher, 38*(1), 37–51.

Johnson, D. W., & Johnson, R. T. (2010). Peace education in the classroom: Creating effective peace education programs. In G. Salomon & E. Cairns (Eds.), *Handbook of peace education* (pp. 223–240). New York: Psychology Press.

Johnson, D. W., & Johnson, R. T. (2014). Constructive controversy as a means of teaching citizens how to engage in political discourse. *Policy Futures in Education, 12*(3), 417–430.

Johnson, D. W., Johnson, R. T., & Holubec, E. (2013). *Cooperation in the classroom* (9th edn.). Edina, MN: Interaction Book Company.

Johnson, D. W., Johnson, R. T., & Johnson, F. (1976). Promoting constructive conflict in the classroom. *Notre Dame Journal of Education, 7*, 163–168.

Johnson, D. W., Johnson, R. T., Pierson, W., & Lyons, V. (1985). Controversy versus concurrence seeking in multi-grade and single-grade learning groups. *Journal of Research in Science Teaching, 22*(9), 835–848.

Johnson, D. W., Johnson, R. T., & Scott, L. (1978). The effects of cooperative and individualized instruction on student attitudes and achievement. *Journal of Social Psychology, 104*, 207–216.

Johnson, D. W., Johnson, R. T., & Tiffany, M. (1984). Structuring academic conflicts between majority and minority students: Hindrance or help to integration. *Contemporary Educational Psychology, 9*, 61–73.

Johnson, R., Brooker, C., Stutzman, J., Hultman, D., & Johnson, D. W. (1985). The effects of controversy, concurrence seeking, and individualistic learning on achievement and attitude change. *Journal of Research in Science Teaching, 22*, 197–205.

Jones, E. E., & Aneshansel, J. (1956). The learning and utilization of contravaluent material. *Journal of Abnormal and Social Psychology, 53*, 27–33.

Judd, C. (1978). Cognitive effects of attitude conflict resolution. *Conflict Resolution, 22*, 483–498.

Kahneman, D. (2003). A perspective on judgment and choice: Mapping bounded rationality. *American Psychologist, 58*, 697–720.

Kalven, H., & Zeisel, H. (1966). *The American jury*. Boston: Little Brown.

Kang, M. J., Hsu, M., Krajbich, I. M., Loewenstein, G., McClure, S. M., Wang, J. T., & Camerer, C. F. (2009). The wick in the candle of learning: Epistemic curiosity activates reward circuitry and enhances memory. *Psychological Science, 20*(8), 963–973.

Kaplan, M. (1977). Discussion polarization effects in a modern jury decision paradigm: Informational influences. *Sociometry, 40*, 262–271.

Kaplan, M., & Miller, C. (1977). Judgments and group discussion: Effect of presentation and memory factors on polarization. *Sociometry, 40*, 337–343.

Keasey, C. (1973). Experimentally induced changes in moral opinions and reasoning. *Journal of Personality and Social Psychology, 26*, 30–38.

Keefer, M. W., Zeitz, C. M., & Resnick, L. B. (2000). Judging the quality of peer-led student dialogues. *Cognition and Instruction, 18*, 53–81.

Kennedy, K. A., & Pronin, E. (2008). When disagreement gets ugly: Perceptions of bias and the escalation of conflict. *Personality and Social Psychology Bulletin*, *34*(6), 833–848.

Kim, I. H., Anderson, R., Nguyen-Jahiel, K., & Archodidou, A. (2007). Discourse patterns during children's online discussions. *Journal of the Learning Sciences*, *16*(3), 333–370.

King-Casas, B., Tomlin, D., Anen, C., Camerer, C. F., Quartz, S. R., & Montague, P. R. (2005). Getting to know you: Reputation and trust in a two-person economic exchange. *Science Magazine*, *308*(5718), 78–83.

Kirchmeyer, C., & Cohen, A. (1992). Multicultural groups. Their performance and reactions with constructive conflict. *Group and Organization Management*, *17*(2), 153–170.

Klaczynski, P. (2000). Motivated scientific reasoning biases, epistemological beliefs, and theory polarization: A two-process approach to adolescent cognition. *Child Development*, *71*, 1347–1366.

Klaczynski, P. (2004). A dual process model of adolescent development: Implications for decision making, reasoning, and identity. In R. Kail (Ed.), *Advances in child development and behavior* (Vol. 31, pp. 73–123). San Diego, CA: Academic Press.

Kleinhesselink, R., & Edwards, R. (1975). Seeking and avoiding belief-discrepant information as a function of its perceived refutability. *Journal of Personality and Social Psychology*, *31*, 787–790.

Knight-Arest, I., & Reid, D. K. (1978). Peer interaction as a catalyst for conservation acquisition in normal and learning-disabled children. Paper presented at the 8th Annual Symposium of the Jean Piaget Society, Philadelphia, May. ERIC Number: ED162489.

Knudson, R. (1992). Analysis of argumentative writing at two grade levels. *Journal of Educational Research*, *85*, 169–179.

Kohlberg, L. (1969). Stage and sequence: The cognitive-developmental approach to socialization. In D. Goslin (Ed.), *Handbook of socialization theory and research* (pp. 347–480). Chicago, IL: Rand McNally.

Kolbert, E. (2014). *The sixth extinction*. New York: Henry Holt.

Kropotkin, P. A. (1902). *Mutual aid: A factor of evolution*. London: William Heinemann.

Krueger, J. I. (2013). Social projection as a source of cooperation. *Current Directions in Psychological Science*, *22*, 289–294.

Kruger, A. C. (1992). The effect of peer- and adult-child transactive discussions on moral reasoning. *Merrill-Palmer Quarterly*, *38*, 191–211.

Kruger, A. C. (1993). Peer collaboration: Conflict, co-operation or both? *Social Development*, *2*, 165–182.

Kruglanski, A. W. (1980). Lay epistemo-logic-process and contents: Another look at attribution theory. *Psychological Review*, 87(1), 70–87.

Kuhn, D. (1991). *The skills of argument*. Cambridge, UK: Cambridge University Press.

Kuhn, D., Langer, J., Kohlberg, L., & Haan, N. S. (1977). The development of formal operations in logical and moral judgment. *Genetic Psychological Monographs*, 55, 97–188.

Kuhn, D., Shaw, V., & Felton, M. (1997). Effects of dyadic interaction on argumentive reasoning. *Cognition and Instruction*, 15, 287–315.

Kuhn, D., & Udell, W. (2003). The development of argument skill. *Child Development*, 74, 1245–1260.

Kuhn, D., & Udell, W. (2007). Coordinating own and other perspectives in argument. *Thinking and Reasoning*, 13(2), 90–104.

Kumpulainen, K., & Wray, D. (Eds.). (2002). *Classroom interaction and social learning: From theory to practice*. London: Routledge-Falmer.

Lampert, M. L., Rittenhouse, P., & Crumbaugh, C. (1996). Agreeing to disagree: Developing sociable mathematical discourse. In D. R. Olson & N. Torrance (Eds.), *Handbook of human development in education* (pp. 731–764). Cambridge, MA: Blackwell.

Langer, E., Blank, A., & Chanowitz, B. (1978). The mindlessness of ostensibly thoughtful action: The role of "placebic" information in interpersonal interaction. *Journal of Personality and Social Psychology*, 36, 635–642.

Larson, J. R. Jr. (2007). Deep diversity and strong synergy. *Small Group Research*, 38, 413–436.

Larson, J. R. Jr., Christiansen, C., Abbott, A. S., & Franz, T. M. (1996). Diagnosing groups. *Journal of Personality and Social Psychology*, 71, 315–330.

Laughlin, P. (1980). Social combination processes of cooperative problem-solving groups on verbal intellective tasks. In M. Fishbein (Ed.), *Progress in social psychology* (Vol. 1, pp. 127–155). Hillsdale, NJ: Lawrence Erlbaum.

Laughlin, P., & Adamopoulos, J. (1980). Social combination processes and individual learning for six-person cooperative groups on an intellective task. *Journal of Personality and Social Psychology*, 38, 941–947.

Lave, J., & Wenger, E. (1991). *Situated learning: Legitimate peripheral participation*. Cambridge, UK: Cambridge University Press.

LeFurgy, W., & Woloshin, G. (1969). Immediate and long-term effects of experimentally induced social influence in the modification of adolescents' moral judgments. *Journal of Personality and Social Psychology*, 12, 104–110.

Legrenzi, P., Butera, F., Mugny, G., & Perez, J. A. (1991). Majority and minority influence in inductive reasoning: A preliminary study. *European Journal of Social Psychology*, 21, 359–363.

Levi, M., Torrance, E. P., & Pletts, G. O. (1955). *Sociometric studies of combat air crews in survival training* (Sociometry Monographs). New York: Beacon House.

Levine, J., & Murphy, G. (1943). The learning and forgetting of controversial material. *Journal of Abnormal and Social Psychology, 38*, 507–517.

Levine, R., Chein, I., & Murphy, G. (1942). The relation of a need to the amount of perceptual distortion: A preliminary report. *Journal of Psychology: Interdisciplinary and Applied, 13*, 283–293.

Lewin, K. (1935). *A dynamic theory of personality*. New York: McGraw-Hill.

Lewin, K. (1948). *Resolving social conflicts*. New York: Harper.

Lewin, K. (1951). *Field theory in social science: Selected theoretical papers*. New York: Harper.

Lewis, C. S. (2010). *The chronicles of Narnia* (Box Set). New York: Harper, Collins.

Leyens, J. P., Dardeene, B., Yzerbyt, V., Scaillet, N., & Snyder, M. (1999). Confirmation and disconfirmation: Their social advantages. In W. Stroebe & M. Hewstone (Eds.), *European review of social psychology* (Vol. 10, pp. 199–230). Chickester, UK: Wiley.

Limon, M. (2001). On the cognitive conflict as an instructional strategy for conceptual change: A critical appraisal. *Learning and Instruction, 11*, 357–380.

Linn, M. C., & Elyon, B. S. (2000). Knowledge integration and displaced volume. *Journal of Science Education and Technology, 9*, 287–310.

Lord, C., Ross, L., & Lepper, M. (1979). Biased assimilation and attitude polarization: The effects of prior theories on subsequently considered evidence. *Journal of Personality and Social Psychology, 37*, 2098–2109.

Lorenz, C. (1963). *On aggression*. New York: Hartcourt, Brace, and World.

Lovelace, K., Shapiro, D., & Weingart, L. R. (2001). Maximizing cross-functional new product team's innovativeness and constraint adherence: A conflict communications perspective. *Academy of Management Journal, 44*, 779–793.

Lowin, A. (1967). Approach and avoidance: alternative modes of selective exposure to information. *Journal of Personality and Social Psychology, 6*(1), 1–9.

Lowin, A. (1969). Further evidence for an approach-avoidance interpretation of selective exposure. *Journal of Experimental Social Psychology, 5*, 265–271.

Lowry, N., & Johnson, D. W. (1981). Effects of controversy on epistemic curiosity, achievement, and attitudes. *Journal of Social Psychology, 115*, 31–43.

Luchins, A. (1942). Mechanization in problem solving: The effect of Einstellung. *Psychological Monographs, 54*(6), Whole No. 248.

Maass, A., & Clark, R. (1984). Hidden impact of minorities: Fifteen years of minority influence research. *Psychological Bulletin, 95*, 428–450.

Mackie, D. M. (1987). Systematic and nonsystematic processing of majority and minority persuasive communications. *Journal of Personality and Social Psychology*, 53, 41–52.

Maggi, J., Butera, F., Legrenzi, P., & Mugny, G. (1998). Relevance of information and social influence in the pseudodiagnosticity bias. *Swiss Journal of Psychology*, 57, 188–199.

Magnuson, E. (1986, March 10). A serious deficiency: The Rogers Commission faults NASA's flawed decision-making process. *Time*, pp. 40–42.

Maier, N. (1970). *Problem solving and creativity in individuals and groups.* Belmont, CA: Brooks/Cole.

Maier, N., & Hoffman, L. (1964). Financial incentives and group decision in motivating change. *Journal of Social Psychology*, 64, 369–378.

Maier, N., & Solem, A. (1952). The contributions of a discussion leader to the quality of group thinking: The effective use of minority opinions. *Human Relations*, 5, 277–288.

Maier, N., & Thurber, J. (1969). Problems in delegation. *Personnel Psychology*, 22(2), 131–139.

Maitland, K. A., & Goldman, J. R. (1974). Moral judgment as a function of peer group interaction. *Journal of Personality and Social Psychology*, 30(5), 699–704.

Ma-Naim, C., Bar, V., & Zinn, B. (2002). *Integrating microscopic macroscopic and energetic descriptions for a Conceptual Change in Thermodynamics.* Paper presented in the third European Symposium, on Conceptual Change, June 26–28, Turku, Finland.

Martin, R., & Hewstone, M. (2003). Majority and minority influence: When, not whether, source status instigates heuristic or systematic processing. *European Journal of Social Psychology*, 33, 313–330.

Martin, R., Hewstone, M., & Martin, P. Y. (2007). Systematic and heuristic processing of majority and minority-endorsed messages: The effects of varying outcome relevance and levels of orientation on attitude and message processing. *Personality and Social Psychology Bulletin*, 33, 43–56.

Maybin, J. (2006). *Children's voices: Talk, knowledge and identity.* Basingstoke, UK: Palgrave Macmillan.

McClelland, D. C., & Atkinson, J. A. (1948). The projective expression of needs. I. The effect of different intensities of the hunger drive on perception. *Journal of Psychology*, 25, 205–222.

McKenzie, C. R. M. (2004). Hypothesis testing and evaluation. In D. J. Koehler & N. Harvey (Eds.), *Blackwell handbook of judgment & decision making* (pp. 200–219). Malden, MA: Blackwell.

McLeod, P. L., Lobel, S. A., & Cox, T. H. Jr. (1996). Ethnic diversity and creativity in small groups. *Small Group Research, 27*(2), 248–264.

Means, M. L., & Voss, J. F. (1996). Who reasons well? Two studies of informal reasoning among children of different grade, ability, and knowledge levels. *Cognition and Instruction, 14*, 139–178.

Mendelberg, T. (2002). The deliberative citizen: Theory and evidence. *Political Decision Making, Deliberation and Participation, 6*, 151–193.

Mercer, N. (1995). *The guided construction of knowledge: Talk amongst teachers and learners*. Clevedon: Multilingual Matters.

Mercer, N., & Littleton, K. (2007). *Dialogue and the development of children's thinking: A sociocultural approach*. London: Routledge.

Merton, R. K. (1957). *Social theory and social structure*. New York: Free Press.

Meyers, R. A., Brashers, D. E., & Hanner, J. (2000). Majority-minority influence: Identifying argumentative patterns and predicting argument-outcome links. *Journal of Communication, 50*, 3–30.

Miell, D., & MacDonald, R. (2000). Children's creative collaborations: The importance of friendship when working together on a musical composition. *Social Development, 9*, 348–369.

Miller, S., & Brownell, C. (1975). Peers, persuasion, and Piaget: Dyadic interaction between conservers and nonconservers. *Child Development, 46*, 992–997.

Milliken, F. J., Bartel, C. A., & Kurtzberg, T. R. (2003). Diversity and creativity in work groups. In P. B. Paulus & B. A. Nijstad (Eds.), *Group creativity* (pp. 32–62). Oxford: Oxford University Press.

Mills, T. (1967). *The sociology of small groups*. Englewood Cliffs, NJ: Prentice-Hall.

Monteil, J. M., & Chambres, P. (1990). Eléments pour une exploration des dimensions du conflit socio-cognitif: Une expérimentation chez l'adulte [Elements for exploring socio-cognitive conflict: An experiment with adults]. *Revue Internationale de Psychologie Sociale, 3*, 499–517.

Mosconi. G. (1990). *Discorso e pensiero [Discourse and thinking]*. Bologna, Italy: Il Mulino.

Moscovici, S. (1980). Toward a theory of conversion behavior. In L. Berkowitz (Ed.), *Advances in experimental social psychology* (Vol. 13, pp. 209–239). New York: Academic Press.

Moscovici, S. (1985a). Innovation and minority influence. In S. Moscovici, G. Mugny, & E. Van Avermaet (Eds.), *Perspectives on minority influence* (pp. 9–52). Cambridge, UK: Cambridge University Press.

Moscovici, S. (1985b). Social influence and conformity. In G. Lindzey & E. Aronson (Eds.), *The handbook of social psychology* (3rd edn., Vol. 2, pp. 347–412). New York: Random House.

Moscovici, S., & Faucheux, C. (1972). Social Influence, conforming bias, and the study of active minorities. In L. Berkowitz (Ed.), *Advances in experimental social psychology* (Vol. 13). New York: Academic Press.

Moscovici, S., & Lage, E. (1976). Studies in social influence III: Majority versus minority influence in a group. *European Journal of Social Psychology, 6,* 149–174.

Moscovici, S., Lage, E., & Naffrechoux, M. (1969). Influence of a consistent minority on the responses of a majority in a color perception task. *Sociometry, 32,* 365–380.

Moscovici, S., & Nemeth, C. (1974). *Social influence: II. Minority influence.* Oxford, England: Rand McNally.

Mouffe, C. (2000). *The democratic paradox.* London: Verso.

Mucchi-Faina, A., & Cicoletti, G. (2006). Divergence vs. ambivalence: Effects of personal relevance on minority influence. *European Journal of Social Psychology, 36*(1), 91–104.

Mugny, G. (1982). *The power of minorities.* London: Academic Press.

Mugny, G., Butera, F., Quiamzade, A., Dragulescu, A., & Tomei, A. (2003). Comparaisons sociales des compétences et dynamiques d'influence sociale dans les tâches d'aptitudes (social comparison of competencies and social influence). *Année Psychologique, 103*(3), 469–496.

Mugny, G., De Paolis, P., & Carugati, F. (1984). Social regulation in cognitive development. In W. Doise & A. Palmonari, *Social interaction in individual development* (pp. 127–146). Cambridge, UK: Cambridge University Press.

Mugny, G., & Doise, W. (1978). Socio-cognitive conflict and structure of individual and collective performances. *European Journal of Social Psychology, 8,* 181–192.

Mugny, G., Doise, W., & Perret-Clermont, A. N. (1975–1976). Conflit de centrations et progrès cognitif. *Bulletin de Psychologie, 29,* 199–204.

Mugny, G., Giroud, J. C., & Doise, W. (1978–1979). Conflit de centrations et progress cognitif. II: nouvelles illustrations experimentales. *Bulletin de Psychologie, 32,* 979–985.

Mugny, G., Levy, M., & Doise, W. (1978). Conflit socio-cognitif et developpement cognitif. *Swiss Journal of Psychology, 37*(1), 22–43.

Mugny, G., Perret-Clermont, A. N., & Doise, W. (1981). Interpersonal coordinations and sociological differences in the construction of the intellect. *Progress in Applied Social Psychology, 1,* 315–343.

Mugny, G., Tafani, E., Falomir, J. M., & Layat, C. (2000). Source credibility, social comparison and social influence. *International Review of Social Psychology, 13,* 151–175.

Murray, F. B. (1972). The acquisition of conservation through social interaction. *Developmental Psychology, 6,* 1–6.

Murray, F. B. (1978). Development of intellect and reading. In F. Murray & J. Pikulski (Eds.), *The acquisition of reading* (pp. 55–60). Baltimore: University Park Press.

Murray, F. B. (1981). The conservation paradigm: Conservation of conservation research. In D. Brodzinsky, I. Sigel, & R. Golinkoff (Eds.), *New directions in Piagetian theory and research* (pp. 143–175). Hillsdale, NJ: Lawrence Erlbaum Associates.

Murray, F. B. (1982). Teaching through social conflict. *Contemporary Educational Psychology, 7*, 257–271.

Murray, F. B. (1983). *Cognitive benefits of teaching on the teacher.* Paper presented at American Educational Research Association Annual Meeting, Montreal, Quebec.

Murray, F. B., Ames, G., & Botvin, G. (1977). Acquisition of conservation through cognitive dissonance. *Journal of Educational Psychology, 69*, 519–527.

Murray, J. (1974). Social learning and cognitive development: Modeling effects on children's understanding of conservation. *British Journal of Psychology, 65*, 151–160.

Mutz, D. C. (2002). The consequences of cross-cutting networks for political participation. *American Journal of Political Science, 46*(4), 838–855.

Narvaez, D., & Rest, J. (1995). The four components of acting morally. In W. Kurtines & J. Gewirtz (Eds.), *Moral behavior and moral development: An introduction* (pp. 385–400). New York: McGraw-Hill.

Nauta, A., De Dreu, C. K. W., & Van Der Vaart, T. (2002). Social value orientation, organizational goal concerns and interdepartmental problem-solving behavior. *Journal of Organizational Behavior, 23*, 199–213.

Neisser, U. (1954). On experimental distinction between perceptual process and verbal response. *Journal of Experimental Psychology, 47*, 399–402.

Nel, E., Helmreich, R., & Aronson, E. (1969). Opinion change in the advocate as a function of the persuasibility of his audience: A clarification of the meaning of dissonance. *Journal of Personality and Social Psychology, 12*, 117–124.

Nemeth, C. J. (1976). *A comparison between conformity and minority influence.* Paper presented to the International Congress of Psychology, Paris, France.

Nemeth, C. J. (1977). Interactions between jurors as a function of majority vs. unanimity decision rules. *Journal of Applied Social Psychology, 7*, 38–56.

Nemeth, C. J. (1986). Differential contributions of majority and minority influence. *Psychological Review, 93*, 23–32.

Nemeth, C. J. (1995). Dissent as driving cognition, attitudes and judgments. *Social Cognition, 13*, 273–291.

Nemeth, C. J. (1997). Managing innovation: When less is more. *California Management Review, 40*, 59–74.

Nemeth, C. J., Brown, K., & Rogers, J. (2001). Devil's advocate versus authentic dissent: Stimulating quantity and quality. *European Journal of Social Psychology, 31*(6), 707–720.

Nemeth, C. J., & Chiles, C. (1988). Modeling courage: The role of dissent in fostering independence. *European Journal of Social Psychology, 18,* 275–280.

Nemeth, C. J., & Goncalo, J. A. (2005). Influence and persuasion in small groups. In T. C. Brock & M. C. Green (Eds.), *Persuasion: Psychological insights and perspectives* (pp. 171–194). London: Sage Publications.

Nemeth, C. J., & Goncalo, J. A. (2011). Rogues and heroes: Finding value in dissent. In J. Jetten & M. Hornsey (Eds.), *Rebels in groups: Dissent, deviance, difference and defiance* (pp. 73–92). Chichester, UK: Wiley-Blackwell Publishing Ltd.

Nemeth, C. J., & Kwan, J. L. (1985). Originality of word associations as a function of majority vs. minority influence. *Social Psychology Quarterly, 48,* 277–282.

Nemeth, C. J., & Kwan, J. L. (1987). Minority influence, divergent thinking and detection of correct solutions. *Journal of Applied Social Psychology, 17,* 788–799.

Nemeth, C. J., Mosier, K., & Chiles, C. (1992). When convergent thought improves performance: Majority versus minority influence. *Personality and Social Psychology Bulletin, 18,* 139–144.

Nemeth, C. J., & Rogers, J. (1996). Dissent and the search for information. *British Journal of Social Psychology. Special Issue: Minority Influences, 35,* 67–76.

Nemeth, C. J., Swedlund, M., & Kanki, B. (1974). Patterning of a minority's responses and their influence on the majority. *European Journal of Social Psychology, 4,* 53–64.

Nemeth, C. J., & Wachtler, J. (1974). Creating the perceptions of consistency and confidence: A necessary condition for minority influence. *Sociometry, 37,* 529–540.

Nemeth, C. J., & Wachtler, J. (1983). Creative problem solving as a result of majority vs. minority influence. *European Journal of Social Psychology, 13,* 45–55.

Nicholls, J. (1983). Conceptions of ability and achievement motivation: A theory and its implications for education. In S. Paris, G. Olson, & H. Stevenson (Eds.), *Learning and motivation in the classroom* (pp. 211–237). Hillsdale, NJ: Erlbaum.

Nijhof, W., & Kommers, P. (1982). *Analysis of cooperation in relation to cognitive controversy.* Second International Conference on Cooperation in Education, Provo, Utah, July.

Nijstad, B. A., Diehl, M., & Stroebe, W. (2003). Cognitive stimulation and interference in idea generating groups. In P. B. Paulus & B. A. Nijstad (Eds.), *Group creativity: Innovation through collaboration* (pp. 137–159). New York: Oxford University Press.

Nisbett, R. E., & Ross, L. (1980). *Human inference: Strategies and shortcomings of social judgement*. Englewood Cliffs, NJ: Prentice-Hall.

Noonan-Wagner, M. (1975). *Intimacy of self-disclosure and response processes as factors affecting the development of interpersonal relationships*. Unpublished doctoral dissertation, University of Minnesota.

Nussbaum, E. M. (2008a). Collaborative discourse, argumentation, and learning: Preface and literature review. *Contemporary Educational Psychology, 33,* 345–359.

Nussbaum, E. M. (2008b). Using argumentation vee diagrams (AVDs) for promoting argument/counterargument integration in reflective writing. *Journal of Educational Psychology, 100,* 549–565.

Nussbaum, E. M., & Schraw, G. (2007). Promoting argument-counterargument integration in students' writing. *Journal of Experimental Education, 76,* 59–92.

Nussbaum, E. M., Winsor, D. L., Aqui, Y. M., & Poliquin, A. M. (2007). Putting the pieces together: Online argumentation vee diagrams enhance thinking during discussions. *International Journal of Computer-Supported Collaborative Learning, 2,* 479–500.

Orlitzky, M., & Hirokawa, R. Y. (2001). To err is human, to correct for it divine. *Small Group Research, 32,* 313–341.

Orsolini, M. (1993). Dwarfs do not shoot: An analysis of children's justifications. *Cognition and Instruction, 11,* 281–297.

Oscamp, S. (2000). Multiple paths to reducing prejudice and discrimination. In S. Oskamp (Ed.), *Reducing prejudice and discrimination* (pp. 1–19). Mahwah, NJ: Lawrence Erlbaum.

Packer, D. J. (2008). On being both with us and against us: A normative conflict model of dissent in social groups. *Personality and Social Psychology Review, 12,* 50–73.

Parker, W. C. (2006). Public discourses in schools: Purposes, problems, possibilities. *Educational Researcher, 35*(8), 11–18.

Paulus, P. B., & Brown, V. (2003). Ideational creativity in groups. In P. B. Paulus & B. A. Nijstad (Eds.), *Group creativity* (pp. 110–136). New York: Oxford University Press.

Paulus, P. B., & Nijstad, B. A. (Eds.). (2003). *Group creativity: Innovation through collaboration*. New York: Oxford University Press.

Pepitone, A. (1950). Motivational effects in social perception. *Human Relations, 3,* 57–76.

Perkins, D. N., Farady, M., & Bushey, B. (1991). Everyday reasoning and the roots of intelligence. In J. F. Voss, D. N. Perkins, & J. W. Segal (Eds.), *Informal reasoning and education* (pp. 83–105). Hillsdale, NJ: Erlbaum.

Perret-Clermont, A. N. (1980). *Social interaction and cognitive development in children*. London: Academic Press.

Perry-Smith, J. E. (2006). Social yet creative: The role of social relationships in facilitating individual creativity. *Academy of Management Journal, 49*, 85–101.

Perry-Smith, J. E., & Shalley, C. E. (2003). The social side of creativity: A static and dynamic social network perspective. *Academy of Management Review, 28*, 89–106.

Persky, H. R., Daane, M. C., & Jin, Y. (2003). *The nation's report card: Writing 2002* (U.S. Department of Education Pub. No. NCES 2003–529). Washington, DC: U.S. Government Printing Office.

Peters, R., & Torrance, E. (1972). Dyadic interaction of preschool children and performance on a construction task. *Psychological Reports, 30*, 747–750.

Peterson, R., & Nemeth, C. J. (1996). Focus versus flexibility: Majority and minority influence can both improve performance. *Personality and Social Psychological Bulletin, 22*(1), 14–23.

Piaget, J. (1948). *The moral judgment of the child*. Glencoe, IL: Free Press.

Piaget, J. (1950). *The psychology of intelligence*. New York: Harper.

Piaget, J. (1964). Development and learning. In R. E. Ripple & V. N. Rockcastle (Eds.), *Piaget rediscovered* (pp. 7–20). Ithaca, NY: Cornell University Press.

Piaget, J. (1985). *The equilibration of cognitive structures: The central problem of intellectual development*. Chicago: University of Chicago Press.

Piolat, A., Roussey, J. Y., & Gombert, A. (1999). Developmental cues of argumentative writing. In J. E. B. Andriessen & P. Coirier (Eds.), *Foundations of argumentative text processing* (pp. 117–135). Amsterdam: Amsterdam University Press.

Ploetzner, R., Dillenbourg, P., Preier, M., & Traum, D. (1999). Learning by explaining to oneself and to others. In P. Dillenbourg (Ed.), *Collaborating learning: Cognitive and computational approaches* (pp. 103–121). Amsterdam/New York: EARLI Pergamon, Elsevier.

Pontecorvo, C., & Girardet, H. (1993). Arguing and reasoning in understanding historical topics. *Cognition and Instruction, 11*, 365–395.

Pontecorvo, C., Paoletti, G., & Orsolini, M. (1989). Use of the computer and social interaction in a language curriculum. *Golem, 5*, 12–14.

Popper, K. R. (1962). *Conjectures and refutations: The growth of scientific knowledge*. New York: Basic Books.

Postman, L., & Brown, D. R. (1952). Perceptual consequences of success and failure. *Journal of Abnormal and Social Psychology, 47*, 213–221.

Postmes, T., Spears, R., & Cihangir, S. (2001). Quality of group decision making and group norms. *Journal of Personality and Social Psychology, 80*(6), 918–930.

Pratto, F., & John, O. P. (1991). Automatic vigilance: The attention-grabbing power of negative social information. *Journal of Personality and Social Psychology, 61* (3), 380–391.

Price, V., Cappella, J. N., & Nir, L. (2002). Does disagreement contribute to more deliberative opinion? *Political Communication, 19,* 95–112.

Putnam, L., & Geist, P. (1985). Argument in bargaining: An analysis of the reasoning process. *Southern Speech Communication Journal, 50,* 225–245.

Ranciere, J. (1995). *On the shores of politics.* London: Verso.

Rest, J., Turiel, E., & Kohlberg, L. (1969). Relations between level of moral judgment and preference and comprehension of the moral judgment of others. *Journal of Personality, 37,* 225–252.

Rilling, J. K., Gutman, D. A., Zeh, T. R., Pagnoni, G., Berns, G. S., & Kitts, C. D. (2002). A neural basis for social cooperation. *Neuron, 35,* 395–405.

Robbins, J. M., & Krueger, J. I. (2005). Social projection to ingroups and outgroups: A review and meta-analysis. *Personality and Social Psychology Review, 9,* 32–47.

Rogers, C. (1970). Towards a theory of creativity. In P. Vernon (Ed.), *Readings in creativity* (pp. 137–151). London: Penguin.

Rokeach, M. (1954). The nature and meaning of dogmatism. *Psychological Review, 61,* 194–204.

Rokeach, M. (1960). *The open and closed mind.* New York: Basic Books.

Roseth, C. J., Saltarelli, A. J., & Glass, C. R. (2011). Effects of face-to-face and computer-mediated constructive controversy on social interdependence, motivation, and achievement. *Journal of Educational Psychology, 103,* 804–820.

Roy, A., & Howe, C. (1990). Effects of cognitive conflict, socio-cognitive conflict and imitation on children's socio-legal thinking. *European Journal of Social Psychology, 20,* 241–252.

Saltarelli, A. J., & Roseth, C. J. (2014). Effects of synchronicity and belongingness on face-to-face and computer-mediated constructive controversy. *Journal of Educational Psychology, 106*(4), 946–960.

Sandoval, W. A., & Millwood, K. A. (2005). The quality of students' use of evidence in written scientific explanations. *Cognition and Instruction, 23,* 23–55.

Sarbin, T. (1976). Cross-age tutoring and social identity. In V. Allen (Ed.), *Children as teachers: Theory and research on tutoring* (pp. 27–40). New York: Academic Press.

Schwarz, B. B., Neuman, Y., & Biezuner, S. (2000). Two wrongs may make a right . . . If they argue together! *Cognition and Instruction, 18*(4), 461–494.

Schwartz, D. L. (1995). The emergence of abstract representations in dyad problem solving. *The Journal of the Learning Sciences, 4,* 321–354.

Sears, D. O., & Freedman, J. L. (1967). Selective exposure to information: A critical review. *Public Opinion Quarterly, 31*(2), 194–213.

Sermat, V., & Smyth, M. (1973). Content analysis of verbal communication in the development of a relationship: Conditions influencing self-disclosure. *Journal of Personality and Social Psychology, 26,* 332–346.

Shalley, C. E., Zhou, J., & Oldham, G. R. (2004). The effects of personal and contextual characteristics on creativity: Where should we go from here? *Journal of Management, 30,* 933–958.

Shipley, J. E., & Veroff, J. (1952). A projective measure of need for affiliation. *Journal of Experimental Psychology, 43,* 349–356.

Shuper, P. A., & Sorrentino, R. M. (2004). Minority versus majority influence and uncertainty orientation: Processing persuasive messages on the basis of situational expectancies. *Journal of Social Psychology, 144,* 127–147.

Sigel, I., & Hooper, F. (Eds.). (1968). *Logical thinking in children: Research based on Piaget's theory.* New York: Holt, Rinehart and Winston.

Silverman, I., & Geiringer, E. (1973). Dyadic interaction and conservation induction: A test of Piaget's equilibration model. *Child Development, 44,* 815–820.

Silverman, I., & Stone, J. (1972). Modifying cognitive functioning through participation in a problem-solving group. *Journal of Educational Psychology, 63,* 603–608.

Silvia, P. J. (2005). Deflecting reactance: The role of similarity in increasing compliance and reducing resistance. *Basic and Applied Social Psychology, 27,* 277–284.

Simon, H. A. (1976). *Administrative behavior* (3rd edn.). New York, NY: The Free Press.

Sinclair, H. (1969). Developmental psycho-linguistics. In D. Elkind & J. Flavell (Eds.), *Studies in cognitive development: Essays in honor of Jean Piaget* (pp. 315–336). New York: Oxford University Press.

Skinner, B. (1968). *The technology of teaching.* New York: Appleton-Century-Crofts.

Smedslund, J. (1961a). The acquisition of conservation of substance and weight in children: II. External reinforcement of conservation and weight and of the operations of addition and subtraction. *Scandinavian Journal of Psychology, 2,* 71–84.

Smedslund, J. (1961b). The acquisition of conservation of substance and weight on children: III. Extinction of conservation of weight acquired "normally" and by means of empirical controls on a balance. *Scandinavian Journal of Psychology, 2,* 85–87.

Smedslund, J. (1966). Les origins social de la decentration [The social origins of decentration]. In F. Bresson & M. de Montmollin (Eds.), *Psychologie et epistemologie genetiques* (pp. 159–167). Paris: Dunod.

Smith, K. A. (1984). Structured controversy. *Engineering Education*, 74(5), 306–309.

Smith, K. A., Johnson, D. W., & Johnson, R. (1981). Can conflict be constructive? Controversy versus concurrence seeking in learning groups. *Journal of Educational Psychology*, 73, 651–663.

Smith, K. A., Johnson, D. W., & Johnson, R. (1984). Effects of controversy on learning in cooperative groups. *Journal of Social Psychology*, 122, 199–209.

Smith, K. A., Matusovich, H., Meyers, K., & Mann, L. (2011). Preparing the next generation of engineering educators and researchers: Cooperative learning in the Purdue University School of Engineering Education PhD Program. Chapter 6 in B. Millis (Ed.), *Cooperative learning in higher education: Across the disciplines, across the academy*. Sterling, VA: Stylus Press.

Smith, K. A., Petersen, R. P., Johnson, D. W., & Johnson, R. T. (1986). The effects of controversy and concurrence seeking on effective decision making. *Journal of Social Psychology*, 126(2), 237–248.

Snell, R. S., Tjosvold, D., & Su, F. (2006). Resolving ethical conflicts at work through cooperative goals and constructive controversy in the People's Republic of China. *Asia Pacific Journal of Management*, 23, 319–343.

Snyder, M., & Cantor, N. (1979). Testing theories about other people: The use of historical knowledge. *Journal of Experimental Social Psychology*, 15, 330–342.

Stanovich, K. E., West, R. F., & Toplak, M. E. (2013). Myside bias, rational thinking, and intelligence. *Current Directions in Psychological Science*, 22, 259–264.

Stasson, M. F., & Bradshaw, S. D. (1995). Explanation of individual-group performance differences. *Small Group Research*, 26, 296–308.

Stavy, R., & Berkovits, B. (1980). Cognitive conflict as a basis for teaching quantitative aspects of the concept of temperature. *Science Education*, 64(5), 679–692.

Staw, B. M. (1995). Why no one really wants creativity. In C. M. Ford & D. A. Gioia (Eds.), *Creative action in organizations: Ivory tower visions & real world voices* (pp. 161–172). Thousand Oaks, CA: Sage.

Steele, C. M. (1988). The psychology of self-affirmation: Sustaining the integrity of the self. In L. Berkowitz (Ed.) *Advances in experimental social psychology* (Vol. 21, pp. 261–302). New York: Academic Press.

Stein, M. (1968). *The creative individual*. New York: Harper & Row.

Stevenson, A. E. (1952). *Major campaign speeches of Adlai E. Stevenson*. New York: Random House.

Sunstein, C. R. (2002). The law of group polarization. *The Journal of Political Philosophy*, 10(2), 175–195.

Swann, W. B. Jr., Kwan, V. S. Y., Polzer, J. T., & Milton, L. P. (2003). Vanquishing stereotypic perceptions via individuation and self-verification: Waning of gender expectations in small groups. *Social Cognition*, 21, 194–212.

Swann, W. B. Jr., & Reid, S. (1981). Acquiring self-knowledge: The search for feedback that fits. *Journal of Personality and Social Psychology, 41*, 1119–1128.

Tanford, S., & Penrod, S. (1984). Social influence model: A formal integration of research on majority and minority influence processes. *Psychological Bulletin, 95*, 189–225.

Taylor, D., Altman, I., & Sorrentino, R. (1969). Interpersonal exchange as a function of rewards and costs and situational factors: Expectancy confirmation-disconfirmation. *Journal of Experimental Social Psychology, 5*, 324–339.

Taylor, S. E. (1980). The interface of cognitive and social psychology. In J. H. Harvey (Ed.), *Cognition, social behavior, and the environment* (pp. 189–211). Hillsdale, NJ: Erlbaum.

Taylor, S. E. (1991). Asymmetric effects of positive and negative events: The mobilization-minimization hypothesis. *Psychological Bulletin, 110*, 67–85.

Teasley, S. D. (1995). The role of talk in children's peer collaborations. *Developmental Psychology, 31*, 207–220.

Teasley, S. D. (1997). Talking about reasoning: How important is the peer in peer collaboration. In L. B. Resnick, R. Säljö, C. Pontecorvo, & B. Burge (Eds.), *Discourse tools and reasoning: Essays on situated cognition* (pp. 363–384). New York: Springer.

Tesser, A. (1988). Toward a self-evaluation maintenance model of social behavior. In L. Berkowitz (Ed.), *Advances in experimental social psychology* (pp. 181–227). San Diego, CA: Academic Press.

Tesser, A., Millar, M., & Moore, J. (1988). Some affective consequences of social comparison and reflection processes: The pain and pleasure of being close. *Journal of Personality and Social Psychology, 54*(1), 49.

Tichy, M., Johnson, D. W., Johnson, R. T., & Roseth, C. (2010). The impact of constructive controversy on moral development. *Journal of Applied Social Psychology, 40*(4), 765–787.

Tjosvold, D. (1974). Threat as a low-power person's strategy in bargaining: Social face and tangible outcomes. *International Journal of Group Tensions, 4*, 494–510.

Tjosvold, D. (1982). Effects of the approach to controversy on superiors' incorporation of subordinates' information in decision-making. *Journal of Applied Psychology, 67*, 189–193.

Tjosvold, D. (1984). Effects of crisis orientation on managers' approach to controversy in decision making. *Academy of Management Journal, 27*, 130–138.

Tjosvold, D. (1988). Effects of shared responsibility and goal interdependence on controversy and decision making between departments. *Journal of Social Psychology, 128*(1), 7–18.

Tjosvold, D. (1995). Effects of power to reward and punish in cooperative and competitive contexts. *Journal of Social Psychology, 135*, 723–736.

Tjosvold, D. (1998a). Cooperative and competitive goal approach to conflict: Accomplishments and challenges. *Applied Psychology: An International Review, 47*(3), 285–342.

Tjosvold, D. (1998b). Making employee involvement work: Cooperative goals and controversy to reduce costs. *Human Relations, 51*, 201–214.

Tjosvold, D. (2002). Managing anger for teamwork in Hong Kong: Goal interdependence and open-mindedness. *Asian Journal Social Psychology, 5*, 107–123.

Tjosvold, D., & De Dreu, C. K. W. (1997). Managing conflict in Dutch organizations: A test of the relevance of Deutsch's cooperation theory, *Journal of Applied Social Psychology, 27*, 2213–2227.

Tjosvold, D., & Deemer, D. K. (1980). Effects of controversy within a cooperative or competitive context on organizational decision making. *Journal of Applied Psychology, 65*(5), 590–595.

Tjosvold, D., & Field, R. H. G. (1986). Effect of concurrence, controversy, and consensus on group decision making. *Journal of Social Psychology, 125*(3), 355–363.

Tjosvold, D., & Halco, J. A. (1992). Performance appraisal of managers: Goal interdependence, ratings, and outcomes. *Journal of Social Psychology, 132*, 629–639.

Tjosvold, D., Hui, C., & Law, K. S. (1998). Empowerment in the manager-employee relationship in Hong Kong: Interdependence and controversy. *Journal of Social Psychology, 138*, 624–637.

Tjosvold, D., Hui, C., & Sun, H. (2004). Can Chinese discuss conflicts openly? Field and experimental studies of face dynamics in China. *Group Decision and Negotiation, 13*, 351–373.

Tjosvold, D., & Johnson, D. W. (1977). Effects of controversy on cognitive perspective taking. *Journal of Educational Psychology, 69*(6), 679–685.

Tjosvold, D., & Johnson, D. W. (1978). Controversy within a cooperative or competitive context and cognitive perspective-taking. *Contemporary Educational Psychology, 3*, 376–386.

Tjosvold, D., Johnson, D. W., & Fabrey, L. J. (1980). Effects of controversy and defensiveness on cognitive perspective-taking. *Psychological Reports, 47*, 1043–1053.

Tjosvold, D., Johnson, D. W., & Lerner, J. (1981). Effects of affirmation of one's competence, personal acceptance, and disconfirmation of one's competence on incorporation of opposing information on problem-solving situations. *Journal of Social Psychology, 114*, 103–110.

Tjosvold, D., Law, K. S., & Sun, H. (2003). Collectivistic and individualistic values: their effects on group dynamics and productivity in China. *Group Decision and Negotiation, 12*, 243–263.

Tjosvold, D., Meredith, L., & Wong, C. (1998). Coordination to market technology: the contribution of cooperative goals and interaction. *Journal of High Technology Management Research, 9*, 1–15.

Tjosvold, D., & Poon, M. (1998). Using and valuing accounting information: Joint decision making between accountants and retail managers. *Group Decision and Negotiation, 7*, 1–19.

Tjosvold, D., & Su, F. S. (2007). Managing anger and annoyance in organizations in China: The role of constructive controversy. *Group and Organization Management, 32*(3), 260–289.

Tjosvold, D., & Sun, H. F. (2001). Effects of influence tactics and social contexts: An experiment on relationships in China. *International Journal of Conflict Management, 12*, 239–258.

Tjosvold, D., & Sun, H. F. (2003). Openness among Chinese in conflict: Effects of direct discussion and warmth on integrative decision making, *Journal of Applied Social Psychology, 33*, 1878–1897.

Tjosvold, D., Wedley, W. C., & Field, R. H. G. (1986). Constructive controversy, the Vroom-Yetton model, and managerial decision making. *Journal of Occupational Behaviour, 7*, 125–138.

Tjosvold, D., XueHuang, Y., Johnson, D. W., & Johnson, R. (2008). Is the way you resolve conflicts related to your psychological health. *Peace and Conflict: Journal of Peace Psychology, 14*(4), 395–428.

Tjosvold, D., & Yu, Z. Y. (2007). Group risk-taking: The constructive role of controversy in China. *Group and Organization Management, 32*, 653–674.

Tjosvold, D., Yu, Z. Y., & Hui, C. (2004). Team learning from mistakes: The contribution of cooperative goals and problem-solving. *Journal of Management Studies, 41*, 1223–1245.

Tolkien, J. R. R. (2012). *The hobbit and the lord of the rings* (Box Set). New York: Del Ray.

Tolmie, A., Howe, C. J., Mackenzie, M., & Greer, K. (1993). Task design as an influence on dialogue and learning: Primary school group work with object flotation. *Social Development, 2*, 183–201.

Toma, C., & Butera, F. (2009). Hidden profiles and concealed information: Strategic information sharing and use in group decision making. *Personality and Social Psychological Bulletin, 35*, 793–806.

Tomasetto, C., Mucchi-Faina, A., Alparone, F. R., & Pagliaro, S. (2009). Differential effects of majority and minority influence on argumentation strategies. *Social Influence, 4*, 33–45.

Torrance, E. P. (1957). *Training combat aircrewmen for confidence in ability to adhere to code of conduct* (ASTIA document). Office for Social Science Programs, Air Force Personnel and Training Research Center.

Torrance, E. P. (1963). *Education and the creative potential.* Minneapolis: University of Minnesota Press.

Torrance, E. P. (1965). *Rewarding creative behavior.* Englewood Cliffs, NJ: Prentice-Hall.

Torrance, E. P. (1970). Influence of dyadic interaction on creative functioning. *Psychological Reports, 26,* 391–394.

Torrance, E. P. (1971). Stimulation, enjoyment, and originality in dyadic creativity. *Journal of Educational Psychology, 62,* 45–48.

Torrance, E. P. (1973). *Dyadic interaction in creative thinking and problem solving.* Paper read at American Educational Research Association, New Orleans, February.

Toulmin, S. (1958). *The uses of argument.* Cambridge, UK: Cambridge University Press.

Treffinger, D. J., Speedie, S. M., & Brunner, W. D. (1974). *Improving children's creative problem solving ability: The Purdue creativity project. Journal of Creative Behavior, 8*(1), 20–30.

Triandis, H., Bass, A., Ewen, R., & Midesele, E. (1963). Teaching creativity as a function of the creativity of the members. *Journal of Applied Psychology, 47,* 104–110.

Trosset, C. (1998). Obstacles to open discussion and critical thinking: The Grinnel College study. *Change, 30*(5), 44–49.

Turiel, E. (1966). An experimental test of the sequentiality of development stages in the child's moral judgment. *Journal of Personality and Social Psychology, 3,* 611–618.

Turiel, E. (1973). Stage transition in moral development. In R. Travers (Ed.), *Second handbook of research on teaching* (pp. 732–758). Chicago: Rand McNally.

Tversky, A., & Kahneman, D. (1981). The framing of decisions and the psychology of choice. *Science, 211,* 453–458.

Vacchiano, R. B., Strauss, P. S., & Hochman, L. (1969). The open and closed mind: A review of dogmatism. *Psychological Bulletin, 71,* 261–273.

Van Blerkom, M., & Tjosvold, D. (1981). The effects of social context on engaging in controversy. *Journal of Psychology, 107,* 141–145.

Van Dyne, L., Ang, S., & Botero, I. C. (2003). Conceptualizing employee silence and employee voice as multi-dimensional constructs. *Journal of Management Studies, 40,* 1360–1392.

Van Dyne, L., & LePine, J. A. (1998). Helping and voice extra-role behavior: Evidence of a construct and predictive validity. *Academy of Management Journal, 41,* 108–119.

Van Dyne, L., & Saavedra, R. (1996). A naturalistic minority influence experiment: Effects of divergent thinking, conflict and originality in work groups. *British Journal of Social Psychology, 35,* 151–168.

Van Eemeren, F. H. (2003). A glance behind the scenes: The state of the art in the study of argumentation. *Studies in Communication Sciences, 3,* 1–23.

Van Eemeren, F. H., & Grootendorst, R. (1999). Developments in argumentation theory. In G. Rijlaarsdam & E. Espéret (Series Eds.) & J. Andriessen & P. Coirier (Vol. Eds.), *Studies in writing, Vol. 5: Foundations of argumentative text processing* (pp. 43–57). Amsterdam: Amsterdam University Press.

Van Eemeren, F. H., Grootendorst, R., Jackson, S., & Jacobs, S. (1996). Argumentation. In T. van Dink (Ed.), *Discourse studies: A multidisciplinary introduction: Vol. 1. Discourse as structure and process* (pp. 208–229). London: Sage Publications.

Vinokur, A., & Burnstein, E. (1974). Effects of partially shared persuasive arguments on group-induced shifts. *Journal of Personality and Social Psychology, 29,* 305–315.

Vollmer, A., Dick, M., & Wehner, T. (Eds.). (2014). *Innovation as a social process: Constructive controversy – a method for conflict management.* Berlin: Gabler/Eiesbaden/Germany Publishers.

Vonk, R. (1993). The negativity effect in trait ratings and in open-ended descriptions of persons. *Personality and Social Psychology Bulletin, 19*(3), 269–278.

Voss, J. F., & Means, M. L. (1991). Learning to reason via instruction in argumentation. *Learning and Instruction, 1,* 337–350.

Vygotsky, L. (2012). *Thought and language.* Cambridge, MA: MIT Press.

Walker, L. (1983). Sources of cognitive conflict for stage transition in moral development. *Developmental Psychology, 19,* 103–110.

Wallach, L., & Sprott, R. (1964). Inducing number conservation in children. *Child Development, 35,* 1057–1071.

Wallach, L., Wall, A., & Anderson, L. (1967). Number conservation: The roles of reversibility, addition-subtraction, and misleading perceptual cues. *Child Development, 38,* 425–442.

Walton, D. N. (1985). *Arguer's position: A pragmatic study of ad hominem attacks, criticism, refutation, and fallacy.* Westport, CT/London: Greenwood.

Walton, D. N. (1999). *The new dialectic.* University Park, PA: Pennsylvania University Press.

Walton, D. N. (2003). *Ethical argumentation.* New York: Lexington Books.

Walzer, M. (2004). *Politics and passion: Toward a more egalitarian liberalism.* New Haven, CT: Yale University Press.

Wason, P. C. (1960). On the failure to eliminate hypotheses in a conceptual task. *Quarterly Journal of Experimental Psychology, 12,* 255–274.

Watson, G., & Johnson, D. W. (1972). *Social psychology: Issues and insights* (2nd edn.). Philadelphia: Lippincott.

Webb, N. M. (1991). Task-related verbal interaction and mathematics learning in small groups. *Journal for Research in Mathematics Education, 22,* 366–389.

Webb, N. M. (1995). Constructive activity and learning in collaborative small groups. *Journal of Educational Psychology, 87,* 406–423.

Wegerif, R., Mercer, N., & Dawes, L. (1999). From social interaction to individual reasoning: An empirical investigation of a possible socio-cultural model of cognitive development. *Learning and Instruction, 9,* 493–516.

Wegerif, R., & Scrimshaw, P. (Eds.). (1997). *Computers and talk in the primary classroom.* Clevedon: Multilingual Matters.

Wells, H. G. (1927). *Outline of history.* New York: Macmillan Press.

Wills, T. A. (1981). Downward comparison principles in social psychology. *Psychological Bulletin, 90,* 245–271.

Wittrock, M. (1990). Generative processes of comprehension. *Educational Psychologist, 24,* 345–376.

Wittrock, M. C. (1992). Generative learning processes of the brain. *Educational Psychologist, 27,* 531–541.

Woholwill, J., & Lowe, R. (1962). Experimental analysis of the development of the conservation of number. *Child Development, 33,* 153–167.

Worchel, P., & McCormick, B. (1963). Self-concept and dissonance reduction. *Journal of Personality, 31,* 589–599.

Zajonc, R. (1965). Social facilitation. *Science, 149,* 269–272.

Zimbardo, P. (1965). The effect of effort and improvisation on self-persuasion produced by role playing. *Journal of Experimental Social Psychology, 1,* 103–120.

Zohar, A., & Nemet, F. (2002). Fostering students' knowledge and argumentation skills through dilemmas in human genetics. *Journal of Research in Science Teaching, 39,* 35–62.

Zou, T. X. P., Mickleborough, N., & Leung, J. (2012). Promoting collaborative problem solving through peer tutoring and structured controversy. Presentation at *2012 Engineering Education Innovation Workshop,* Hong Kong University of Science and Technology, Clearwater Bay, Hong Kong.

Zuckerman, M., Knee, C. R., Hodgins, H. S., & Miyake, K. (1995). Hypothesis confirmation: The joint effect of positive test strategy and acquiescence response set. *Journal of Personality and Social Psychology, 68,* 52–60.

Index